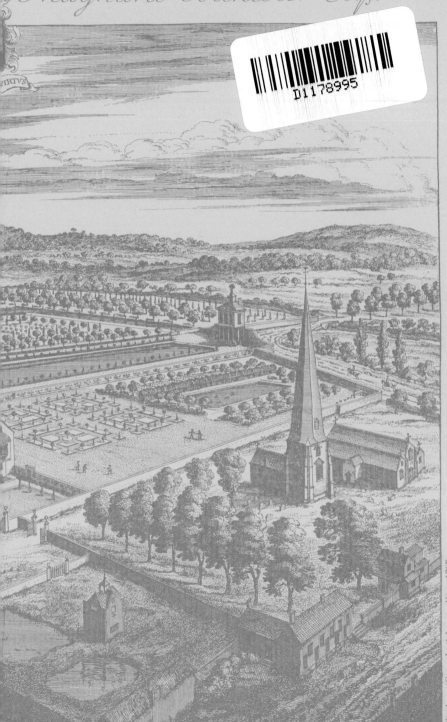

Maynard Colchester Esq.

VIRTVS

I. Kip delin. et Sculp.

West Country Gardens

To Lyn

West Country Gardens

The Gardens of Gloucestershire, Avon, Somerset and Wiltshire

John Sales

ALAN SUTTON

1980

Alan Sutton Publishing Limited
17a Brunswick Road
Gloucester GL1 1HG

First Published 1980

BRITISH LIBRARY CATALOGUING IN PUBLICATION DATA

Sales, John
   West Country gardens.
   1. Gardens – England – West Country
   I. Title
   712'.6'09423   SB451

   ISBN 0-904387-55-0

Typesetting and origination by
Alan Sutton Publishing Limited.
Photoset Bembo 10/11
Printed in Great Britain
by Redwood Burn Limited
Trowbridge & Esher

Contents

List of Black and White Photographs

List of Colour Photographs

County Maps

List of Garden Plans

Preface

This book is primarily about private gardens, gardens created and maintained by individuals for their own pleasure and now generously shared with others, either as one means of the gardens' survival or as a uniquely British way of raising money for worthy charities.

Gardens of the National Trust are included because of its private charitable status and because its intention is always to maintain its properties in the spirit of private ownership, taking into account the inevitable effects of increased visiting.

There is, happily for the visitor, a wonderful choice of gardens; the selection I have made here (given the consent of the owners) is the result of my lifelong interest in horticulture and professional interest in gardens, but I don't imply anything by my omissions. I have deliberately not written at the length one might have done about some of the world famous gardens so as to say more about the less well known but equally deserving ones. I hope readers will agree with me that this makes for a more informative and, at the same time, a more stimulating guide.

Inevitably there are changes from time to time in the details of which gardens are open, so you might like to keep at hand the latest edition of such publications as the National Gardens Scheme *Yellow Book* and *Historic Houses, Castles and Gardens.*

I am much indebted to garden owners for their interest and help so freely given and for their kindness and hospitality; evidence, if any was needed, of the affinity that always exists between gardeners of all kinds. As well as its obvious use as a guide in planning visits to gardens, I hope this book will serve in some way as a tribute to their owners; also, that it may be a source of ideas for people planning their own gardens and that as a record of the gardens of the late 1970s it will be of historical interest in the future.

Acknowledgements

I am grateful to the many people who have given freely of their time to assist with the preparation of this book; in particular the owners who have made their gardens available and have kindly commented on the draft descriptions sent to them. I would also like to record special thanks to my wife Lyn, for typing the whole book, for various corrections and for preparing the index; also to Doris Twigg who read the draft and to Paula Shea for editing it. My thanks are also due to Bridget Wainwright, Wendy Luttley, Cy Bartlett, Roy Cheek, Peter Thoday and Graham Thomas, all of whom helped in various ways in reading parts of the manuscript and helping in the choice of gardens to visit; also to my three sons Nicholas, Richard and Simon, for their forbearance while I visited and wrote.

I would like to record particularly thanks to John Anthony for producing the garden plans with much clarity and professionalism despite considerable difficulties and to C. Patrick Smith for his delightful line drawings.

Introduction

Britain holds horticultural riches unparalleled elsewhere in the world. Within a few hundred miles there is a diversity of gardens, plants and styles expressing, as eloquently as anything can, our history and culture and our horticultural skill over the past several hundred years. In their variety they reflect not only the complexity of the soil and climate but also the interests and tastes, even eccentricities, of those who own them. Gardening has been our national obsession for centuries and never more than now.

Garden visiting is now a major national pastime ranking well ahead of all summer sports in popularity. Each year an estimated 7,000,000 paid visits are made primarily to gardens, quite apart from the far larger number made where a house and garden are open jointly. Like our great houses, our gardens are a major tourist attraction and with the country house they are our most important national contribution to world culture and art. But these qualities are not concentrated wholly in the larger gardens of our great houses. Although the English Landscape style — as expressed in great gardens and parks like Stourhead, Bowood and Longleat — is rightly regarded throughout the world as the supreme English innovation of the eighteenth century, in more recent times it has been in gardens of more modest size that we have led the world. Gardens like Hidcote, Kiftsgate, Tintinhull — and more recently Alderley Grange, The Dower House, Badminton and Barnsley House — mark high points in a style which is truly English, relying for its effect not only on a firm framework of formal spaces and predetermined series of colour schemes but also on an originality in the planting that comes from a real knowledge and love of plants. Its apparent casualness is derived from the English habit of understatement: trying hard without seeming to do so. Here is the true English character expressed in its gardens.

Everyone sees a garden with different eyes and according to his interest appreciates one aspect or another. The purpose of this book, is to introduce gardens to the visitor in the hope that, in seeing the garden through the eyes of another, the visit will be enriched and the experience deepened.

Although a great deal of pleasure can be had from seeing any plant well grown, gardeners soon find that there is more to it than making the biggest show from the most colourful plants or even assembling the greatest number of rarities. But the 'collectors' interest in gardening should not be underestimated and many gardens described in this book have at least an element of collecting in them. The potential range is so wide, however, that even in the largest gardens selection becomes inevitable sooner or later. Sometimes the limits of space or of site and soil impose a discipline which may in itself create a kind of unity, but usually it is the owner who makes a selection and an arrangement according to his taste and the fashion of the time.

A garden can be the statement of a particular personality or more frequently the expression of two in combination, e.g. designer and client or husband and wife. Sometimes a garden will show the imprint of successive generations of the same family, giving evidence of the remarkable continuity in the ownership of great houses and gardens which is so rare elsewhere and so relatively common in Britain.

With the ebb and flow of civilization and the evolution of cultural ideals on the one hand and changes in internal security and social structures on the other, styles of gardening have undergone enormous changes over the centuries. The gardens of Gloucestershire, Wiltshire, Avon and Somerset illustrate these changes. Almost every style and influence on gardens in the past 300 years is represented, together with traces of earlier gardens, right through to the present 'garden-centre' style with its over-emphasis on ornaments, concrete, conifers and colour.

It is axiomatic that the older the style the less likely it is to have survived. Hence little genuine planting of earlier than c.1700 remains. Nothing of the garden of the Roman villa at Chedworth exists although the empty enclosure amid the buildings is presumably one of the oldest garden sites in the country. Medieval gardens were usually sited within the curtilage of religious buildings or closely associated with them and perhaps the cloistered court at Lacock Abbey and the garden of the Bishop's Palace at Wells once contained herbs and simples, and maybe even some vegetables and flowers. Almost certainly there would have been gardens within the fortified area of ancient castles like Berkeley and Dunster but of necessity they would have been small, and little is known of their layout and content.

In 1511 the Duke of Buckingham began Thornbury Castle, enclosing a delightful courtyard garden, much larger and more elaborate than anything seen before within castle walls and more Elizabethan than medieval. The site of the knot garden can still be distinguished below an elegant oriel window from which it was viewed. That many of the Tudor houses mentioned in this book had elaborate gardens is sometimes confirmed by contemporary descriptions and surveys but none of the planting has survived. At Montacute the exquisite pavilions and the walled enclosures of the Elizabethan garden have been preserved, and at Sheldon Manor the forecourt garden may be even older. At Sudeley Castle and Owlpen Manor there are nineteenth-century restorations of Elizabethan gardens.

Although nothing of it remains, the Renaissance garden at Wilton, the first great formal garden in England, was recorded in all its complex detail by its designer, Isaac de Caus. It was made by the fourth Earl of Pembroke between 1623 and 1635. The formal gardens of late seventeeth-century Gloucestershire were recorded in engravings by Kip (probably from paintings by Knyff) in *The Ancient and Present State of Glostershire* (1712) by Sir Robert Atkyns, whose own house at Sapperton was illustrated. It was later destroyed by the first Earl Bathurst, the stone being used to make the first-ever gothic folly, in Cirencester Park. Most of the other gardens drawn by Kip have gone but the remains of George London's and Henry Wise's stupendous layout for Dyrham can still be detected in the avenues and in the garden. The most remarkable survival is the small water garden of Dutch inspiration at Westbury Court. The prevailing French fashion in gardens was reflected in immense formal schemes by London and Wise for Badminton and Longleat, both of which have been swept away.

It would require a much larger book than this to describe the history of the English Landscape Movement of the eighteenth-century. The counties of Gloucestershire, Wiltshire and Somerset were closely associated with its development through Henry Hoare's Stourhead, C.P. Bampfylde's Hestercombe, William Kent's work at Badminton and Alexander Pope's musings in Cirencester. Lancelot Brown worked at a number of places including Badminton, Corsham, Dodington, Kings Weston (now built-over but the house remains), Longleat, Prior Park, Wilton and not least Bowood, which is one of his greatest surviving works.

Humphry Repton was employed at Blaise Castle and his Blaise Hamlet remains as an elegant example of his skill on a small scale. His larger commissions were fewer than Brown's but included Corsham Court and Longleat and he gave advice at Sezincote. But there was no single style of gardening in the eighteenth-century any more than there is today. While Henry Hoare was making Stourhead, Earl Bathurst was laying out his predominantly formal park at Cirencester and later in the century William Beckford created his extraordinary, gothic, Fonthill Abbey with a garden which even today, long after the demise of the house, still retains elements of the sublime in the form of 'a rude erection in the imitation of a Cromlech' — a rocky cave covered in ivy, designed by Josiah Lane in the 1790s.

Probably because of its relative isolation from the Industrial Revolution of the nineteenth-century the region lacks many grand examples of high Victorian gardening. Bowood has its mid-nineteenth-century Italianate terraces; also in Wiltshire, Longleat has its formal flower garden and Wilton its Italian garden (not open). Most Victorian gardening was on a more modest scale like the layout at Orchardleigh Park, its terraces with urns from the former house and its pleasure-grounds in the gardenesque style of J.C. Loudon. James Shirley Hibberd was a great exponent of the Victorian Italianate Garden, 'Let the terrace be truly Italian . . .' he said, and later admitted, 'Wealth is certainly a blessing'! Hibberd had a great influence on the development of late-Victorian taste in gardens through his books, especially *Rustic Adornments for Homes of Taste* but the writings of his contemporary, Canon Henry N. Ellacombe, who gardened at Bitton near Bristol, also made a considerable local and national impression. His book *In a Gloucestershire Garden* is full of first-hand observations and loving descriptions of plants and their uses. He enjoyed simplicity in gardens and extolled the more natural use of plants and shrubs. He disliked 'the bedding craze' and in this his philosophy was close to that of William Robinson. The latter led the revolt against the artificiality of carpet bedding and pioneered the 'Wild Garden' which has its echo in woodland gardens at Bowood, Broadleas, Marlands, Lydney Park, Batsford Park and even in the 'Westonbirt' part of Hidcote.

The great plant hunters, who sent back a stream of new plants from abroad in the nineteenth-century, were patronized by R.S. Holford and his successors in the development of one of the nation's greatest arboreta at Westonbirt. Other great historical collections include the pinetum at Bowood, Batsford Park, Stourhead and, on a different scale, Hidcote and Kiftsgate. At Colesbourne, Henry Elwes' arboretum is still intact and the present owner, Mr. H.W.G. Elwes, opens it for special parties from time to time. The arboretum at Tortworth Court, now Leyhill Open Prison, although for good reason not open to visitors, is of the highest quality. It was planted by Lord Ducie who vied with the Holfords for the rarest and the best in trees and shrubs.

If William Robinson prepared the way for the great revolution in garden taste early in the twentieth-century, it was Gertrude Jekyll who brought it about. She developed colour schemes and textural associations in gardens and achieved the ideal partnership in planting Sir Edwin Lutyens' architectural designs. Her influence on gardens in the region has been immense and outstanding examples of her style have been preserved at Hestercombe where she worked with Sir Edwin, and at Barrington Court where Forbes and Tate were the architects. Sir Edwin also designed the outline of the formal garden at Abbotswood where that great gardener Mark Fenwick was responsible for the planting. Ammerdown Park near Radstock is another of Lutyens' most successful gardens but it is not normally open.

The English garden style of this century reached its climax in the work of Lawrence Johnston at Hidcote Manor and has been developed in countless variations to become the dominant influence on gardens in the region. The making of Kiftsgate Court was deeply influenced by that of Hidcote, and vice-versa, and some intriguing gardens of similar character, like Snowshill Manor, Rodmarton Manor and Lyegrove, were being developed at the same time. But whether they were part of the cause or a symptom of the effect is not clear. However Tintinhull and The Courts, Holt, are distinctive and highly original variations on the Hidcote theme while Sezincote and Hadspen House make use of the principles of colour and texture of Jekyll and Johnston in the context of a freer and more informal arrangement.

Particularly in Somerset but also, because of her writings, throughout the country Margery Fish has been a considerable influence in the arrangement of plants according to the 'Cottage Garden' style. This deliberately unsophisticated development of the Jekyll principles depends for its effect upon the careful selection of plants and their use in conjunction with gardens like Mrs Fish's at East Lambrook. Many will regret the passing of Mrs Patrick Saunders, whose lovely little garden is at Orchard Cottage, Gretton, near Winchcombe. Sadly most gardens tend to die with their owners because they rely on constant personal attention. Of course there are other influences including the work of Russell Page and other garden designers, especially Harold Peto in an earlier generation. The effect of Graham Thomas' books on the wider use of herbaceous and ground-covering plants and old-fashioned roses has been considerable and in some cases his advice has been more direct. Nor is it difficult to detect Keith Steadman's effect on gardens in his immediate vicinity, an influence that is entirely desirable because it makes gardens of that area distinctive. Less desirable is the ever-increasing conformity in gardens that is encouraged by the mass media and the ever-narrowing range of plants offered by nurserymen and garden centres. We now see gardens polarizing into identifiable types according to the social ambitions, magazine reading, television interest and buying habits of the owners!

Among them the gardens in this book contain excellent examples of the whole range of garden features. Fine stonework, statuary and ornaments exist in too many gardens to mention but are a particular feature at The Courts, Iford Manor, Montacute and Orchardleigh Park. Although fewer in number, the grottoes include some of the finest in the country. As well as the famous examples at Stourhead and Bowood, there is the spectacular Goldney's Grotto in Bristol, which is open sometimes, a remarkable and seemingly little-known gothic grotto at Bowden Park and even a brand-new one at Bradley Court.

Somerset, Avon, Wiltshire and particularly Gloucestershire contain a vast range and number of gardens open to visitors at one time or another. In the summaries for each garden an abbreviated reference is given for further information on opening:

NGS — The National Gardens Scheme, 57 Lower Belgrave Street, London SW1W 0LR, publish annually the yellow book *Gardens Open to the Public in England and Wales,* containing information on over 1,250 gardens open primarily in aid of the Benevolent Funds of the Queen's Nursing Institute and also for the National Trust. The booklet is sold by most leading booksellers.

GS — The Gardeners' Sunday Organization, White Witches, Claygate Road, Dorking, Surrey, publish annually the green book *Gardens to Visit.* Gardens are open in aid of The Gardeners' Royal Benevolent Society and The Royal Gardeners' Orphan Fund and the booklet is also sold by booksellers and newsagents.

RC — The Red Cross, particularly Gloucestershire Branch, Red Cross House, Cainscross, Stroud, Glos., GL5 4JQ, is active in organizing the opening of gardens for its own funds. Also The British Red Cross Society, 9, Grosvenor Crescent, London, SW1X 7EJ.

HHCG — The booklet *Historic Houses, Castles and Gardens* is published annually by Historic Publications, Oldhill. London Road, Dunstable Beds., and contains details of opening for most properties regularly open, including those of the National Trust.

NT — The National Trust publishes its *Opening Arrangements* annually, free to members and also available to others from NT shops or from the National Trust, 42 Queen Anne's Gate, London SW1H 9AS. Membership of the National Trust entitles the member to free admission to all its properties in England, Wales and Northern Ireland, including more than 100 where there is a garden. A few gardens are open for local charities or in aid of such organizations as the Council for the Protection of Rural England.

SOILS AND GEOLOGY

The most notable characteristic of the soils of the region is their extreme diversity. The geological map shows that rocks from five major periods outcrop in the counties dealt with in this book. The formations are comprised of many and various sedimentary deposits laid down over a period spanning 265 million years. As a result of weathering, each type of rock has given rise to its own range of soil types thus creating an enormous diversity. Superficial deposits left by the action of wind and water play a smaller part than in most other regions of the country and glacial-derived soils are generally absent since the ice cap hardly penetrated into north Gloucestershire. Nevertheless there are alluvial deposits of sandy and silty soils along most of the river valleys, particularly in the Severn Vale and along the north coast of Somerset. The peaty soils formed in the bogs of the Somerset Levels add to the diversity of parent material.

The most recently-formed rocks are in Wiltshire where chalk covers almost the whole of the southern part, including Salisbury Plain. These scenically beautiful but often exposed downlands do not carry naturally fertile soils and most gardens in this area occur either in the river gravels of the Avon valley, where water is not far below the surface, or on the edge of the chalk where an entirely different type of rock outcrops. This is the Upper Greensand which forms an irregular western edge to the chalk, zigzagging from south of Swindon via Chippenham into the Vale of Pewsey, taking in parts of Bowood and Broadleas. It then swings out south-west to include Longleat and Stourhead, then south-east along the River Wylye almost to Salisbury before cutting back into Dorset. The soils derived from this form of sandstone are, from a horticultural point of view, in great contrast to the neighbouring chalk. They are generally deep, well drained and lime-free and particularly suitable for trees and shrubs, especially rhododendrons. The results of man's settlement has left the whole Greensand Ridge noticeably more densely wooded than the chalk and this produces the kind of dramatic scenery change that characterizes the English landscape.

Much of Gloucestershire, parts of Wiltshire, eastern Somerset and the Blackdown Hills in south Somerset are composed of the great belt of oolitic limestone that stretches from north Yorkshire via Lincoln, Northampton and Oxford and which has been so widely used as a building material. This Jurassic rock provides the single most important parent material for the soils found in gardens listed in this book. The soils derived from it vary from quite heavy and near neutral in the high north Cotswolds — at Hidcote, Kiftsgate and Abbotswood, where much of the lime has been leached out — to thin alkaline soils over broken limestone brash. This brash has a considerable water-holding capacity and is explored by the root systems of many plants but such soils are noticeably better in the valleys and produce good gardens when well worked and enriched.

Another group of Jurassic rocks are the Lias Clays of the upper Severn Valley and much of central Somerset where they are often covered with alluvial deposits of sand or silt. The Keuper Marls of an older geological period stretch over the lower Severn Valley and much of Avon and link up with the Lias Clays to create the impermeable bed of Sedgemoor in central Somerset. Once drained, these former peaty swamps become some of the richest agricultural land but they rarely contain good gardens, presumably because of the area's limited scenic value. Unlike farms, gardens tend to be made where people choose to live and the quality of the soil is usually fortuitous.

Carboniferous limestone outcrops in Avon and the Forest of Dean and forms the Mendip Hills. The Quantocks and the Brendon Hills of west Somerset are part of the even older Devonian period whose Old Red Sandstone makes up much of Devon. These rocks invariably give rise to lime-free soils but their fertility is very variable.

A brief description of the soils in each garden is given in the summary preceding each garden description.

Although the topography of the area is extremely varied few hills rise to more than 300m (about 1,000 ft). Only a few gardens are situated above 150m (about 500 ft) and these are mostly confined to the relatively shelter-ed north Cotswolds. The summary at the beginning of each garden account includes its approximate mean height above sea-level expressed in metres and feet.

The degree of exposure to wind, especially to westerly gales and to freezing north-easterlies, is one of the major limiting factors for plant growth and survival. Obviously this is affected by altitude and orientation but much more by the immediate surroundings, the 'microclimate', in which the plant lives. Choosing the ideal place, the perfect niche in the garden for each plant is one of the challenges that make gardening so absorbing. The close proximity of other plants not only gives shelter but also raises the humidity, this combined effect being most noticeable in woodland.

CLIMATE

The relatively mild maritime north temperate climate of the region combined with its wide range of soils makes it possible for an enormous variety of plants to be grown.

Perhaps the most critical limiting factor determining a plant's range is winter temperature. This is usually expressed as the average air temperature during the coldest month, i.e January, and by the length of the growing season. 'Growing season' is defined by the Ministry of Agriculture as those days in the year when the soil temperature at 300mm (1 ft) exceeds 6°C (42.8°F). Average values over ten seasons have been calculated for both of these measures of severity of climate.

Area	January average air temperature	Length of 'growing season'
1. Somerset	3.9°C (39°F)	269 days
2. Severn Valley of Glos., Avon and N.W. Wilts.	3.6°C (38.5°F)	263 days
3. Remainder of Wiltshire	3.4°C (38.1°F)	256 days
4. Cotswolds	2.9°C (37.2°F)	246 days

The sharp difference between the Cotswolds and other areas is an outstanding feature of the temperature pattern. A difference in the growing season of more than three weeks can be expected in Somerset compared with the Cotswolds, as well as a difference of 1°C between their average air temperatures in January. These factors have a profound effect upon plant growth and survival and account for considerable differences in the character of gardens east and west of the Cotswold scarp. The figures quoted are area averages but local variations of microclimate affect growing conditions to an even greater degree, thereby intensifying or modifying the regional trend. The proximity of the sea usually raises the average temperature and a south slope will give an extra 20 days growing season as well as a higher temperature. Dunster Castle is an example where these effects combine to modify further an already mild climate, making it possible to grow mimosa and even more tender plants outside and a lemon with only cold glass protection. At the other extreme every 100m (about 350ft) rise in altitude reduces the annual growing season by 20–25 days and the average temperature by O.6°C (1.8°F). The increased incidence of damaging late spring frosts in 'frost hollows' (where cold air comes in from higher levels and cannot drain away to lower levels) has to be taken into account and in some places, such as in Elwes' arboretum at Colesbourne between Cirencester and Cheltenham, it is common to experience ground frost in every month of the year.

Rainfall is locally highly variable. It is expressed in mm and inches as part of the summary at the beginning of each garden account. Here again average patterns are noticeable.

Area	Average annual precipitation
1. Somerset	865mm (34.06in.)
2. Severn Valley of Glos., Avon and N.W. Wilts	775mm (30.5in.)
3. Remainder of Wiltshire	799mm (31.45in.)
4. Cotswolds	726mm (28.6in.)

Not only is Somerset the warmest but it is also the wettest part of the region under consideration. The rainfall shows a similar progression as that for temperature from Somerset to the Cotswolds. Indeed the Cotswolds experience an altogether much sharper and more 'continental' climate which is as cold as Norfolk and as dry as east Kent.

The Gardens of Gloucestershire
and
North Avon

Hereford and Worcester

Bromesberrow Place

M50

Sheld
Nurse

Gloucest

·Amberley House
· Courtfield and Home Farm

WESTBURY COURT

M5

Painswick Garde
and House

Clearwell
Castle

·THE LEVEL

·FRAMPTON COU

Gwent

LYDNEY PARK

The Lammas, Hya
St. Francis Lamma

·BERKELEY CASTLE

·Owlpen M
BEVERSTON CAS
·BRADLEY COURT
Lasborough
Manor

STANCOMBE PARK·

ALDERLEY GRANGE →

M4

WESTONBIRT ARBORETUM & HOUS
WESTEND HOUSE· ·HILL HOUSE

ESSEX HOUSE, DOWER
HOUSE and Badminton
· Garden

Algars.
Manor

Oaklands·

River Severn

M5

LYEGROVE HOUSE
DODINGTON PARK

·VINE
HOUSE

M32

M4

·DYRHAM PARK

Bristol

Avon

· Springfield Barn

Bath

The map shows the following locations:

KIFTSGATE COURT
·HIDCOTE MANOR·
·HIDCOTE VALE
Burnt Norton·
Willersey House·
·The Grey House
Warmington
Grange
Stanton Gdns·
·SNOWSHILL
Stanway House· MANOR
·BATSFORD PARK ARBORETUM
·Little Orchard
BOURTON HOUSE·
shbury House SEZINCOTE·
·Little Barrow
Windy·
·SUDELEY Ridge ·Broadwell Manor·
Celtenham CASTLE and Lodge
ABBOTSWOOD· ·NEWLANDS
·Bledington Village Gardens
Brook Cottage·
Upper Slaughter·
Manor House
·Notgrove and
Leygore Gdns.
·GREAT RISSINGTON MANOR
be Park Withington Gardens
Stowell Park · ·Sherbourne House
Fossbridge Gardens· ·Eastington Gardens
DEN PARK ·Winson Mill Farm Oxfordshire
ld Farm· North Cerney Gdns.
bourne·
Gardens ·Bagendon House
CIRENCESTER ·BARNSLEY ·Colne St. Aldwyns Gardens
Gardens HOUSE & PARK ·Southrop Gardens
·PARK
·Barton ·YEW TREE COTTAGE
Mill ·Paulton House
RODMARTON
·MANOR ·Ewen Manor ·Marston Meysey Gardens
SOM
TCOURT GRANGE Wiltshire
GES BARN and
Cottage and Idlwyld

Scale: 0   5   10   15   20   25   30 kilometres
        0   5   10   15 miles

The Gardens of

GLOUCESTERSHIRE
AND NORTH AVON

Abbotswood

Dikler Farming Co. (Mr R.F. Scully)

1.6 km (1 Mile) from Stow-on-the-Wold on B4077 Tewkesbury Road in Lower Swell. Extensive garden of about 4 ha (10 acres); formal terraces, herbaceous borders, large rock garden, trees and shrubs, park and lake, surrounding 1867 house altered by Sir Edwin Lutyens in 1902. Open at least three times a year in spring for NGS, GS and RC. Heavy clay soil over N. Cotswold limestone but leached and not highly alkaline. On south-west slope at 167mm (550ft). Rainfall 787mm (31ins.). Maintained at a high standard by a head gardener, Mr Smalley, three full-time assistants, and two part-time helpers.

Early in the century the late Mark Fenwick employed Sir Edwin Lutyens to alter Abbotswood, a manor house of warm-coloured north Cotswold stone. The architect extended the house and created a series of broad, dignified terraces to link the house brilliantly to the sloping site. The lines of the house are projected with such skill and the whole composition of walls, steps, pools and summerhouse so finely balanced and detailed that this must rank among the most successful of Lutyens' garden works.

Mr Mark Fenwick was one of the great gardeners of the period between the wars. On this superb site, with its magnificent Cotswold view towards the Slaughters and the upper reaches of the River Windrush, he created a garden of immense variety and cohesion.

Although exposed to the south, much of the garden is protected by a belt of tall beech trees to the north and east and by a spinney of oaks, beeches, ashes and evergreens to the west, straddling the stream below the rock garden. The park below the garden is finely grazed by sheep among venerable oaks, and a broad tributary of the Windrush flows through a well-formed lake (made by Mrs Harry Ferguson in the late 1950s when she owned the house) glints in the valley.

From the car park the garden is approached by way of a copse west of the house in which the banks of a splashing stream are massed with naturalized bulbs, well-planted drifts of *Narcissus* cultivars including 'Bartley', *Scilla* spp. and *Anemone appenina*, and wild colonies of bluebells, primroses and Wood Anemones. At the stream edges the bold yellow tongues of the Bog Arum, *Lysichitum americanum*, are a striking accent in spring while higher up the bank are Japanese Maples for autumn colour. Look out for the lavender-coloured *Lathraea clandestina*, a dwarf parasitic plant growing on the roots of ash.

Eventually the stream emerges into the open where it has been cunningly employed in an extensive rock garden which straddles the drive north and west of the house. Below the drive the water cascades steeply into two pools formed with Cotswold limestone and planted with more Bog Arums and the contrasting leaf shapes of *Peltiphyllum peltatum*, bamboos, dwarf junipers and other conifers, azaleas and *Bergenia cordifolia*. Above the drive the rock garden proper is of Westmorland limestone and with its expertly arranged outcrops of rock and scree set in an alpine meadow and linked by meandering streams, it must rank high among the many fine examples made between the wars when rock garden construction was at its highest level in art and craftsmanship. The grass is thick with fritillaries, squills, anemones, dwarf narcissus, crocuses and snowflakes, *Leucojum vernum* and *L. aestivum*. Heathers are a feature and acid soil areas have been made to accommodate the lings and *Erica vagans* as well as the winter-flowering kinds. Also in peaty beds are acid-loving dwarf rhododendrons, *R. scintillans* and *R. impeditum, Pieris floribunda* and *Lithospermum diffusum*. All this and much more leads up to a thatched hut of sandstone surrounded by the fragrant white *Osmanthus delavayi*; a splendid place to rest and admire the view.

Surrounding the rock garden and house both to the west and to the north and east is a well-stocked arboretum, now becoming somewhat overcrowded, containing a remarkable collection of trees and shrubs. Here grow many fine conifers: *Calocedrus decurrens*, Blue Atlantic Cedars, Monterey Pine, Dawn Redwood, the gracefully pendulous *Picea brewerana* and *Chamaecyparis nootkatensis* 'Pendula'. There is interest for every season, with cherries including the early-flowering *Prunus yedoensis*, many magnolias, the Handkerchief Tree and the Judas Tree for spring; *Acer griseum, Gleditsia triacanthos, Liquidambar styraciflua* and *Parrotia persica* for autumn. There is a fine specimen of the Southern Beech, *Nothofagus procera* and east of the formal garden the rare Willow Oak, *Quercus phellos*, and several other unusual species. Below this the planting grades down to a heather garden, now rather overgrown, overlooking the formal terraces and the elegant conservatory.

The house, which is covered with wistaria, Virginia Creeper and *Clematis montana*, opens south on to an upper terrace with sun-loving irises, Rosemary and *Nerine bowdenii* against the house walls. The rectangular middle terrace on the second level is the width of the house and each quarter is arranged in a pattern of heart-shaped beds around clipped yews and planted with herbaceous subjects, roses, bedding plants and

bulbs. In the centre is a fine sundial of which the gnomon is supported by three cherubs. On either side of this terrace stand narrow rectangular sections each planted as a knot of dwarf box-edged beds surrounding a stone jar and an urn, with roses and bedding. I remember a striking combination of purple-tipped clary with silver *Senecio cineraria* in these beds.

The lowest terrace is much wider and in simple contrast to the others, being dominated by a central, long rectangular pool with apsidal-shaped ends, a central statue and two small fountains. Around the edge a low wall supports a terrace walk decorated with aubrietias, pinks and veronicas. In front of this lie herbaceous borders for mixed summer and autumn effect: campanulas, Michaelmas Daisies, phloxes, delphiniums, Day Lilies, Globe Thistles and *Alchemilla mollis*. Roses and vines have been used to embellish the finely-dressed, capped stone walls. In the south-west corner and balancing the natural fall of the land in this direction is a charming gazebo, a cool spot on even the hottest day.

The west lawn is clumped with hardy hybrid rhododendrons no doubt growing in imported soil and peat. But as at Hidcote the soil here, although on limestone, is near neutral. The lawn is linked imaginatively to the house by means of a walled canal garden that can also be viewed from the terrace above. Here a Keystone fountain in the wall dips into a small circular pool to make dancing, reflected patterns on the concave shape inset into the house wall behind. Extending from this is a narrow canal with small groups of irises and water lilies at the edges. Sheltered by flanking walls, the effect is tranquil and lovely — possibly the true genesis of gardening.

Alderley Grange
Mr Guy and the Hon. Mrs Acloque

At Alderley, 3.2km (2 miles) equidistant from Upton, Hawkesbury and Wotton-under-Edge, turn NW off A46 Bath-Stroud Road at Dunkirk. Open twice in summer for NGS and local charities. Intensively-planted walled garden of about 0.8ha (2 acres) around Jacobean house with classical facade. Situated at 122m (400ft) on well-drained heavy soil over Cotswold limestone. Rainfall 838mm (33in). One full-time gardener.

It is one thing to make a garden but quite another to take over a highly personal and intensively planted garden and keep it lively and fresh, especially when the style is such that constant reworking and rethinking are essential for success. In ten years after 1961 Alvilde Lees-Milne created the garden at Alderley Grange brilliantly in a development of the Hidcote/Sissinghurst style and the new owners have succeeded in the difficult task of continuing where she left off. Garden conservation demands an eye sensitive to the happy accident and, most difficult of all, to the gradual changes of scale that come from overgrowth and maturity. It needs a streak of ruthlessness and a willingness to keep experimenting within a given theme of colour and form. But Mr and Mrs Lees-Milne also took over a legacy of the past in that the eminent botanist B.H. Hodgson, of *Rhododendron Lodgsonii* fame, lived here for 30 years in the mid-nineteenth century and no doubt some of the older trees are of his planting.

The garden is enclosed by walls and sheltered by trees especially on the western road boundary in front of the house where tall birches, poplars, yews and Holm Oaks have been supplemented with cherries, variegated maples, *Liquidambar styraciflua* and *Parrotia persica.*

On the enclosed south side the best advantage has been taken of a small but sunny spot for a tiny paved sitting-place surrounded by the cool whiteness of rose 'Iceberg', white Rugosa roses, Madonna Lilies and white variegated *Aralia elata* with a lavender hedge. The white and silver theme is repeated all around with purple, mauve and pink for contrast. A striking border of silvers, Cotton Lavender, Lad's Love, *Anaphalis margaritacea* and *Senecio* 'Sunshine' contrasts with clipped balls of box. Recently the much maligned and neglected Evening Primrose has been justly included for its long succession of pale yellow flowers.

The main lawn is east of the house and enclosed by high walls entirely covered by climbers, old roses like 'Madame Grégoire Staechelin', clematises, *Ceanothus* spp., the blue potato-like flowers of *Solanum crispum*, the dusky purple *Vitis vinifera* 'Purpurea' and many others with shade-loving *Hedera canariensis* 'Variegata' and climbing hydrangeas conspicuous on the north-facing wall. Shrubs like the Mexican Orange, Laurustinus, *Garrya elliptica* and the lustrous-leaved *Viburnum cinnamomifolium* form bold buttresses with *Geranium macrorrhizum*, bergenias, hostas and ferns between. Here is wall gardening at its best. Facing south with a wall behind is a broad border of roses and shrubs edged sensibly with paving to allow the front plants to sprawl. The colours are soft — pink, white, mauve and pale yellow — with purple and silver foliage: a favourite and successful theme for gardens of this style. It is applied here with great skill and imagination using mostly Hybrid Musk roses, Gallicas and other shrub roses with a few larger shrubs such as *Abutilon vitifolium* and *Mahonia lomariifolia* and purple foliage. *Alchemilla mollis*, *Ballota pseudodictamnus*, *Santolina neapolitana* and campanulas spill over at the front.

A large Indian Bean Tree, probably planted by B.H. Hodgson, dominates the lawn. Many other trees have been planted and some thinning will be needed to prevent the bigger trees like poplar and maple swamping all. The old apples, some used as supports for vigorous climbing roses, are gradually reaching the end of their lives to make way for flowering trees, magnolia and mulberry.

Through a gate in the wall on the south side is a total change of atmosphere with narrow paved paths edged with a collection of old pinks and lined with pleached limes that are also trained across to form living arches. Fragrance is everywhere and between the limes glimpses of full-blown shrub roses can be seen. At the crossing of paths the impossible choice is presented of either enjoying the charming little lily pool surrounded by camomile and paving with sunloving *Cistus* spp. behind or of opting for the fascinating star-like herb garden. Although small in scale this herbary must rank among the finest of its kind, being simple in concept, original in design, superb in detail and meticulous in upkeep. The design consists of eight segments edged with dwarf box radiating from a central sundial with narrow brick paths. The planting includes an enormous range of herbs and builds up in height from the centre to the outside where 'Isphahan' roses, one in each bed, lend unity to the scheme.

An intriguing little gate leads on into a charmingly unsophisticated cottage garden where the gardener grows splendid roses and sweet peas among his broad beans and enjoys the finest view out into the valley beyond the garden.

There is also a little kitchen garden to admire, and other borders and small enclosed gardens north of the house to explore, all full of stimulating ideas for the discerning gardener. For Jubilee year (1977) and to recall the days of the first Queen Elizabeth a little orchard of medlars, filberts and quinces was planted.

Enclosed gardens are necessarily introspective and deliberate but the danger of the planting appearing too obviously self-conscious has been cleverly offset by allowing an apparently casual profusion.

Algars Manor

John M. Naish Esq.

Open for NGS in spring. At Iron Acton, 4.8km (3 miles) W of Yate; N of Bristol. Informal and woodland garden of 1.2ha (3 acres) beside the River Frome and around unpretentious Jacobean house and barn of great beauty. Fine gates and ball-topped gate posts. Mill-race and leat from adjacent Mill through water meadow.

Despite loss of elms there are fine trees, including Weeping Silver Lime, Atlas Cedar, Red Oak and many young ones planted. On the acid soil and steep slopes to the river a wide range of flowering trees and shrubs have been planted, e.g. magnolias in variety, camellias, rhododendrons and azaleas, all among wild and naturalized plants in an atmosphere of relaxed informality.

Amberley House

Mrs Brookbank

Open for GS in summer. At Hasfield 12.8km (8 miles) W of Gloucester. Small garden of shrubs, shrub roses and ground covers made since 1973 in a setting of mature trees around a Georgian house.

Badminton Gardens

A group of gardens open for NGS in summer, including THE DOWER HOUSE and ESSEX HOUSE (see under Dower House, Badminton). BADMINTON HOUSE (The Duke and Duchess of Beaufort) has large ornamental grounds including some fine trees — especially Copper Beech, Oriental Plane and conifers — and a Victorian layout incorporating a classical Orangery by John Webb (1818), where tea is served.

The magnificent and historic park was altered from the G. London and H. Wise geometrical layout, illustrated by Kip in Atkyns' *The Ancient and Present State of Glostershire* (1712), by William Kent just before the middle of the eighteenth–century. Kent also built the spectacular Worcester Lodge which can be seen from the Tetbury road, at the end of the 4.8km (3 mile) ride, directly in line with the north front of the house. The park is said to have been further altered to the English Landscape style by Lancelot Brown later in the eighteenth-century. It is not open except on the annual occasion of the Horse Trials, but the house is open (see HHCG). THE OLD VICARAGE (Colonel and Mrs Guinness) has a pretty walled garden in a picturesque setting.

Bagendon House

Mr and Mrs C.G. Leach

Open for NGS in summer. At Bagendon, 3.2km (2 miles) N of Cirencester. Garden of 1.9ha (4.7 acres) on south slope surrounding Cotswold stone late-Georgian house, formerly the Rectory.

The attractive cream-painted house with its overhanging eaves and stone quoins is dominated by two splendid trees, a magnificent Cedar of Lebanon on one side and a huge Copper Beech, of which there are more in the garden, on the other. From here is a lovely view over the valley while a beautiful stone summerhouse, facing east, affords a sheltered place to sit. Contiguous with the house is a conservatory, crammed Victorian style with all kinds of treasures in pots; a large Bougainvillaea revels in the sun and Cherry Pie scents the air.

The garden would seem to have been laid out after the house was extended in 1846. East of the house the steep bank has been embellished with new borders in colours of gold and purple and silver and *Cupressus sempervirens*, the tender Italian Cypress, rises up behind. On the slope above, the Victorian character is most evident. Mysterious narrow paths edged neatly with Dagham stone wind through shrubberies and laurels, all in the melancholy shade of Copper Beeches. Best of all is a Victorian fern dell with a pool and rocky grotto and winter heliotrope all around. Nearby is a little formal rose garden with the beds edged in Dwarf Box.

Right at the top is a colourful rose and herbaceous walk and a very well cultivated kitchen garden with excellent vegetables and a glasshouse surrounded by *Crinum powellii* and auriculas.

Barnsley House

Mr and Mrs David Verey

At Barnsley, 6.5km (4 miles) NE of Cirencester, on east side of A433 Burford Road. For opening arrangements see HHCG, NGS and GS; every Wednesday throughout the growing seasons. Intensive garden of about 1.4ha (3½ acres) around beautiful late-seventeenth-century former rectory of Cotswold stone, altered in 1830. Well-drained alkaline soil over Cotswold limestone, partly terraced on a westerly slope at 137m (450 ft). Rainfall 813mm (32 ins). Mrs Verey and one full-time gardener. Many unusual plants for sale.

With gardening, as with other great arts, there is danger in generalization. Yet how often one hears the facile observation that all gardeners fall into one of two categories: plantsmen and designers. It is often those who consider themselves to be in the latter category who repeat this threadbare notion, perhaps as a means of justifying the poverty of their own schemes. Certainly it is possible to create fine designs, both formal and informal, with a minimum of variety and this has been proven by the great names of the eighteenth-century. But the real challenge in gardening is to achieve a satisfying, coherent design while using a large variety of plants; to make each interesting detail read as part of the whole. This is the great achievement of the British artist-plantsmen and women of the twentieth-century: Gertrude Jekyll, Lawrence Johnston, Vita Sackville-West and others. It is the reason why they stand head and shoulders above those who think solely in terms of clipped bay trees and pleached limes and those who classify plants arbitrarily into those that are design-worthy and those that are not.

Rosemary Verey is indeed a worthy successor in the honourable British tradition of artist-gardeners. But more than that she has a strong feeling for history both in her garden and as revealed in her wonderful collection of ancient gardening books. Perhaps this is why the garden at Barnsley House so successfully combines a respect for the achievements of past owners with a variety of new features added since 1960. Like many other great gardens this one was made by a combination of talents: David Verey contributing his architectural concern for the structure and progression of spaces and with the incorporation of garden buildings, and Rosemary Verey exercising her adventurous talent for designing with plants.

The Vereys would be the first to acknowledge their debt to the past. There is the house itself, so long a rectory, with its charming castellated verandah; the superb eighteenth-century summerhouse; also the large trees, especially the limes, planes, oaks and beeches which shelter the garden and frame the approach. A succession of clergymen each made

Above: Barnsley House. Profuse planting spills onto the paving from borders and tubs around the garden door.

Left: Berkeley Castle. The formal lily pool garden with a glimpse of the castle beyond. *Iris Hardwick*

their own contribution until it was bought by Mr Verey's father in 1939. After Mr and Mrs Verey took up residence in 1951, garden development began slowly while they learned more about gardening and while their young family grew up. But during the 1960s and 1970s the pace quickened; as they gained expertise so their enthusiasm grew until now they have a garden which is crammed with plants and which reflects a wealth of ideas.

From the road the house is made to seem taller by its position above a bank. This vertical effect is emphasized by a pattern of alternate 'Ellwoodii' cypresses and Cotton Lavenders planted below the higher of two terrace walls built by the Vereys immediately under the house to replace a series of small terraces. The approach has been kept simple and park-like with the house framed by magnificent trees under which early bulbs, cyclamen and hellebores grow. The grass sweeps up the slope past a picturesque False Acacia to the side of the house where the 'Strawberry Hill gothic' summerhouse acts as a focal point.

Beyond the lush green lawn on this south-western side of the house Mr and Mrs Verey have planted an interesting mixture of more unusual trees including maples and rowans and the sumptuous *Paulownia tomentosa*. A new addition is a stone sculpture by Simon Verity of a lady in hunting clothes, placed apparently casually in the shrubs but actually aligned with great cunning to give an exciting peep between hedges from the flower garden. Near the house, and related in shape and size to the castellated verandah, is Mrs Verey's knot garden: two intricate designs from her library worked in box and *Teucrium chamaedrys* and set appropriately in a clipped outer hedge of Rosemary. The verandah is roofed with the Strawberry Grape and the house walls are generously draped with climbing roses, wisteria, clematises, honeysuckles and *Solanum crispum* in controlled disarray. This exuberance is repeated in the borders below, which overflow on to the terrace, and in the fascinating variety of tubs and pots which spill their fragrant confections of geranium, Lemon Verbena and the like on to the paving.

The main flower garden is south-east of the house. A paved path, too flowery with Sun Roses to walk upon and guarded by pairs of Irish Yews, links the door of the house to a gate in the garden wall and gives the lawn a backbone. Always there are these firm, orderly vistas drawing together the extraordinary complexity of the planting. The borders all around burgeon with beautiful things arranged with that apparently casual elegance that distinguishes the highest skills of the English cottage-garden style. That most elusive of objectives, the all-seasons border, is here achieved but not without diligence. At any time of the year the garden is of interest because not an inch is wasted and the principle of succession is practised as well as understood. Like all good gardens it is always developing and a recent addition is a little geometrical herb plot set sensibly and effectively in paving.

The other main axis of the flower garden, at right angles to the Irish Yews, is also arranged with considerable cunning to make it look much longer than it is in reality. At one end is a fine Tuscan Doric Temple of 1787 brought from Fairford Park and re-erected in 1962, with a lily pool containing goldfish set before it for reflections. This paved area is rich with a variety of mostly yellow and white flowered plants and the pool is furnished with irises and bergenias and with other waterside plants for foliage contrast. The effect is light and open; it is a place to sit and enjoy the afternoon sun. The vista along which it looks begins with low hedges of Miss Jessop's Rosemary and Lad's Love but beyond the flagged path there are pleached limes on one side and a progressively higher border of gold and green with deep purple accents on the other. This subtle use of the false perspective also has the effect of reducing the apparent scale at the end, around Simon Verity's fountain piece, a tablet of fossil-filled Purbeck stone depicting a pair of rams. In contrast to the opposite end all around is cool and moist with big-leaved *Ligularia*, *Senecio*, *Hosta*, Tree Paeonies and variegated ivies.

Running almost parallel is, in season, perhaps the most spectacular feature in a garden of surprises. Pleached limes close in and lead to a tunnel of *Laburnum* 'Vossii' dripping with gold, underplanted with a mass of white-variegated hostas and the tall lavender-flowered *Allium aflatunense* — an inspired piece of planting.

But there is much more to see: a new potager, the nursery, roses and clematises. Every corner and every wall is planted and every plant is loved and cherished. This is a true gardeners' garden, inward looking and expressing the enthusiasm of the owners. It is a garden for continuous enjoyment and always worth another visit.

Barnsley Park
The Lord Faringdon

NE side of Barnsley village, 7.2km (4½ miles) NE of Cirencester on A433 road to Bibury. Open once a year in summer for NGS. Formal garden of 4ha (10 acres), Orangery and walled garden around important Georgian baroque house. Situated at 152m (500ft) in landscaped park, well-drained heavy soil over limestone. Rainfall 813mm (32 ins). Maintained by two gardeners.

Lord and Lady Faringdon have wisely made a garden to complement, rather than to compete with, the exquisite Vanburgh-like house of the early-eighteenth-century. Each of the three principal fronts has been given a different formal layout as a fitting transition to the late-eighteenth-century landscaped park beyond the ha-ha.

The west entrance front is framed by ancient yew trees and has tubs of Agapanthus and a border of coloured foliage — gold, purple and silver — nearby. It looks out down a broad vista of splendid young beeches to a parkland valley beyond the ha-ha.

Facing south is the most beautiful garden front of the house where there are splendid urns and Victorian cast-iron fern seats on the shallow terrace, and croquet on the lawn gives a pleasing country-house touch. Beyond is a trim vista of beech hedges backed by trees and bordered by rose beds of 'Queen Elizabeth' and 'Iceberg'. The hedges have niches for statues and open into a curving amphitheatre studded with mature limes and a fine old walnut. Crossing this main avenue are smaller *allées* forming a 'goose foot' of linked walks with ornaments at each *rond-point*.

The east front faces a rectangular lawn leading to a narrow vista of poplars through the apsidal-shaped far end and nearby there is a shady duck-pond. The classical Orangery near the house is amply stocked with superb fruiting orange-trees and a variety of tender plants and climbers: trumpet-flowered *Datura suavolens*, the sky-blue of *Plumbago capensis*, Passion Flowers and fuchsias.

The separate walled garden brims full of flowers for cutting and vegetables among box hedges and roses. It also manages to accommodate tennis-courts and a swimming-pool. The lean-to greenhouse range is a joy with expertly-grown geraniums arranged on tiered shelves, orchids, houseplants, fuchsias and vines.

Barton Mill House
Mrs Mullings

Open for NGS in summer. In Cirencester; Barton Lane, off Gloucester Street. Medium-sized garden with wildfowl, and the river running through, around old Cotswold mill-house, part of which is also opened. This is a colourful garden with streamside planting, herbaceous plants, dahlias and roses.

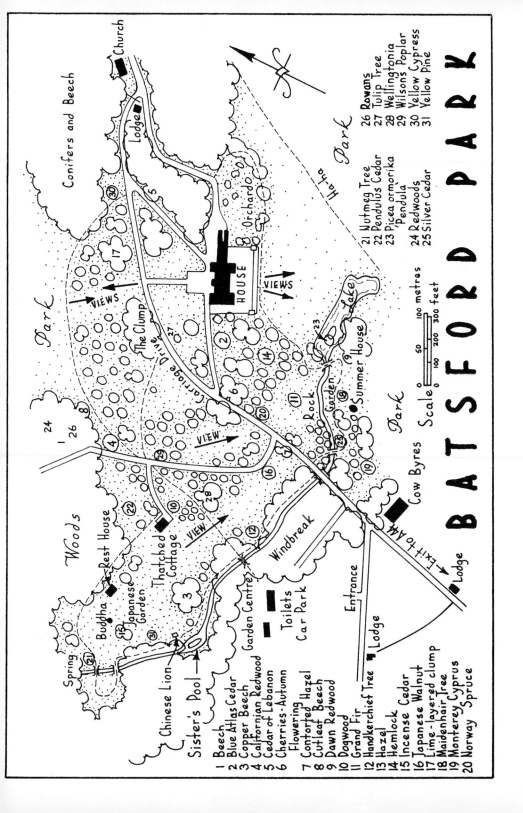

BATSFORD PARK

1 Beech
2 Blue Atlas Cedar
3 Copper Beech
4 Californian Redwood
5 Cedar of Lebanon
6 Cherries - Autumn
   Flowering
7 Contorted Hazel
8 Cutleaf Beech
9 Dawn Redwood
10 Dogwood
11 Grand Fir
12 Handkerchief Tree
13 Hazel
14 Hemlock
15 Incense Cedar
16 Japanese Walnut
17 Lime-layered clump
18 Maidenhair Tree
19 Monterey Cyprus
20 Norway Spruce

21 Nutmeg Tree
22 Pendulus Cedar
23 Picea ormorika
   'Pendula'
24 Redwoods
25 Silver Cedar

26 Rowans
27 Tulip Tree
28 Wellingtonia
29 Wilsons Poplar
30 Yellow Cypress
31 Yellow Pine

Scale

0   50   100 metres
0 100 200 300 feet

Batsford Park Arboretum

Batsford Estates Company and Lord and Lady Dulverton

2.4km (1½ miles) NW of Moreton-in-Marsh, park drive on north side of A44 Evesham road near Bourton-on-the-Hill. Opening arrangements in HHCG normally April-October daily; also for NGS, GS and RC. 20ha (50 acre) garden arboretum around large Elizabethan-style house of late-nineteenth century by Sir Ernest George and Harold Peto. Situated at 229m (750ft) on south-facing slope overlooking the Vale of Evenlode. Free-draining alkaline soil over Cotswold limestone on high ground becoming heavy clay in the valley. Rainfall 762mm (30in.). Good guide book available. Garden Centre in walled garden. Three gardeners.

Although the Freeman family had owned the estate since the fifteenth-century, it was Algernon Bertram Freeman-Mitford, later Lord Redesdale, who around 1890 rebuilt the house and laid out the extensive garden. He had been an attaché in the British Embassy in Tokyo where he was influenced by the Oriental approach to garden design and by the mountain landscape and rich flora of Asia Minor and Japan. This inspired him to create a picturesque garden landscape comprising carefully-composed groupings of rock and water, and buildings and ornaments embellished by a remarkable range of trees and shrubs, including many natives of China and Japan. Not for him the stiff formality of the Victorian bedding schemes with their ostentatious displays of tender exotics; indeed Lord Redesdale was part of the reactionary school of thought (of which William Robinson was *the* exponent) who upheld the naturalistic use of plants. At Batsford the 'Wild Garden' was taken further than the mere use of plants according to their natural requirements: an inspired composition of plant form and variety enhanced the natural advantages of the site. Behind the house, trees were grouped to emphasize the hillocks and to frame a splendid view of the house seen against the hazy Evenlode valley in the distance. In an area high to the north-west Lord Redesdale made a Japanese garden around a Japanese Rest-house, a bronze Buddha and several Japanese animals in bronze. He linked this to the rest by taming a stream along the south-west boundary and leading this through a rock garden to a lake below the house. Beyond the stream he wisely planted a thick shelter belt of trees to break the south-west winds to which the garden would otherwise be exposed. This enabled the cultivation of a wide range of trees many of which have now matured into immense specimens and impressive groups. He also planted many shrubs, especially bamboos, for which the garden became famous. Lord Redesdale wrote an essay on Wild Gardens which explains the philosophy behind his highly successful work.

Between 1920 and the outbreak of war in 1939 the garden was cared for by the late Lady Dulverton, who made a number of additions. But thereafter and until 1956, when the present Lord Dulverton succeeded, it fell into a state of considerable neglect. He courageously decided to reclaim the wilderness and expand the tree collection into what has become an outstanding arboretum. Building upon the framework of Lord Redesdale's, and even older, trees he reclaimed overgrown areas, opened vistas and planted many hundreds of species and varieties particularly of maples, oaks, limes, spruces and pines. An enormous wealth of trees is here, including many beautiful and unjustly neglected subjects as well as the rare and the curious. It is now a living catalogue and an ideal reference collection for students of horticulture and arboriculture. Lord Dulverton is confident that the open spaces, which are so well in scale with the older specimens, can be retained by pruning and thinning but any possible loss here is amply offset by the interest and excitement of seeing so much variety in such close proximity.

The guidebook gives a good description of the garden arboretum and is an ample guide to its contents. It is worth visiting at any season, even in winter when the conifers can be enjoyed to the full. There is a superb cluster of Wellingtonias, and of Blue Lebanon Cedars, Californian Redwoods, a splendid group of *Chamaecyparis lawsoniana* 'Erecta Viridis', Grand Firs, Incense Cedars, Western Hemlocks, *Pinus parviflora*, *P. ponderosa* and *P. excelsa*, and many more evergreens contrasting with the bark and stem effects of birches and dogwoods. Spring is of course a joy in any arboretum but especially at Batsford when the many Japanese Cherries, over forty species of *Magnolia*, the Handkerchief Tree, *Davidia involucrata*, and masses of naturalized bulbs are coming into bloom. But my favourite time to visit is October when the whole place lights up against the sombre background of conifers to give one great spectacle of autumn tints; scarlet and orange from Japanese Maples; burnt umber from Red Oaks; pure gold from the Maidenhair Tree; the pale yellow tracery of *Cercidiphyllum japonicum*; an enormous scarlet vine, *Vitis coignetiae*, clambering through a yew; and many more shades of colour from oaks, chestnuts, beeches, Tulip Tree and walnuts, not forgetting a group of the Autumn Cherry, *Prunus subhirtella* 'Autumnalis', seen against a background of Blue Atlas Cedars.

Berkeley Castle
Mr and Mrs R.V. Berkeley

S edge of the town of Berkeley, N of A28 road midway between Bristol and Gloucester. For opening arrangements see HHCG, normally daily except Mondays but afternoons only in spring and autumn. Terraced garden of 3.2ha (8 acres) around twelfth-century fortified castle commanding the Severn Vale; at 30-46m (100-150ft) on heavy soil made up on terraces facing south and east. Windy but otherwise favourable site for tender plants. Rainfall 838mm (33in.). Maintained by a staff of two. Good general guidebook to the Castle available.

The terraces at Berkeley Castle were planted by the present owner's father, Major Robert Berkeley, who also developed the plant collection at Spetchley Park, one of the great gardens of Worcestershire. Both gardens are a testimony to his zeal as a collector and his skill as a plantsman. That Ellen Willmott of Warley Place, Essex, was his aunt, and that Gertrude Jekyll and Vita Sackville-West were visitors, all show in the disposition of the wide range of plants, making the most of every opportunity to embellish this romantic place.

From the car park the approach is beneath walnuts and mature beech trees underplanted with yews, all of which form valuable shelter north of the garden. Entry from the town would be up a long ramp past the church and through the Gatehouse to the gravel forecourt. To the south — below the ramp, forecourt and Castle walls — are the garden terraces overlooking the water-meadows of the Berkeley Vale where the gothic stables of the Berkeley Hunt catch the eye.

The fascinating variety of the plants is lent unity by the simplicity of the layout, three terraces falling away steeply to the south. Exotic plants bask in the reflected warmth of the ancient walls and flow from the borders on to the path. The top border has climbing roses including 'New Dawn', hardy fuchsias, yuccas, tobacco plants and *Ceanothus thyrsiflorus* 'Repens', and in a specially sheltered corner are tender *Cestrum* spp. and *Corokia cotoneaster*.

The second terrace border billows out over the gravel path with bergenias, tree paeonies and *Salvia haematodes* and is dominated by a venerable fig and the large-leaved *Magnolia grandiflora*. This terrace leads west to the sheltered bowling-alley protected on one side by a high hedge and on the other by the high wall of the gatehouse ramp which also supports an exotic profusion of high-climbing plants such as *Rosa banksiae*, *Vitis coignetiae*, climbing hydrangea, large-leaved ivies, clematises and *Eucalyptus globulus*. In front is a mixed border where the hardy orange *Poncirus trifoliata*, the dwarf pomegranate *Punica granatum* 'Nanum' and fragrant evergreen *Osmanthus delavayi* are prominent. The second terrace also leads right around the Castle to the east where the planting is truly inspired, there being striking associations of bold-leaved plants entirely in scale with the rugged Castle walls: Red-hot pokers and *Yucca filamentosa* bristle next to the silvery softness of *Cytisus battandieri* and the broad-leaved pattern of *Acanthus mollis*. Many *Cistus* spp. revel in the hot sun with prickly *Colletia* spp. and an enormous wistaria with an equally tall *Magnolia delavayi* tower over all. There are more delights in store on the east-facing side with broad buttresses of *Choisya ternata*, buddleias, *Escallonia* and *Olearia* spp. and *Clerodendrum bungei* scenting the air and *Macleaya cordata* filling the spaces between.

The third terrace is wider and grassier and at the corner of the Castle a fine old fallen mulberry crouches over a well. The buttressed walls are decorated with *Ceanothus* in many species and cultivars, and there is a jolly mixture of the Mexican Orange with *Clematis* 'Jackmanii' and *Hedera colchica* 'Dentata Variegata' by the steps. This terrace leads west into the formal water garden which was once a swimming-pool and now sports water lilies and goldfish, and gives fine reflections and one of the best views of the Castle with church and old Scots Pines in the foreground. The balustraded terrace leads to steps dignified by a formal arrangement of Irish Yews but sadly the topiary elephants that once loomed over the pool have gone.

At the bottom is a broad tilt-yard lawn enclosed by a vast hedge of Handsworth box with towering Wellingtonias at one end and old Holm Oaks at the other. All around are groups of shrubs and specimen trees such as *Acer hersii*. From here Gertrude Jekyll's description of the Castle still rings true '. . . it looks like some great fortress roughly hewn out of natural rock. Nature would seem to have taken back to herself the masses of stone reared seven-and-a-half centuries ago. The giant walls and mighty buttresses look as if they have been carved by wind and weather out of some solid rock-mass, rather than wrought by human handiwork'.

Beverston Castle

Major and Mrs L. Rook

At Beverstone, 2.4km (1½ miles) W of Tetbury on A4135 road to Dursley. Mainly informal garden of 1.25ha (3¼ acres), mostly south of seventeenth-century Cotswold stone house and remains of thirteenth and fourteenth-century Castle and Gatehouse. Open two or three times per year in summer for NGS and RC Situated at 153m (500ft) on well-drained soil over limestone. Rainfall 813mm (32in.). Maintained by the owners and one full-time gardener.

One quality of the corporate English character, which comes through in its gardens, is the ideal of achieving much without seeming to try too hard. At Beverston Castle the atmosphere of antiquity is strengthened by the presence of fine mature beeches and yews and given charm by the seemingly casual but sensitive planting. The free and unforced effect is entirely successful, especially near the house.

Along the approach, past ponies and the clustered barns of a working farm, is a splendid first view of the Castle Tower through an old gateway decorated with 'François Juranville' roses. The verge widens into a green, shaded by ancient walnuts, leading to the fourteenth-century gatehouse and courtyard, south of which is the seventeenth-century house and then the garden.

Undoubtedly the most beautiful part of the garden is the paved terrace which faces south and occupies the interval between house and what remains of the Castle moat. Sheltered by a venerable old yew wreathed with the autumn-colouring vine *Vitis coignetiae* on one side and beeches to the west, it is a haven of fragrant peacefulness. The soft-leaved *Alchemilla mollis*, with thymes and species of *Sisyrinchium* and *Campanula* fill the crevices, building up to a scattering of shrubs, all distinguished by their long period of decorative effect: *Choisya ternata*, purple *Cotinus coggygria*, *Senecio* 'Sunshine', *Potentilla fruticosa* and *Hebe rakaiensis*. On the house wall, in well-planned disarray, are magnolias, summer Jasmine, clematises, honeysuckles and old roses like 'Albertine', while tumbling over the edge of the moat are the huge leaves of *Actinidia chinensis* and *Rosa paulii*.

Enjoying the dampness of the moat, which curves around to the west are dogwoods and yellow flag irises with the vigorous *Rosa brunonii* 'La Mortola' smothering an old holly, and lilacs and buddleias on drier ground. Overlooking the moat is a small eighteenth-century gazebo with a pyramidal roof and beyond is the fourteenth-century tower of Lord Berkeley's castle. A climb affords an exciting diversion and fine views of the garden and surrounding country.

Beyond the moat to the east are two vast beeches screening an old nut walk and, nearby, the garden wall provides a background for a raised border of old roses, Tree Paeonies, catmint and potentillas. To the south the large lawn contains another ancient walnut, a Weeping Ash and a Deodar and the shelter-belt to the west protects large shrubs and small trees like rose 'Nevada', the shaggy-barked *Acer griseum* and *Parrotia persica*, angular in growth and spectacular in autumn.

Further south beyond the grass tennis-court, enclosed at either end by groups of flowering cherries, a long curving border separates the garden from the roadside paddock beyond. Here is a fine range of old roses, shrubs and hardy flowers well arranged but struggling a little to seem significant against the larger scale of the surroundings. Rose 'Blanc double de Coubert' and variegated weigela associate well with a background of purple nuts and further along there is another good combination of rose 'Frühlingsgold' with golden variegated weigelas and dogwoods and purple *Cotinus coggygria* 'Foliis Purpureis' underplanted with *Alchemilla mollis*. Hybrid musk roses such as 'Felicia' are prominent with paeonies, *Sedum telephium* and white violas.

Rounding off the garden is a neat and productive walled kitchen garden where sometimes there are spare plants for sale.

Next door THE OLD RECTORY, BEVERSTONE, is sometimes open for Red Cross in late June when the fine display of roses assembled by Lt. General Sir Terence and Lady McKeekin are at their best. The cream-painted house with stone quoins sits well amid a variety of fine trees, False Acacias, Holm Oaks, Sweet Chestnuts, limes and beeches and the garden is well endowed with an interesting series of levels and a variety of flowering shrubs. Furthest from the road is a raised area containing a spectacular show of 'Iceberg' and other bush roses successfully associated with catmint and Snow-in-Summer, and with a seat arbour. Climbing roses such as 'Zephirine Drouhin', 'Albertine' and 'New Dawn' grow on the walls here as well as behind the herbaceous border leading back to the house and on the house walls themselves.

Bisley Gardens

Two groups of small gardens open for NGS, one group in spring and the other in summer. At Bisley, 6.4km (4 miles) NE of Stroud

Bledington Village Gardens

A group of village gardens of mixed size and character. Open for NGS in summer. 7.2km (4½ miles) SE of Stow-on-the-Wold.

Blockley Gardens

Village gardens open for NGS in spring and again with others for RC in summer. 6.4km (4 miles) NW of Moreton-in-Marsh.

That three are mill gardens and another adjoins the river gives the gardens an added attraction. There are fine conifers and coloured foliage trees.

Bourton House

Mr and Mrs E.M. Watson-Smyth

At Bourton-on-the-Hill, 2.4km (1½ miles) W of Moreton-in-Marsh on the road Evesham A44. Outstanding eighteenth-century house in 4.8ha (12 acre) garden and orchard within the curtilage of an earlier seventeenth-century house. Open for NGS and RC Well-drained soil over Cotswold limestone. Rainfall 760mm (30in.) On E slope below the village, 167m (550ft). Maintained by one gardener with help from the owners.

Within the garden enclosures of the former Jacobean house, part of which was incorporated into the present very beautiful Queen Anne mansion, Mr and Mrs Watson-Smyth have a garden of great interest and charm. They have wisely retained simple large lawns that are in scale with the house. More than anything it is the balance of simple open space and mature trees that gives the sense of dignity and repose so complementary to fine buildings. With its glorious views to the south over the valley towards Batsford Park and Sezincote the garden, designed by Lanning Roper, is worthy of a visit at any time.

The garden entrance is downhill from the house and visitors are greeted by borders of yellow 'Canary Bird' and other shrub roses and one of the Tree Paeonies, *Paeonia lutea* 'Ludlowii', its pale-green contrasted against the purple foliage of *Berberis thunbergii* 'Atropurpurea' and *Prunus* 'Cistena'. The magnificent sixteenth-century tithe-barn was built by Richard Johnson and is the largest in Gloucestershire. As if to gild the lily, it is decorated on the outside with climbing roses 'Etoile de Holland', 'New Dawn' and 'Lady Hillingdon Climbing'. Through the wide gabled porch the original roof timbers can be seen still functional and beautiful after 400 years. Beyond is an old orchard, full of daffodils in April. A broad grass walk crosses east/west and forms the main axis through the garden. At its lower eastern end is an eye-catching arbour of white-painted trellis making a *trompe-l'oeil* to end the vista. Turning west towards the house the path leads up steps flanked with *Euphorbia veneta* and through cypress hedges screening the walled kitchen garden, with colourful annuals in front. The greenhouse is planted with varieties of *Camellia japonica* and tuberous begonias.

The main axis becomes a terrace near the house, paved with random rectangular York stone and with colourful planting spilling on to it from the south-facing border: *Skimmia japonica* and *Sarcococca humilis* in the shade of a yew and annual flowers and bergenias in the sun. The superb main south facade of the house overlooks a simple rectangular croquet-lawn enclosed at the sides by walls and old yew trees. At the far end is a formal terrace walk, no doubt surviving from the Jacobean garden, in which they were a common feature to give views out over the secure boundary walls.

By the east wall is a border of annual flowering plants with pyramid Sweet Bays and a superb seventeenth-century lead tank planted with clematis and fuchsias. On the west side a deep, mixed border is designed to give interest and colour from flowers and foliage through the year. There is a rich textural combination of the horizontally branched *Prunus* 'Zabeliana' with *Euphorbia robbiae*, bergenias and flag irises and further along the border turns to flowering plants in the softer colours with silver foliage. Prominent are shrub roses such as 'Nevada'; Silver Pear, purple *Cotinus coggygria*, lavenders, irises, paeonies, phloxes and Jackman's Rue. These borders flank steps to enclose a raised area further west in which a formal rose garden, all in white 'Iceberg', has been made. Here is a clever contrast from the open spaces of the lawn to the intimate scale in which roses can be better enjoyed. As dual focal points there are charming rose arbours with climbing roses trained over the white metalwork to shelter matching white painted seats.

Close to the west side of the house, and partly enclosed by it, is a small but effective knot garden made around a two-tier medieval fountain set in cobbles. Low box hedges and clipped box balls form a satisfying pattern with the paved paths edged with cobbles and aubrietia. All around are evergreens to give a rich furnished appearance all the year; *Osmanthus* × *burkwoodii*, *Mahonia japonica*, Laurustinus, Sweet Bay and *Magnolia grandiflora*.

In the centre of the forecourt is a large stone basket presented to the owner by Queen Mary. This basket was originally in the Great Exhibition of London in 1851. Framing the north front of the house are fine large lime trees and the gravel forecourt is bordered by shrubs — 'Zabeliana' laurel, buddleias, hydrangeas and skimmias — with clipped bays in Versailles cases and two clipped holly cones giving shape and pattern. This is the combination of firm evergreen shapes and profuse flowery planting that is the theme of the garden.

Bradley Court

Mr and Mrs A. Garnett

At Bradley Green, 1.6km (1 mile) NW of Wotton-under-Edge, S of B4060 Dursley road. Open for NGS in late June. Mainly formal garden of 1.2ha (3 acres) around 1567 house with eighteenth-century additions at the rear. Heavy alkaline soil. On westerly lower slope of the Cotswold escarpment with views over the Severn Vale and of the Cotswold edge, at 106m (350ft). Rainfall 813mm (32in.). Owners and one part-time gardener.

The Kip engraving of Bradley Court as it was in 1707 shows the south front of the house much as it is today although now it is swathed in roses and Virginia Creeper. Facing the road its six irregular gables and two projecting staircase towers contrast with the symmetrical arrangement of drive and trees, where once no doubt there was an enclosed front court.

The land falls away to the west and here the original terraced, walled garden remains. The beautiful 1702 gazebo with its ogee roof, also shown in the Kip engraving, was placed centrally on the terrace wall so that its occupants could look back towards the house and out over the kitchen garden into the country. The gazebo is flanked by yew hedges and the enclosure thus formed is now a croquet-lawn surrounded by carefree mixed borders of summer flowers, entirely in keeping with the old-English atmosphere. Here is the typical country-house mixture with roses like the Hybrid Musk 'Penelope' and 'Buff Beauty', also *R. rubrifolia* and 'Iceberg' mixed with purple *Cotinus coggygria*, *Cistus* spp., sages, Tree Lupins and Seakale backed by larger shrubs, Sweet Bays and a large *Magnolia* × *soulangiana*. On one wall is a vast *Clematis montana* and on the house a magnificent old Wisteria.

From here this garden of many parts begins to unfold. Almost too discreetly tucked away behind hedges is an effective secret garden of white flowers and silver foliage set in a formal pattern, a simple cross of paving, with a fine stone urn in the centre. This garden is lovely in late June when the White Rose of York and *Crambe cordifolia* are flowering and the silver foliage shrubs are at their best. At each of the four corners is a huge 'Wickwar' rose, an excellent silvery foliage shrub raised by Keith Steadman, whose influence is rightly very strong in these parts.

Having found one piece of hidden treasure the game of garden hide-and-seek continues. North of the house, one is led along a grassy vista to a statue of Diana and a fine view to the hills and the Tyndale Monument at North Nibley, framed by a superb group of Scots Pines. At the end is the richest and best-hidden treasure in the garden. A narrow opening leads to an artificial ravine, overhung with evergreens, winding its way ever deeper between ferns and periwinkle to an astonishing grotto complete with a pool and trickling water. As in the best traditions of grottoes, the light is dim and dramatic and an atmosphere of dark melancholy prevails. The arching roof is reflected in the pattern of the paving and the pool to create an entirely convincing design.

Nearby the main lawns, decorated with groups of roses and shrubs, lead to a ha-ha. Here there is a remarkably tall Judas tree and the choice of newer shrubs shows Keith Steadman's discriminating influence, with flowering privets, Firethorns and *Hypericum* 'Hidcote' combined with some of the characteristic Wickwar foliage plants like *Elaeagnus* × *ebbingei* and *E. angustifolia, Pyrus salicifolia*, the Camellia-leaved Holly and Portugal Laurel.

Last in the treasure-hunt is the swimming-pool, almost as difficult to find as the rest but a contrast is provided by its brightness. The pool is completely surrounded by high banks of roses: a mass of pink and white climbing and scrambling roses starting with 'Paulii' and 'Max Graf' and working up the scale to 'New Dawn', 'Alberic Barbier' and *R. filipes*.

In the short time, by gardening standards, since 1970 Mr and Mrs Garnett have created an imaginative garden full of originality and surprise.

Nearby is TALBOT END HOUSE at Talbot End, near Cromhall, 8.8km (5½ miles) SW of Wotton-under-Edge, where Mr G.E.C. Dougherty has created a charming cottage-style garden from an original Edwardian layout. The old yews and fruit trees give a sense of maturity and he has added old roses, borders of old cottage-garden flowers and big groups of *Aruncus dioicus*, bamboos and Pampas Grass in the lawn. Beyond a low wall is the original formal rose garden with lovely Madonna Lilies, a kitchen garden and — set into the wall — a telephone! Nearby a former rock garden was cleared and this and the old orchard used to accommodate groups of shrubs and trees. Here again the influence of Keith Steadman shows in the willows, poplars, *Elaeagnus, Sorbaria* and *Kolkwitzia* spp.

Broadwell Manor

I.N. Maitland Hume Esq.

Open for RC in summer. At Broadwell, 2.4km (1½ miles) N of Stow-on-the-Wold. An old-fashioned garden with a large herbaceous border and lawns surrounding a classic Georgian house of 1757, parts of which date from Jacobean times.

Bromesberrow Place

Miss D.G. Albright

Open for GS in May. At Bromesberrow, 6.4km (4 miles) SE of Ledbury, 1.6km (1 mile) from junction 2 on M50. Flowering trees and shrubs, including rhododendrons and azaleas and species of Kalmia and Pieris. Adjacent to Bromesberrow Place Nurseries which is well known for its orchid collection as well as for fuchsias, pelargoniums and houseplants for sale.

Brook Cottage

Miss G. Wright

Open for NGS by appointment March-October. At Sevenhampton, 11.2km (7 miles) E of Cheltenham and 3.2km (2 miles) NE of Andoversford via A436. Charming small alpine garden with fast-flowing stream around lovely old scheduled Cotswold cottage, set in beautiful surroundings. Wide variety of alpines, bulbs and waterside plants lovingly cared for. Also nearby Church Garden of rare quality with rose and alpine beds (open in aid of church roof).

Burnt Norton

(Viscount Sandon)

Open for GS several times. Aston Subedge, 2.4km (1½m) N of Chipping Campden. Part formal, part woodland garden of 4.85ha (12 acres) on N-facing Cotswold escarpment, with panoramic views of the entire Vale of Evesham. Part seventeenth-century house converted by Sir Guy Dawber in 1902. For a fuller account see Edward Malins, "Burnt Norton", Garden History, vol. VII, no.1.

In 1740 Norton House and its 2-2.4ha (5-6 acres) garden was thought to be part of the finest estate in the district. Sir William Keyt had spent many years and £10,000 in building the house and laying out the garden "in Building or Removing Mountains for Order and Ornament". Sir William had become notorious for heavy drinking, womanising and gambling and on this account his wife left him. Eventually he set light to the house and to himself with grisly results; hence Burnt Norton, although this name was not used until 1919/20. The main part of the house was left as a ruin and not demolished until nearly a century later. However the older part, built mainly in 1620, remained and the formal garden, mostly south of the house, was kept up reasonably well by the Ryder family (later the Earls of Harrowby) who purchased the estate in 1753. It was the fifth Earl who converted the house in 1902 and the architect Sir Guy Dawber, a personal friend of the family, also designed a large terraced extension to the garden westwards incorporating a rose garden, tennis lawns and at the far end an impressive amphitheatre containing a swimming pool, which can still be seen today. It was a visit by T.S. Eliot in 1935 that gave the place fame, for it was this garden that inspired his *Four Quartets* of which *Burnt Norton* is the first

> . . .'Dry the pool dry concrete, brown edged,
> And the pool was filled with water out of sunlight'.

Today the garden retains its romantic atmosphere in a period when only minimum maintenance is possible. Traces of the whole of its fascinating history are there for the curious to discover.

Cirencester Park

Earl Bathurst

Open throughout the year to pedestrians free of charge and to vehicles at a fee for special events. Situated on the western side of Cirencester and contiguous with it.

Thanks to the generosity of the family a stroll in the park has been an everyday possibility for residents and visitors alike since 1714. It is the finest surviving example in England of a large scale park in the Baroque, pre-landscape manner. It was planted by Allen, first Earl Bathurst, an accomplished forester and gardener, between 1714 and 1775, against the prevailing English Landscape style of the time and with the help of Alexander Pope who wrote: 'I am with Lord Bathurst at my bower . . . draw plans for houses and gardens, open avenues, cut glades, plant firs, contrive waterworks, all very fine and beautiful in our own imagination'.

Unusually for an English house (Petworth is another example), the house is sited on the edge of the town separated from it only by the famous yew hedge of record size. The best place to see the layout of the park is from the top of the church tower of St John the Baptist on which the 8km (5 mile) long Broad Avenue, a grand vista of Horse Chestnuts and beeches, is focused. Another axis from the Church passes through the house to Queen Anne's Monument with clumps of trees on either side and an irregular lake to the south. Bathurst did not then entirely reject the new landscape fashion, as Pope recorded: 'There is something in the amiable simplicity of unadorned nature . . .'. Cirencester Park is an eclectic fusion of the two styles of gardening and architectural taste. Bathurst adorned the park with a variety of buildings including Alfred's Hall, the first of all romantic castellated follies, a building that belongs more to the second half of the eighteenth-century and to the English Landscape style than to the symmetry of the formal park. But the main structure of the park is distinctly geometrical with a succession of features along the Broad Avenue. Three rides meet at Lord Bathurst's Hexagon, a covered sitting-place in rusticated stone. The next is Pope's Seat, another small stone pavilion where seven rides meet. The great *rond-point* of rides is near the Polo

Ground, where another folly, Horse Guards, consists of two ornamental arches. The whole park is clad in mature beechwoods of the highest quality, all husbanded to this day with skill and care. As Pope also wrote:

'Who then shall grace or who improve the soil,
Who plants like Bathurst or who builds like Boyle'.

Clearwell Castle
B. Yeates Esq

For opening see HHCG. At Coleford, 32km (20 miles) W of Gloucester and 8km (5 miles) SE of Monmouth. 3.2ha (8 acre) formal garden on five different levels, in process of restoration.

Coln St Aldwyns Gardens

A group of village gardens open for NGS in spring and for RC in summer. 3.2km (2 miles) N of Fairford. An interesting selection of gardens including riverside planting, unusual foliage and flowering plants and shrubs.

Cotswold Farm
Major and Mrs P.D. Birchall

Open for NGS in early summer and by appointment for parties. At Duntisbourne Abbots, 8km (5 miles) NW of Cirencester on A417.

The house is important, having been altered and enlarged by Sidney Barnsley in 1926, and is a prime example of the work of the Cotswold Craftsmen. It has a lovely position and the garden is of the highest quality with terraces, mixed borders of shrubs, herbaceous and ground-cover plants and bulbs, and rock borders with alpines. Shrub roses are a speciality.

Courtfield

S.T. Skelton Esq.

Open jointly for GS in summer. At Longhope, 16km (10 miles) W of Gloucester on A4136.
COURTFIELD is a 1.2ha (3 acre) mixed garden with stream, rock garden, unusual shrubs and
with special emphasis on plants for the flower arranger. HOME FARM Mrs E. Howard Jones and
Miss Brenda H. Jones is a cottage garden with a wide variety of plants and lovely views.

Dodington Park

Major S.F.B. Codrington

West of the A46 Stroud-Bath road, 4.8km (3 miles) S of the A432 junction and 200m N of M4
junction 18 at Tormarton. For opening arrangements see HHCG. 240ha (600 acres)
eighteenth-century park by L. Brown. Small formal garden. Classic house by James Wyatt 1790-
1817. Situated at 122-152m (400-500ft) in two converging valleys forming the source of the
River Frome. Neutral and slightly acid fine sandy soil. Rainfall 787mm (31in.). Guidebook and
guided-walk leaflets available.

Dodington is a day out for the family. As well as a lived-in great house, as
beautiful inside as it is out, there is a host of attractions in the grounds,
many of which would have surprised Sir William Codrington, who in
1764 engaged Lancelot Brown to lay out the park. Among the welter of
exhibitions and souvenir shops, adventure playground, children's farm,
miniature railway, Red Indian village, etc., lies a great English Landscape
park made by 'Capability' Brown at the very height of his fame. It is a
tribute to him that his work has been able to absorb, although not completely unscathed, the ever-quickening changes of recent years. Views
remain where the full majesty of his conception can be realized despite the
filling-in of part of the upper lake after the First World War and the paraphernalia of twentieth-century tourism.

Brown designed the landscape to surround the earlier sixteenth-century
house and the present house and associated buildings were built more than
30 years later in the mature setting by James Wyatt for Christopher Bethell
Codrington. All the elements of the English Landscape style — woods,
undulations and water — were to hand. In 1728 Alexander Pope described
the setting as 'pretty enough, romantic, covered with woody hills, stum-
bling upon one another confusedly, and the garden makes a valley betwixt
them with some mounts and waterfalls'.

Brown's firm touch and great foresight are evident even now. True to form he opened up the valleys, leaving the best oaks and beeches as specimens and small groups on the slopes, and planted new beech woods on the boundaries and on the higher ground to emphasize the changes of level. Flowers were banished to the walled garden and the park was taken right up to the house. In Brown's own words: 'All obdurate lines softened into curves, the terrace melted into a swelling bank and the walks opened to catch the vicinal country'.

The approach is past Bath Lodge, Wyatt's classic rotunda, through an impressive semicircle of railings and massive gate piers. The drive, at first through woods recently replanted, was made with all the eighteenth-century principles of variety and gradual revelation in mind. After woods it opens out into pasture and then skirts the valley among scattered clumps of limes, beeches and oaks to give diagonal glimpses of the house with its immense classic portico, till finally arriving past big rhododendrons at the forecourt.

South of the house Brown harnessed the source of the River Frome, to make a narrow lake now much reduced in size, and a much broader one with an island in the valley NE of the house. He planted trees and bushes to disguise the awkward conjunction of the two lakes and exploited the change of level brilliantly by making a castellated gothic cascade fed by a curving aqueduct from the upper lake. With its doves and mossy splash it was clearly designed to be seen from the east side of the lake where there is a magnificent Lebanon Cedar, no doubt of Brown's planting. But the finest view is from the far northern end where the cascade closes a vista along the whole length of the lower lake. Near the cascade Brown made an icehouse with a matching castellated gothic tower, now sadly ruinous, a vantage-point for superb views in all directions: back toward the house, across the upper lake, along the lower lake and north-eastwards into the second valley. The drive goes out through this valley among superb Turkey Oaks to Wyatt's neo-Greek Chippenham Lodge and gateway surmounted by the Codringtons' winged dragon.

As well as the magnificent Lebanon Cedar and its timely replacement nearby, many fine trees furnish the lower lake. These are several enormous Copper Beeches, no doubt planted in the nineteenth-century, an old Lucombe Oak and many Holm Oaks. A superb Fern-leaved Beech and two big walnuts stand on the lawn below the east front of the house, the Chapel and the Dower House.

At the north end of the lake are the remains of a garden pavilion with delicate fluted columns, built here by James Wyatt as an eye-catcher from the house and to take advantage of the long vista between the island and the east bank. Nearby is a fine old variegated sycamore, *Acer pseudoplatanus* 'Albo-Variegatum' which gives just the right touch of lightness among the heavy greens of late summer. Further along there is a magnificent grove of Corsican Pines whose rough-barked stems of silvery grey soar to a great height.

Wyatt's main horticultural contribution was the beautiful, curved Conservatory facing south-west with the Chapel behind it. This is an early example of the Regency taste for integrating the garden with the house. With its long orangery windows and glass roof the effect is light and airy. At the back the gallery, with its pretty iron trellis, provides an effective additional way of viewing the plants. Here is a selection of plants and tender climbers including the clear pale-blue *Plumbago capensis*, ivies and geraniums on the walls with daturas, oleanders, *Agapanthus* and *Pittosporum tobira* below. Two large specimens of the Norfolk Island Pine, *Araucaria excelsa*, are prominent.

During the 1930s the present owner's father, Sir Christopher Codrington, Bart., went full circle by restoring on the south side of the house some terraced flower gardens of the kind that Lancelot Brown had 'melted into a swelling bank' almost two centuries earlier. Low-walled in limestone to match the house, they form two enclosures with paved paths leading to the remains of a summer-house facing east near a Weeping Willow. The rectangle nearest the forecourt has a central fountain pool and colourful borders of hardy herbaceous and bedding plants. The other enclosure is axial to the south front and its terrace and has borders of shrub and climbing roses like 'Nevada', 'Marguerite Hilling', 'Roseraie de l'Hay' and 'Sanders' White', leading to a little gate into the park where resides the lasting beauty of Dodington.

The Dower House (The Cottage) Badminton

The Lady Caroline Somerset

In Badminton, 8km (5 miles) E of Chipping Sodbury. Garden of about 1.2ha (3 acres) divided into formal enclosures in the Hidcote manner; complex informal planting with colour schemes in the Gertrude Jekyll tradition. Ornamental kitchen garden and herb garden. Open occasionally for NGS with Badminton House and Essex House. On heavy but well-drained soil over limestone. On southern tip of the Cotswold at 122m (400ft). Rainfall 787mm (31in.). Maintained by the owner and one gardener, full time and another part time.

With English gardens the very finest results seem often to come from a combination of talents. An imaginative ideal of the owners can be turned, with the help of a great designer, into a work of art; a basic concept into a well-worked whole, designer and client each stimulating the other. Such is the garden at The Cottage where, since 1964, Mr David and Lady Caroline Somerset have created a completely satisfying garden with the help of Mr Russell Page. But gardens do not remain static and it is in the sensitive quality of the upkeep that this garden stands out from others. By knowing when to prune and when to allow a plant to sprawl; when to be ruthless and when to allow self-sown seedlings to remain, the most contrived schemes can achieve that sense of casual elegance which is the genius of English garden style. The strong formal outline bounded by neat hedges and climber-covered walls; the clever variety of intimate enclosures; the wide range of plants used at the same time; it is all here, a worthy development of the Hidcote style and a rare achievement in every way.

The layout, mostly west of the house, is extensive but appears the more so because of the imaginative succession of spaces, linked by intriguing Vistas, luring the visitor on from one delight to the next, each area a new surprise.

The garden is entered on the north side of the house passing a small, box-hedged front garden with climbing roses and *Hydrangea petiolaris* on the house walls and fuchsias in front. On a low wall is the pink climbing rose 'New Dawn'. North of the house is a paved area for eating outside in summer with white Valerian and Lilies-of-the-Valley around, and more climbing hydrangeas and rose 'Gloire de Dijon' on the walls. Opposite is a curving south-facing wall painted deep apricot like the house with sun-loving climbers and shrubs like *Carpentaria californica*.

A path bordered with silver *Stachys lanata* and Sun Roses leads to a small winter garden enclosed by walls where the fragrance and quiet charm of *Garrya elliptica, Mahonia japonica, Lonicera fragrantissima*, jasmine and Wintersweet with hellebores, cyclamen and dwarf bulbs can be enjoyed.

The west front and library opens on to a paved terrace given a sense of enclosure by a low wall and provided with steps to the gently rising ground beyond. A profusion of white valerian, *Alchemilla mollis*, thymes and wild strawberries are allowed to encroach, and clipped box balls in square white tubs give formal contrast. Fragrance from Lemon Verbena, thyme and roses fills the air and the house is covered with climbers: roses including 'Easlea's Golden Rambler' and the incomparable 'Climbing Lady Hillingdon', with the big-leafed vine *Vitis coignetiae*.

Through a small gate to the south is a small herb garden of novel design set in a pattern of paving around a central clipped bay tree. Here, close to the kitchen, are all the culinary herbs and their decorative derivatives with sweetbriar to give colour, fragrance and usefulness for a long period. Nearby is a small orchard and a border of flowers for cutting, paeonies, lilies, irises, delphiniums and *Cephalaria tartarica*.

The main axis west from the house leads up steps flanked by clipped yew pyramids to a square grass plat bordered by mixed plantings of soft blue, purple, pink and pale yellow with silver foliage: paeonies, geraniums, flag irises, *Macleaya (Bocconia) cordata*, sages, lavenders and grasses between a framework of shrub roses including 'Nevada' 'Fantin-Latour', 'Gipsy Boy', 'Blanc Double de Coubert', 'Golden Wings' and *R. × cantabrigiensis.*

The next area west is dominated by a short avenue of quinces with a large Indian Bean Tree, *Catalpa bignonioides,* balancing an established Red Horse Chestnut on the other side of the axis. Cunningly concealed on the north side behind a yew hedge decorated with everlasting sweet peas is a swimming-pool, designed with great simplicity and restraint to be a positive feature in the garden plan and sheltered on the north side by a great mounded yew hedge of great age, which has evolved by years of clipping into smooth abstract shapes of great character. This forms the main spine about which the garden is arranged. A path leads through it into the kitchen garden but let us continue along the main west prospect from the house. Flanking the next opening, which consists of a stone gateway, are double borders with more shrub roses including 'Roseraie de l'Hay' and 'Aloha' with phloxes, Michaelmas Daisies, *Lavatera olbia* and the giant thistle *Onopordon acanthium* making its mark.

Through the arch is a complete change to restful greenery and disciplined formality. Trim, pleached limes form a circle with Indian Bean Trees behind, eventually to overtop them. The vista is finished convincingly with a white gate set against an old orchard. Continuing north along a young lime avenue on the second side of a large rectangle which encompasses the garden one is tempted back to the east through a charming arched gate by another long east/west axis roughly parallel to the first. The first square is the pond garden with yew hedges around a circular central fountain pool enclosing densely-planted secret corners with narrow paths and neat box hedges in a strong pattern of interlocking L shapes. Here are many shrub roses, paeonies, lilies, Masterwort, irises and *Acanthus mollis* with *Ceanothus* 'Gloire de Versailles', the purple vine, a fig and roses 'Lady Waterlow', 'François Juranville' and 'Paul's Lemon Pillar' on the thickly-clad walls.

Eastwards through an arch of rose 'Christine White' is the final surprise of this charming garden. A walled kitchen garden has been converted into a 'potager' of great beauty and interest. Indeed, a French influence pervades the whole garden. The focal point is a central arbour of white-painted wood designed by Mr Russell Page, with climbing roses, clematises and *Solanum crispum*, and this is linked to the box-edged perimeter paths by espalier apples and an avenue of standard 'Iceberg' roses bedded beneath with pansies, lobelias and snapdragons. Neat rows of vegetables and soft fruits contribute both to the pattern and to the interest; asparagus and globe artichokes show what we are missing if we ignore useful plants for decorative effect.

And back through that venerable old yew hedge, more than satisfied.

ESSEX HOUSE*(Mr and Mrs J. Lees-Milne). Open with The Dower House and other Badminton gardens in early summer. 8km (5 miles) E of Chipping Sodbury.* Since 1975 that accomplished gardener, Alvilde Lees-Milne, has been making a new garden. Although much smaller than Alderley Grange, it is predictably full of beauty and originality.

In a south-facing angle of the seventeenth-century house she has made a charming sunken paved area for sitting out, surrounded by climbing roses, wistaria and *Solanum crispum*. The garden is dominated by three magnificent Cedars of Lebanon at the far end and the lawn has been given significance by making a firm central feature of paving strewn with pinks and other dwarf plants around a copper urn, all enclosed by a box hedge and 'Golden King' hollies to mark the corners.

Facing west is a separate enclosed area with a pond and raised borders of shrub roses with purple and silver foliage and a seat facing west. There are Weeping Silver Pears and a statue of Apollo draped in variegated *Hedera colchica*

Despite its small size an immense amount has been fitted in without the garden seeming to lose its sense of space. Here is the essence of good design.

Duntisbourne Valley Gardens

Several gardens in the villages of Duntisbourne Abbots, Duntisbourne Leer and Duntisbourne Rous. 6.4km (4 miles) NW of Cirencester. With the joy of seeing superb unspoilt scenery and the chance of visiting the Saxon Church of Duntisbourne Rous, this is possibly the pick of the village openings in Gloucestershire.

Dyrham Park

The National Trust

---

*At Dyrham village, 19.2km (12 miles) E of Bristol, 12.8km (8 miles) N of Bath; entrance from
A46 Bath-Stroud road, 3.2km (2 miles) S of Tormarton M4 interchange. For opening dates and
times see HHCG and NT opening arrangements; normally daily June-Sept., daily except Mons
and Tues April and May, and Sats and Suns only in Oct. and Nov. Part late-seventeenth-century
and part late-eighteenth-century deer park of 105ha (263 acres) and garden of 2.4ha (6 acres)
mainly W of late-seventeenth-century house. Set on a westerly slope at 122-183m (400-600ft).
Thin alkaline soil over limestone in park, deeper in garden. Rainfall 787mm (31in.) Garden west
of house maintained by one gardener with some assistance. Guidebook gives history and description
of house and grounds and there is a fuller account by A. Mitchell in the NT Yearbook for 1977-78.*

William Blathwayt, Secretary of State to William III, built the house and
Orangery of Bath stone between 1691 and 1704, looking east on to a deer
park, which slopes dramatically down to it. The west front, formerly the
entrance, creates a picturesque group with the church and stable block and
looks across the garden to a superb view over the Severn Vale towards
Bristol. The celebrated firm of London and Wise was employed to devise
the extraordinarily extensive formal layout on both sides of the house,
recorded in detail in Kip's engraving in Sir Robert Atkyns' *The Ancient and
Present State of Glostershire* (1712). George London ingeniously used the
stream, which rises high to the east, to make fountains and a cascade,
similar to that at Chatsworth, leading through a canal to more formal
waterworks west of the house. All this was linked to a uniquely complex
layout of terraces, formal gardens and great avenues stretching out above
the scarp.

By 1780 the formal layout had become neglected and the park immediately east of the house was 'reconciled to the modern taste', to the
idealized 'natural' style of the English Landscape school. These changes
were wrought by a Bath surveyor called C. Harcourt Masters, and his
gently flowing turf and tree clumps persist today. But those parts of the
park out of sight of the house were largely left unchanged and the ancient
avenues of elms survived until Dutch Elm disease struck in 1976 at the
time when the National Trust acquired the park. The avenues have now
been replanted, mostly with the limes.

The main lines of the London and Wise layout can still be discerned in
the present garden west of the house but it has been much simplified.
Humphry Repton was employed at Dyrham but not until after the main
changes to the park had taken place. His contribution is not clear but he
may well have planted the cedars north–east of the house and the splendid

leaning Holm Oaks, *Quercus ilex*, in the garden and he probably reshaped the garden ponds.

The garden is now entered from the house on to the terrace where thyme and musk grow in cracks in the paving. Facing south is a border with old Gallica roses. *Daphne* 'Somerset' and *Convolvulus cneorum* enjoy the reflected warmth and on the walls are the large lemon-scented flowers of *Magnolia grandiflora*, a pomegranate and a myrtle. The vista in front is framed by Holm Oaks; some old leaning trees have been removed but there are young ones planted by the Trust for the future.

The tall south-facing wall, with the tiny Church perched above, is 'supported' by clipped yew buttresses and covered with climbing roses, including 'Mermaid' and 'Gloire de Dijon', and the blue-flowered *Solanum crispum*. Sheltering between buttresses is the exotic *Magnolia delavayi* with its enormous but tender leaves and fragrant flowers. The border is furnished with colourful, mainly summer-flowering shrubs: Rugosa roses, Mexican Orange, *Hypericum* 'Hidcote', lavenders, potentillas and *Senecio* 'Sunshine', with *Cotoneaster horizontalis* filling the niches.

The border beyond begins with a flourish of magnolias and lacecap hydrangeas edged with *Bergenia cordifolia*; here also is *Viburnum plicatum* and the semi-shrubby *Clematis × jouiniana* clambers over the Spotted Laurel. But the path soon plunges into the cool shade of the giant ilexes pushed forward by the enormous old limes along church walk. The shady bank is a tamed woodland of hollies, variegated elders, periwinkles, cotoneasters, *Cornus mas* and the unusual late-flowering privet *Ligustrum quihoui*.

Near the west gates, once a main entrance, are borders of shrubs and Hybrid Musk roses, hebes and weigelas, with a young Tulip Tree, *Liriodendron tulipifera* — one of the species planted at Dyrham by William Blathwayt in the late-seventeenth century.

The east-facing boundary wall close to the lake contains seat niches planted on either side with aromatic plants and overhung with vines. Fringing the water is a large group of *Peltiphyllum peltatum*, its umbrella-shaped leaves contrasting with bamboo, the prostrate *Ceanothus thyrsiflorus* 'Repens', and a Weeping Hornbeam. South of the lake a young nut-walk backed by limes, *Tilia × euchlora*, leads back in the direction of the house to the east end of the lake where a bank, which screens the lake from the house, carries a gushing cascade discharging into a small pond and eventually into the lake. Nearby are dogwoods, several *Salix elaeagnos,* other willows including the unusual *Salix babylonica* 'Annularis' ('Crispa') on the little island, an old Mulberry and a fine Manna Ash, *Fraxinus ornus.*

The extreme southern side of the garden has been developed comparatively recently. Some interesting trees and shrubs have been planted mainly for summer and autumn effect, sheltered by tall beeches and

Portugal Laurels. Here are some of the plants mentioned as having been planted by William Blathwayt and Thomas Hurnall, the head gardener, on the advice of George London in the late-seventeenth-century: 'Phillirea, Piracantha, Yew, Virginia Pine and Tulip Tree'. There are also the Indian Bean Tree and *Ligustrum lucidum* of later introduction and a small orchard of Perry Pears.

Before leaving, do not miss a visit to the Orangery, one of the earliest of its kind, where you can take tea surrounded by tubs of oranges and climbers such as the lovely pale-blue *Plumbago capensis* and its white form, *Cassia corymbosa* and Passion Flowers.

Eastington Gardens

Three gardens in a quiet Cotswold village. Open for NGS in spring and summer.

MIDDLE END is the largest with an attractive terraced garden built into a slope to the east and views into the valley. A good range of ornamental trees and unusual shrubs have been well arranged with herbaceous plants and ground covers between. One border has a purple and gold theme and another has silver and white. There is an extensive and productive kitchen garden overlooking the valley and the house is covered with an excellent form of the Virginia Creeper, *Parthenocissus tricuspidata* 'Lowii'. YEW TREE COTTAGE is a tiny garden on a shady bank. Not an inch is wasted and it is an excellent illustration of what can be achieved without much sun. Best of all is BANK COTTAGE, a small garden on an almost impossibly steep slope. It is the garden of real enthusiasts, crammed from one end to the other with a glorious mixture, including many rarities which jostle for space with bedding plants and annuals in profusion. Alpines are a speciality and you can buy plants, very reasonably priced, near the glasshouse.

Elm Cottage
Dr and Mrs Patrick Hardie

Two small gardens open together for NGS in summer. At Shipton Moyne, 4km (2½miles) S of Tetbury.

ELM COTTAGE has spring flowers, bulbs and flowering cherries, climbing and old-fashioned shrub roses, clematis and cottage-garden annuals. IDLWYLDE *Mr and Mrs R.B. Weaver* is a tiny garden for flower arrangers with an 'overflowing' greenhouse.

Essex House
See The Dower House, Badminton

Escourt Grange
Mr and Mrs O.C.S. Lamb

In Escourt Park, 2.4km (1½ miles) SE of Tetbury via B4042 to Malmesbury, turning off south-west at Newton Lodge. Open twice a year for NGS and RC Garden of 1ha (2½ acres) around Elizabethan former farmhouse situated in a valley at 91m (300ft) beside a stream, with terraces rising steeply on the west side. Mostly free-draining alkaline soil over limestone. Rainfall 864mm (34in.). Maintained by the owners and one full-time gardener.

This lovely Elizabethan house sits close to a stream, an early stage of the Bristol Avon, but curiously enough the former owners, Lady Helena and Colonel Gibbs, who designed the present layout from 1918 onwards, largely ignored its presence. They preferred instead to build a fascinating series of terraces facing east and south, between the house and Slad Farm. The large formal garden in the valley due south of the house is almost as plain and featureless as the terraces are full of interest.

The north forecourt surrounds an old cider press and a young Weeping Silver Lime bodes well for the future. On the house is the old climbing rose 'Etoile de Holland' and little terraces rise up steeply to the west crammed with all kinds of roses including forms of the Scotch Rose, *R. spinosossima,* and *R.* × *cantabrigiensis* with *R. longicuspis* growing on a lilac. *Buddleia alternifolia* and the Corkscrew Hazel higher up. At the very top is a hedged orchard full of bulbs and wild flowers with mown paths cut through.

Descending back towards the house on the south side of these terraces is the finest feature of the garden: a long flight of Cotswold stone steps hedged with lavender and carpeted with a gloriously rich mixture of the Bloody Cranesbill, *Geranium sanguineum*, and thymes enlivened here and there with patches of the light acid-yellow of *Alchemilla mollis*. The top of the steps provides the best view of house and garden and every visitor's spot for a photograph. A long walk extends from the steps to a mixed border of strong foliage effects of texture and colour, as well as the fragrance of Gallica and Rogosa roses. The golden foliage of *Juniperus* × *media* 'Pfitzerana Aurea' contrasts with purple *Berberis* and Silver Willows, a recurring feature of the garden, and spears of *Curtonus paniculatus* combine with *Acanthus spinosus*, catmint, sages and *Cotoneaster horizontalis*.

More terraces with roses and shrubs fall away to the lower lawns where an inviting sitting-out area facing south has been created, sheltered and surrounded by *Ceanothus* 'Gloire de Versailles', *Phlomis fruticosa*, purple nuts and three old specimens of the rock garden form of the Norway Spruce, *Picea abies* 'Clanbrassilliana'.

Ewen Manor

Colonel and Mrs M. St J.V. Gibbs

Open for RC and NGS in early summer. 6.4km (4 miles) S of Cirencester. Medium-sized varied garden with herbaceous border, lily pool, sunk garden, cedars and yew hedges around Georgian Cotswold stone manor house.

Fossebridge Gardens

Open for NGS in spring and summer. 11.2km (7 miles) NE of Cirencester. Two contrasting gardens, THE MANOR *is smart and trim with well-drilled roses, colourful herbaceous plants, river, lake, ducks and donkeys.* THE OLD FORGE *is small and intimate with old-fashioned cottage-style planting and lovely views.*

Left: Frampton Court. The formal canal leading to the Strawberry Hill Gothic orangery. *H. Clifford*

Below: Hidcote Manor. From the Red Borders the main vista passes between the two garden houses and the Stilt Garden to the distant view, framed by wrought iron gates. *Iris Hardwick*

Frampton Court

Major and Mrs Peter Clifford

In Frampton-on-Severn 14.4km (9 miles) SW of Gloucester, 3.2km (2 miles) W of junction 13 on the M5, signposted, east side of wide village green. Garden and house open by written appointment to Mrs Clifford. 2ha (5½ acres) of mainly informal and woodland garden surrounding Vanburgh-style house, ornamental canal and orangery. Low-lying site near the river below. At 15m (50ft) on heavy, slightly alkaline soil of the Severn Vale. Rainfall 787mm (31in.). Leaflet about house available. Maintained by the owners. Also Frampton Manor opposite and Keeper's Cottage on edge of lake which is part of the Frampton Court estate.

Family ownership traces an unbroken descent, but twice by the female line, since William the Conqueror. The splendid house with its huge arched chimneys on the rather plain wings was built in 1732 for Richard, son of Nathaniel Clutterbuck who had come from a Gloucestershire weaving family and married Mary Clifford, heir to the estate. It was arranged with the west front facing the road and the east front looking out over the parkland to a large lake, now well stocked with waterfowl and only a short walk from the house.

An old wall separates the garden from the village green and elegant gates lead to a drive through a light woodland of beeches, Holm Oaks, False Acacias and Scots Pines carpeted with spring bulbs. The lawn west of the house and the fine trees that fringe it — Austrian Pines, more Holm Oaks, a Blue Spruce, *Picea pungens glauca*, the variegated *Populus* × *candicans* 'Aurora' and a splendid Weeping Ash — are superbly in scale with the house. South of the house is a charming octagonal Jacobean dovecote with white doves and ornamental pea fowl.

Flower gardening is reserved largely for the Victorian terraces on the east front which are hedged with beech and studded with Mediterranean Cypresses and Irish Yews. Here are beds of hybrid tea roses, and an edging of 'The Fairy' by the stone steps, climbers like 'Albertine' and the vigorous *Rosa soulieana* on the house. Also on the walls are wistaria, clematis and *Lonicera* × *americana*. The view to the lake over the lovely park through groups of limes and White and Weeping Willows is stunning.

Undoubtedly the most important garden feature is Horace Walpole's unique 'Strawberry Hill' gothic orangery and garden house. Built in 1760 it finishes a vista created by a formal canal, similar in style to the much earlier one at Westbury Court across the river. Its south-facing front is romantically framed by beech and sycamore and reflected in the calm, black waters of the canal, disturbed only by the still blacker Australian

Barnsley House. The Laburnum Walk. *Laburnum* 'Vossii' is underplanted with one of the flowering onions *Allium aflatunense*.

Above: Hidcote Manor. The colour scheme in Mrs Winthrop's garden is green and gold with bronzy foliage and touches of violet purple here and there.

In the foreground is *Asphodeline lutea* and *Agave americana* 'Variegata'; at the back the Golden Hop, *Humulus lupulus* 'Aureus' is prominent.

Below: Westonbirt Arboretum. Autumn colour among the Japanese Maples.

swans, tame mallards and the occasional golden carp.

Nearby, the borders are in cool colours. White flowers predominate with touches of blue, mauve and purple and silver foliage: 'Iceberg' and other roses, *Crambe cordifolia, Elaeagnus* spp., *Onopordon acanthium*, catmint and paeonies. But this is a garden for those interested in seeing beautiful buildings in an equally beautiful setting; for here we have garden history, superb trees and landscape, rather than flowers and plants for their own sake.

FRAMPTON MANOR across the road is a black and white twelfth-century and Elizabethan house with an attractive garden of old-fashioned plants; a charming lavender garden, stone paths, staddle stones, herbaceous border full of valerian, old roses; all surrounded by lovely old capped walls.

Gloucestershire College of Agriculture
Glos. County Council

Open for NGS in spring. Hartpury House, 8km (5 miles) N of Gloucester. 1.6ha (4 acres) garden with large lawns, trees, shrubs and terraces, glasshouses, kitchen, demonstration and ornamental gardens.

Great Rissington Manor
D. Godman Esq.

In the village of Great Rissington, 4km (2½ miles) SE of Bourton-on-the-Water. Part terraced and part informal garden and arboretum of about 1.25ha (3 acres) in the Lutyens-Jekyll style around beautiful Elizabethan Cotswold stone manor house. Open for NGS in mid-summer. On varied, part lime-free soil over Cotswold limestone at 152m (500 ft) on a westerly slope below the village, overlooking pasture. Rainfall 787mm (31in.). Owners plus one gardener.

The manor house is a charming complement to the village church and the approach, through well-trimmed pleached limes, gives a hint of the garden. On its east front the house has a simple gravelled forecourt enclosed by a handsome railed wall with ball-capped piers.

The garden leads off to the south where a York stone walk is enclosed by a heavy pergola with massive timbers and round pillars of Cotswold stone, reminiscent of Hestercombe, leading to a curved seat and niche, which dates the garden at 1922. This pergola carries the purple Teinturier Grape and the large-leaved *Vitis coignetiae* as well as climbing rose 'New Dawn'. The paved terrace-walk south of the house is bordered by paeonies and overlooks a lawn and apple trees; originally it led directly to the steep-pitched summerhouse on the terraces but now a border intervenes.

The main terraces lie west of the house, which enjoys a splendid view into the valley and to unspoilt pasture beyond. An attractive loggia faces south at right angles to the house to create a sheltered corner. This top terrace is perhaps a little too broad for the scale of the house but otherwise the four terraces are well arranged with the gazebo-style summerhouse acting as the cornerstone. High to the north-west the former rock garden has understandably given way to a new swimming-pool, the surroundings of which have been arranged for utility rather than to match the original scheme. Circular steps from the top terrace lead past the swimming-pool and a lily pond to the unusual rose garden, which is designed with a central seat recess as its focal point, the beds radiating out in a half-circle within a complex arrangement of yew hedges. As well as roses there is a large False Acacia and a Maidenhair Tree.

Returning to the house, the beautifully varied arrangement and planting of the terraces can be appreciated. From the plain top terrace, central steps descend to a terrace occupied almost entirely by an herbaceous border, then to a narrow E-shaped terrace with topiary yews and red floribunda roses which finishes with steps at the southern end to the gazebo. Finally one emerges down superbly detailed convex stone steps to a plain lawn with the sheep only a ha-ha away.

South of the terraces is a small valley, once an elaborate water garden. Now there are some fine trees here: the 'Goldsworth Purple' form of the Norway Maple; a Sweet Gum, *Liquidambar styraciflua; Cercidiphyllum japonicum*; a Dawn Redwood, *Metasequoia glyptostroboides*; two large birches, and a fine mulberry. The stream is now carried in a stone channel through to a small bog garden — where the leaves of *Peltiphyllum peltatum* and *Rheum palmatum* contrast with crocosmias and Martagon Lilies — and via a waterfall into the duck-pond.

All gardens must adapt to the times and to balance the loss of the labour-intensive rock and water gardens Great Rissington has been given a new dimension. Beyond the duck-pond with its ornamental water fowl is a young arboretum. With spruces, larches, Scots Pines and Lawson's Cypresses for shelter, a variety of trees have been planted with large drifts of vigorous shrubs and winding rides, like a small, immature Westonbirt. Already some fine associations are manifest: *Sorbus hupehensis* with Fire Thorns and Blue Cedars, and purple maples with *Amelanchier laevis* and Silver Willows. The soil is evidently neutral or slightly acid here making it possible for rhododendrons, *Embothrium coccineum lanceolatum* and *Eucryphia glutinosa* to thrive — a rare sight in the Cotswolds.

After that feast of arboriculture a final pleasure awaits when the terraces and house can be viewed across the duck-pond; a better balanced composition of house, terraces and garden would be difficult indeed to find.

The Grey House
Mr and Mrs C. Taylor

Open for NGS in spring and for RC with Blockley Gardens in summer. In Paxford 3.2km (2m) NE of Blockley and 3.2km (2m) E of Chipping Campden. 0.8ha (2 acre) garden of mature trees and shrubs with water garden on Knee Brook.

Hidcote Manor
The National Trust

At Hidcote Bartrim, 6.4km (4m) NE of Chipping Campden; signposted from the A46 and B4081. Open every day except Tuesday and Friday, April–October; see NT Opening Arrangements. Manor House not open. Teas available; no dogs. Garden of 4.5ha (10 acres), owned by the National Trust, presented in 1948 by Major Lawrence Johnston, who created it during the previous 40 years. Situated at 183m (600ft) in the Cotswold Hills on heavy soil overlying oolitic limestone, but leached and not strongly alkaline. Cold, exposed site modified by shelter-belts and high hedges. Rainfall 635mm (25in.). Six gardeners. Excellent guidebook available, also a full account of the garden in **Gardens of the National Trust** *by G.S. Thomas (Weidenfeld and Nicolson, 1979).*

Perhaps we shall never know whether Lawrence Johnston made a garden at Hidcote despite the limitations of the site or because of them. Undoubtedly the views appealed to him, for he used them to such great effect in the design; but that he should have deliberately selected such an exposed position on heavy alkaline soil to create the most important English garden of the twentieth-century seems improbable. We know that in 1902, after service in the Boer War, he went to Northumberland to learn farming, partly at least because the North was thought to be good for his 'weak lungs'. When his mother, Mrs Winthrop, bought him a farm, the choice of a cool and breezy situation high in the Cotswolds would have been logical.

Apart from a fine old Lebanon Cedar and a clump of beech trees there was little established garden. There is no evidence of a master plan. The garden grew gradually as Lawrence Johnston's interest in gardening grew, stimulated by his developing circle of gardening acquaintants: Major Mark Fenwick of Abbotswood, the Hon. Robert James of St Nicholas,

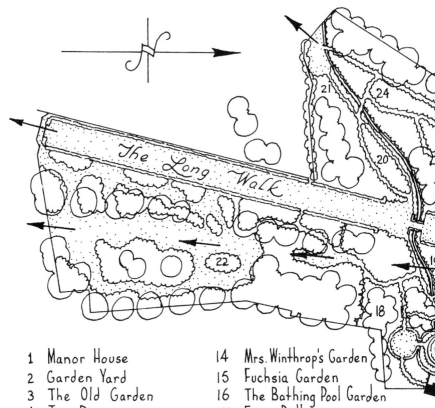

The Long Walk

1 Manor House	14 Mrs. Winthrop's Garden
2 Garden Yard	15 Fuchsia Garden
3 The Old Garden	16 The Bathing Pool Garden
4 Tea Rooms	17 Fern Dell
5 The White Garden	18 Back Border
6 The Maple Garden	19 Upper Stream Garden
7 The Circle	20 Central Stream Garden
8 The Red Borders	21 Lower Stream Garden
9 Garden Houses	22 'Westonbirt'
10 Stilt Garden	23 The Rock Bank
11 The Pillar Garden	24 The Spring
12 Terrace Garden	25 Camellia Corner
13 Winter Garden	26 The Pine Garden

← Notable views

Scale

0 ___ 30 ___ 60 metres
0 _ 50 _ 100 _ 75 _ 200 feet

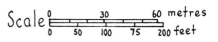

HIDCOTE MANO

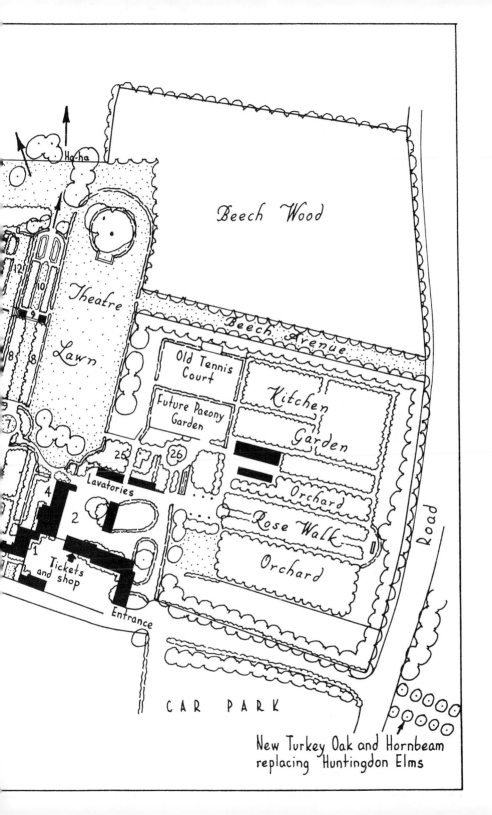

Ha-ha

Beech Wood

Theatre

Lawn

12

10

9

8 8

7

Beech Avenue

Old Tennis
Court

Future Paeony
Garden

Kitchen

Garden

25

26

Orchard

Lavatories

Rose Walk

4

2

Orchard

1

Tickets
and shop

Entrance

Road

CAR   PARK

New Turkey Oak and Hornbeam
replacing Huntingdon Elms

near Richmond, Yorkshire, the Vicomte de Noailles and others. Later there was Norah Lindsay, and then the Muirs who came to live at nearby Kiftsgate. He also had contacts with artists and artist-craftsmen of the day through his friends, the Navarros, at Broadway. Great gardens are rarely created by one person alone and there can be little doubt that his mother, Mrs Winthrop, had as much influence over his gardening as she had over other aspects of his life.

Hedges were needed for shelter and, like all great designers, Johnston made a virtue out of necessity. He planted them with originality and brilliance to create a series of interconnecting spaces, outdoor rooms and corridors, each 'furnished' to a carefully contrived theme but planted with disarming informality in what has been called rather simplistically the English cottage garden style. In fact he combined patterns of paving and topiary with planting according to Gertrude Jekyll's principles to make exciting and original schemes: the Red Borders with purple foliage; the Old Garden of light blues, pinks and silvers — schemes which are now copied in countless flower borders and cut-flower arrangements throughout the country.

He collected plants avidly, both in the wild in South Africa and China and by exchange with friends and visitors. The garden became, and still remains, a remarkable plant collection, always changing as gardens must. It has been said that he even imported lime-free soil by the train-load to extend the range to camellias and rhododendrons. But there are lime-free parts in several of the hill-top gardens of the north Cotswolds and he used sawdust widely. Although new plants poured in, their use was never indiscriminate, each instead being blended with others to create an intended effect, often against the sombre background of hollies, yews and Holm Oaks. The old French roses were much favoured and the garden became famous for them. Paeonies, hydrangeas, maples and magnolias are among the other specialities and several plants have been named after the garden and its creator.

Johnston's great genius lay not only in his ability to use plants but above all in the way that he was able to contrast the disciplined use of clipped architectural shapes with areas of profuse planting. The restful calm of the plain lawns and crisp hedges of the Long Walk acts as a foil to the intricate and sophisticated planting of Mrs Winthrop's Garden and the Pillar Garden. All is tied together with strong axial vistas rising at their ends to enigmatic views of the sky.

The visitor is always drawn on to explore further; a new delight is around every corner. Johnston spent much of his childhood in France and made another garden at Serre de Madone, near Menton, which he bought in the early 1920s. The Gallic influence at Hidcote is clear but the firm architectural lines of France have been softened and enriched by planting which is truly English in style and content.

The garden is not composed entirely of formal enclosures, hedged around. It is a fusion of styles with William Robinson's influence most apparent in the freedom and informality of the Stream Garden and Westonbirt.

The immense influence of Hidcote on gardens of this century is manifest both here and abroad. Sissinghurst Castle, Tintinhull House, Crathes Castle, Newby Hall — and, more recently, Barnsley House and The Dower House, Badminton — all owe much to Lawrence Johnston. Indeed it is difficult to find a country house garden where his ideas have not been used, consciously or unconsciously.

After it had become inevitably run down during the Second World War, the garden was given to the National Trust in 1948. Such gardens can only thrive on constant revision and replanting and the National Trust always takes a positive line, continually restoring the structure and rethinking the planting within the themes envisaged by its creator. It is no easy task to keep the personal touch in a garden made entirely for the enjoyment of its owner and his friends but now seen by tens of thousands every year. This brings problems Lawrence Johnston would never have foreseen but the standard of upkeep remains as high as ever.

Hidcote Vale

One mile away towards Chipping Campden where Miss B.C. Muir gardens on the same breezy ridge as does her sister at KIFTSGATE *q.v. Although only about 0.4ha (1 acre) in extent, the garden is of full interest for the plantsman.*

There is a remarkable collection of unusual and tender plants, all labelled, and everything is in impeccable order. Thanks to deep loamy soil which varies in heaviness across the garden, Miss Muir has found suitable places to grow an enviable range. To temper the wind she has planted hedges of Leyland Cypress and *Elaeagnus* × *ebbingei* but above head height only the most wind-firm trees survive. Near the gate some Italian Cypresses of many years' standing show that, like Kiftsgate and Hidcote, the site is not subject to the most intensive cold despite the altitude. Another legacy of the past is a magnificent pair of silver variegated hollies, probably 'Argenteomarginata', tall and well-shaped.

Miss Muir has sensibly made the framework of the borders with dependable hardy shrubs, especially roses like *R. rubrifolia*, *R. moyesii*,

'Fritz Nobis', 'Sarah van Fleet', 'Highdownensis' and the hybrid China Rose *R. chinensis mutabilis* which she considers 'the best in the world'. But she believes in being adventurous and among them a great range of reputedly tender plants are tried with much success. Although the bitter winter of 1978/79 took its toll there were also major triumphs including *Ceanothus prostratus*, *Olearia* 'Zennorensis', *Ozothamnus ledifolius (Helichrysum ledifolium)* and even the rare broom-like New Zealand shrub *Chordospartium stevensonii*. In the bright and airy conditions silver plants do well and they are a theme in the garden. But this is not just another plantsman's mixture; the whole garden is carefully thought out for colour and for foliage and textural effects. One corner is devoted to silver foliage and orange flowers with *Artemisia ludoviciana*, Cotton Lavender, *Glaucium flavum* and the large-flowered *Zauschneria* 'Glasnevin'.

There are untold treasures to linger over and many examples of how to make the most effective use of a garden of modest proportions.

Hill House

Sally, Duchess of Westminster

At NW edge of Wickwar, 6.4km (4m) N of Chipping Sodbury towards Wotton-under-Edge; west of B4060 on road signposted to Gloucester. Mostly informal garden of approx. 1.6ha (4 acres) around stone-coloured house. Open for NGS and GS late June early July. Heavy, alluvial, slightly alkaline soil. Rainfall 813mm (32in). Mainly level site on slight eminence in the Severn Valley at 60m (200ft). One half-time gardener and two half-time pensioners with considerable help from the owner.

Some gardens are made slowly and deliberately, with as much sense of finality as is possible with growing things. Other gardeners, equally successfully, make a virtue out of change, aiming to create an always developing scene. At Hill House, Sally, Duchess of Westminster has chosen the latter course, using plants with great imagination and freedom to create a beautiful garden in record time. It is not easy to accept that, apart from the framework of walls and trees, this garden has virtually been created since 1968. With great energy the Duchess has planted and altered the garden, extending it in some parts and contracting it in others, each year a new excitement. Meanwhile the garden has evolved into what it is today.

The drive rises steeply from the road beneath fine beeches, ashes, Corsican Pines, a Copper Beech, a fine Weeping Silver Lime and an enormous *Ailanthus altissima*, all giving shelter from the north and east where many new young trees have wisely been added.

The garden lies mainly west of the house where a striking sweep of lawn is fringed with shrubby borders that advance and recede like stage wings to create a series of intriguing spaces. The planting is rich and mixed and recognizably of the 1970s with clever colour blending and frequent use of plants for foliage effect, especially silver and gold. Small trees, shrubs, roses and herbaceous plants for colour and ground-cover rub shoulders to fill every space and leave no room for the weeds. The effect is stimulating and full of interest.

Against the house is a gravel terrace over which sprawl scented sages, rosemary, lavenders and dwarf junipers with roses on the house walls, 'Mermaid' and 'Mme Alfred Carrière'. On the 'cottage' is a superb mixture of rose 'New Dawn' and the clematis 'Jackmanii'. Nearby is a small pool with a cherub fountain almost enveloped in willows, especially the Silver Willow, *Salix alba* 'Sericea' and the fine-foliaged *Salix eleagnos*. The dwarf *S. repens* 'Argentea' is contrasted with the purple filbert and *Buddleia* 'Lochinch' and a Weeping Larch has *Clematis viticella* 'Minuet' rampaging through it.

Beyond an old apple smothered by the climbing rose 'Mrs Honey Dyson', white-flowering *Escallonia* 'Iveyi' combines with the Mexican Orange, *Hypericum* 'Hidcote' and the pineapple-scented *Cytisus battandieri*, with an ancient Mulberry beyond. Other successful associations include an enormous *Abutilon vitifolium* (a favourite plant in the garden) with golden variegated dogwood, and rose 'Nevada' with *Philadelphus coronarius* 'Aureus'. Hebes are plentiful and 'Midsummer Beauty' combines well with roses 'Chinatown' and 'Cecile Brunner'.

There are all kinds of shrub roses; *Rosa alba* and the pale pink 'Fantin-Latour' associated happily with the silver form of *Buddleia alternifolia* and the Plume Poppy, *Macleaya cordata*.

At the end of the main expanse of lawn there is a natural division formed by an old cedar and other trees where a row of fifteenth-century Veronese columns brought from Eaton Hall have been erected, forming at the same time an eye-catcher and an inviting gateway to the newer garden beyond. This area has been developed since 1970 in total contrast as a series of island beds, concentrating on foliage colour, and specimen trees in grass. It is now again in the process of being changed and simplified to reduce work but some of the many choice young trees are likely to remain, including the bold-leaved silver *Sorbus* 'Mitchellii', the variegated Tulip Tree, *Koelreuteria paniculata*, and several *Nothofagus* spp. including an extraordinary horizontal-growing *N. antarctica*. The south-facing wall of this part of the garden supports roses including: Wolley-Dod's Rose, *Rosa villosa* 'Duplex'; 'Dortmund'; 'Wickwar', a cross between *R. brunonii* and

R. soulieana retaining the grey foliage of the latter; the rare and voluptuous 'Souvenir de l'Impératrice', 'Josephine', 'Paulii' and 'Agnes'. Also enjoying the warmth are *Buddleia colvilei* and *B. crispa, Itea illicifolia, Carpentaria californica,* several *Ceanothus* cultivars and clumps of *Agapanthus.*

Returning towards the house along the sheltered south-facing side the way leads to a total surprise: a straight walk of pleached limes, completely concealed by the luxuriant shrub borders. The limes are trained across the path at intervals to make green arches and also along the wide borders to create picture-frames within which a series of well-planned schemes are presented; here there are many more shrub and climbing roses, ornamental grasses, hydrangeas, hollyhocks, geraniums, Russian Sage, penstemons, lilies, catmint, foxgloves and great clumps of Goat's Beard, *Aruncus dioicus.*

The pleached-lime walk leads to a small aviary made in an old greenhouse and back to the main lawn past more large, flowing, groups of sun-loving shrubs: cultivars of *Hebe* including 'Mrs Winder' and 'Midsummer Beauty' with species of *Cistus* and Jackman's Rue, and the quick-growing evergreen *Elaeagnus* × *ebbingei* and the Smoke Bush, *Cotinus coggygria,* are both prominent too. As a final flourish in this garden of exciting and original plant associations, an old golden holly stands surrounded by *Senecio* 'Sunshine', the soft silver leaves a perfect foil to the glistening prickliness above and the golden flowers in their season picking up the colour of the holly foliage.

Hodges Barn

Mr and Mrs C.N. Hornby

At Shipton Moyne, on the Malmesbury side; 4.8km (3m) S of Tetbury. Open two or three times in spring and summer for NGS Varied garden of 3.2ha (8 acres) around unusual and beautiful house (not open) converted from a sixteenth-century barn and two dovecotes by Lawrence Methuen in 1939. Situated in an open park-like setting on good medium-to-heavy soil over Cotswold limestone at 91m (300ft). Rainfall 864mm (34in.). Maintained by the owners and one gardener.

The most satisfying gardens are those where beautiful buildings and a profusion of fine plants are combined with that unity that comes from a strong sense of design; such is the garden at Hodges. From 1949 until she died in 1976, the Hon. Mrs A. Strutt created a layout at Hodges of exceptional charm and surprising maturity around an exquisite house. Such a personal creation might have been totally lost but the present owners, Mr and Mrs C.N. Hornby, have maintained the tradition of good gardening here while shaping the garden to their own taste.

The original sixteenth-century house was burnt down in 1556, leaving the columbary, consisting of a stable barn and two square-built dovecotes with Cotswold stone domed roofs, rising from finely moulded and shaped cornices. Nearby are the stew ponds for carp which with the pigeons formed an important part of the diet in Elizabethan days. After the estate had become derelict the buildings were converted in 1939 with great success, using Queen Anne-style fenestration and doorways.

It was not until 1949, when Mrs Strutt bought the property, that gardening began in earnest. The site, amidst rolling pasture, is open and windy and this must have caused problems. Mrs Strutt wisely planted shelter-belts of birches, pines and Norway Maples and established the garden woodlands around the house. Apart from some hedgerow elms, now sadly all gone, a few fine specimen trees already framed the house — notably two enormous London Planes, one east and one west of the house, two old limes and a huge oak — all of which remain.

The rectangular, walled garden on the south front, through which garden visitors enter, overlooks the park. The Hornbys have fenced in a semicircular apron outside and planted it attractively with groups of daffodils and a pattern of flowering crabs leading to a stone seat. The layout of the enclosed area is attractively simple, being mainly lawn with borders and flowering cherries, including the ever-popular 'Kanzan' and *Prunus serrula* for its shining bark and attractive fruits. Otherwise colours are mostly pale and restrained with white, green, pale blue and pink flowers and silver foliage predominating. Here are white Polyanthus, Hellebores and Solomon's Seal. A curved house terrace echoes the shape of the dovecote roof and looks entirely appropriate. Its foundations were uncovered by German prisoners-of-war when they were clearing the site in 1948 and the part of the enclosing balustrade was found in a ditch, enabling its restoration. In setting, proportion and planting the terrace is perfect, and is a wonderfully warm and sheltered spot to sit out. Aubrietia, Grape Hyacinths and the little silver cushions of *Chrysanthemum haradjanii* soften the paving while the house walls behind provide sheltered support for climbing roses, including the white 'Félicité et Perpétue' and orange-red 'Danse du Feu', and Climbing Hydrangea.

Crossing at right angles to the south front is a spectacular vista through opposite openings in the flanking walls. One way leads west to a simple grass area hedged around with yew. This whole side of the house is dominated by an enormous old London Plane with a splendid soaring bole and cyclamen at its feet. Eastwards gives a tempting view through the pond garden to the woodland garden beyond. In spring well-planned drifts of cream and white daffodils pick up the silver of the birch stems to give a delightfully light and harmonious effect. The pond garden has a

canopy of trees formed from the original oak, plane and limes supplemented by a Weeping Willow, the unusual Red Buckeye, *Aesculus
pavia*, and a fine *Acer griseum*. For background there is a generous shrubbery with more flowering cherries, lilacs and sweetly-fragrant Mock
Orange. Near the water extensive plantings of moisture-loving plants
provide summer flowers and soften the hard pond edge with their lush
foliage. Here the large-leaved *Ligularia dentata, Rheum palmatum* and
glaucous *Hosta sieboldii* are contrasted with Day Lilies, the fiery *Curtonus
paniculatus* and the prickly-leaved evergreen *Helleborus corsicus*. The Red
Bistort, Yellow Loosestrife and candelabra primulas are massed around.
Two successful new beds have been filled entirely with the best of the
Rugosa roses underplanted with Lenten Roses, Forget-me-Nots, bulbs and
grey plants to give interest from March to November.

It seems incredible that the woodland garden further east has grown up
in little over 30 years. In the deep moist soil the Norway Maples, poplars,
birches and Western Red Cedars are still growing quickly and, despite the
demise of the elms, continual thinning will be needed to retain the now
delightfully open effect. The Hornbys have already removed over one
hundred trees and planted a variety of replacements: Whitebeams,
including *Sorbus aria* 'Lutescens', *S. aria* 'Decaisneana' and *S.* 'Mitchellii',
Rowans, *S. commixta* and *S.* 'Joseph Rock', and magnolias in several forms
of M. × *soulangiana* and M. × *loebneri* 'Merrill'. Groups of pale daffodils are
followed by bluebells in the dappled shade. Beyond the woodland, beside a
cottage, is an open croquet-lawn with big walnuts and more groups of
daffodils and *Erythronium* 'White Beauty' around the fringe. This is the site
of the sixteenth-century house. For summer there are borders of roses and
shrubs.

The walled kitchen garden and the orchard alongside have been adapted,
as all gardens must if they are to survive, to the needs of the new owners
with tennis-courts and a swimming-pool and pavilion replacing much of
the former labour-intensive vegetable and fruit production. Many of Mrs
Strutt's collection of rare shrub roses have had to go but borders for cut
flowers and a plant-crammed glasshouse remain.

Perhaps the most flowery and beautifully arranged part of the garden at
Hodges is that which lies north of the house where the ground rises
beyond the gravel of the entrance forecourt. A broad flight of steps,
guarded by topiary pieces, interrupts the stone retaining wall to create a
main axis from the front door. This is a vista full of promise giving a
glimpse between topiary peacocks and through hedges to an eye-catching
stone seat. The stone walls are hung with a rich tapestry of aubrietia,
valerian and catmint with climbing roses cascading here and there. Up the
steps the grass terrace is dominated by flowering cherries and *Magnolia* ×
soulangiana and the borders are profuse with shrubs including some of the

older roses underplanted with hellebores, primroses and Plantain Lilies. The way leads into an *allée* of tapestry hedges and out into an avenue of young Irish Yews, a good choice to replace the avenue of *Chamaecyparis lawsoniana* 'Fraseri' planted by Mrs Strutt. The view from the stone seat to the beehive dome and tower of pale Cotswold stone, framed in the darkly contrasting yew foliage, is a prospect of unique beauty worth travelling a long way to see.

Home Farm
See Courtfield

Hyam
See The Lammas

Ilsom
Sir Kenneth Preston

1.6km (1m) NE of Tetbury on A433 Cirencester road. Open for NGS in late spring. Garden of 2ha (5 acres) around Cotswold stone house designed by Maurice Chesterton in 1922 and extended by him in 1936. In small-scale hilly country at 106m (350ft) on rich alkaline soil over Cotswold limestone. Rainfall 864mm (34in.). One gardener.

Once the modest farmhouse of Hillsome Farm, the house seems to have been extended as much as the name has been abbreviated. Sir Kenneth Preston's father employed Maurice Chesterton, architect of the Stratford-on-Avon Memorial Theatre, not only to extend the house after the First World War and again just before the Second World War but also to design the main framework of the garden. Although the layout was intended for days when more gardeners could be afforded, the 'bones' of the garden are of unusual quality with good stonework and an interesting variety of features held together by connecting vistas.

Extensive accommodation for, at one time, many horses is a feature and the north side of the house is dominated by the impressive stable block with only an herbaceous walk leading to a semicircular stone arbour with a matching seat, under the trees, as a gesture to gardening.

The main garden lies to the south but the best approach is along the west side of the house which looks out over a ha-ha to the adjoining paddock. Here a little crazy-paved terrace has a mass of *Nerine bowdenii*, flag irises and two beds of 'Hugh Dickson' roses meticulously pegged down to encourage flowers down the length of their long stems.

Through the garden gate is a long view to a big Copper Beech past a border of shrub roses and Tree Paeonies sheltered by the west boundary wall. At right angles is the house terrace of crazy-paving full of aubrietia and clumps of flag irises, the wider, square-paved central part being enclosed by a short balustrade and lavender. A big wistaria enjoys the southerly aspect. Sited conveniently at the junction of these two walks is another stone alcove of concave design complete with ivy-leaved geraniums in niches and a complementary curved seat. Here is a place to sit and look out over the extensive lawn to the tall sycamores and a well-shaped walnut tree beyond.

Across the lawn is the little 'piggery garden' with a low shelter covered in *Hedera canariensis* 'Variegata'. This tiny paved area, which was converted from a former pigsty, is surrounded by raised beds overflowing with vigorous alpine plants in relaxed confusion: dwarf geraniums, aubrietia, campanulas, Snow-in-Summer, *Iberis sempervirens* and that fine viola called 'Huntercombe Purple'.

This leads east along another axis through a cruciform rose garden and an elaborate arch topped grandly with an urn and covered with the old rose 'Frau Karl Druschki'. Beyond is a long herbaceous border backed by a high wall designed to screen the tennis-courts. The walk leads to a raised platform of ingenious design with a bench seat invaded by aubrietia where there are views out over the fields to the old railway line along which the famous *Tetbury Flier* once puffed to Cirencester and back.

But the greatest horticultural excitement is still felt on entering the two kitchen gardens, both immaculately maintained in the original style. The first is a walk through borders of sky-high delphiniums and equally vigorous flag irises and pyrethrums, forming a flowery border to neat rows of vegetables and well-established beds of rhubarb, Globe and Jerusalem Artichokes and Asparagus. The main walled garden is beyond and this is a rare treat with its generous herbaceous borders and broad grass path leading to a bench seat backed by a stone wall smothered in 'Albertine' roses. Here are superbly grown salad crops and luscious-looking soft fruits; everything as it should be.

Kemble Gardens

Three gardens open for NGS and RC in early summer. KEMBLE HOUSE (Mrs Donald Peachey) also open through June and July on Wednesday afternoons. 6.4km (4 miles) SW of Cirencester. All three gardens have wonderful roses, especially old-fashioned kinds as well as many other attractions.

Kiftsgate Court

Mrs D.H. Binny

NW of the village of Hidcote Bartrim, 4.8km (3 miles) NE of Chipping Campden, 1.6km (1 mile) E of A46 Chipping Campden to Stratford Road, and B4081. For opening arrangements see HHCG; usually Easter to end September, Weds, Thurs, Sunday afternoons and Bank Holidays. Intensively-planted garden of 1.2ha (3 acres) with a further 1.4ha (3½ acres) of lawns and curtilage. Late nineteenth-century classical house in Cotswold stone. Situated at 167m (550 ft) on a ridge exposed to the N and W; with free-draining alkaline soil over limestone. Rainfall 737mm (29in.). Maintained by the owner and two gardeners. Excellent garden guide and comprehensive lists of plants available. Selection of unusual plants for sale.

Through Mrs Binny's mother, Heather Muir, Kiftsgate played a key part in that great gardening movement that arose as a reaction to the stiff ostentation of high Victorian gardening and culminated in the English garden style of Hidcote and Sissinghurst. It began with the writings of William Robinson who preached the matching of plant to site in as natural a way as possible; it continued with Gertrude Jekyll who developed colour and textural associations of plants and who furnished so subtly Sir Edwin Lutyens' architectural layouts; it reached its climax in the work of Lawrence Johnston at Hidcote, and it has been developed in countless variations since then.

Movements of such artistic magnitude do not happen in isolation and, as close neighbours and friends, Heather Muir and Lawrence Johnston must have helped and inspired one another. Compared with Hidcote, Kiftsgate's garden layout relies more on its close affinity with the house but there is greater freedom and profusion in the planting. The colour schemes are a delight and rank alongside those at Hidcote. In many ways the two gardens are complementary; Hidcote with its unified and original structure and planting, Kiftsgate with its less ambitious but more personal luxuriance and its inspired essays in colour.

The garden sits astonishingly on the very edge of the northern

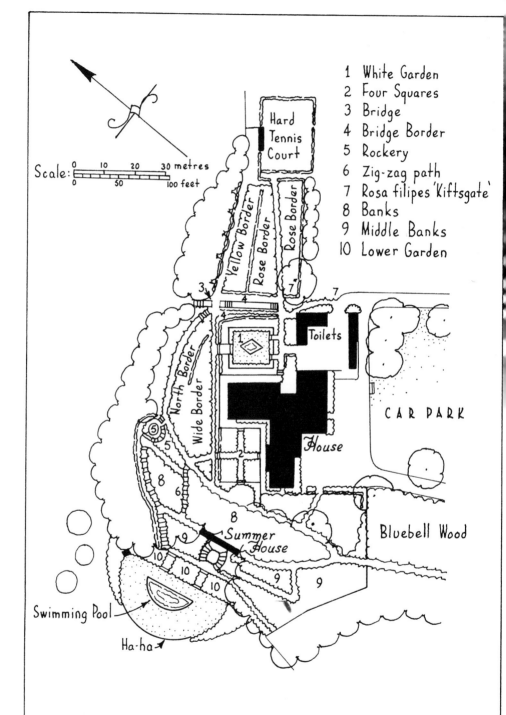

Scale: 0 10 20 30 metres
0 50 100 feet

1 White Garden
2 Four Squares
3 Bridge
4 Bridge Border
5 Rockery
6 Zig-zag path
7 Rosa filipes 'Kiftsgate'
8 Banks
9 Middle Banks
10 Lower Garden

Hard Tennis Court

Yellow Border
Rose Border
Rose Border

Toilets

North Border
Wide Border

House

CAR PARK

Summer House

Bluebell Wood

Swimming Pool

Ha-ha

KIFTSGATE COURT

Cotswold scarp with breathtaking views to the west and north over the Vale of Evesham. Here, between 1920 and 1954, Heather Muir made her garden, sheltered from the wind only by the hedges she planted and trees she augmented. Partly, then, for practical reasons the garden is arranged as a series of outdoor 'rooms' enclosed by hedges and linked sometimes by galleries of the utmost splendour and sometimes by intriguing doors in shady corners.

By contrast the surrounding steep banks carry winding paths and steps through informal shrubs and woodland. No doubt these thickly-planted slopes absorb much of the force of the winds, which would otherwise be deflected upwards with gathering speed into the garden.

As the garden is so well described in the illustrated guide book and a comprehensive list of plants is also available, this account is confined to impressions, the most powerful being the sense of profusion. The plants jostle for space almost as they would in nature. Shrubs are grown to their full stature with climbers through them and bulbs pop up among the weed-smothering groundwork.

The colour schemes are progressive: the blue-shot reds and pinks of old roses, with purples and blues and silvers, in the 'four squares' and similar summery colours, with white and light yellow in the 'wide borders'. The white garden is a cool interlude before exploring new excitements. Beyond the chestnut is the yellow border with gold and sulphur-coloured flowers set against deep-purple foliage, with contrasting touches of strong blue and purple flowers giving a rich and exotic effect.

The collection of old roses is well known for its range and for the immense proportions to which each bush is grown. Largest of all is the famous 'Kiftsgate' rose, *Rosa filipes* Kiftsgate', which has engulfed several trees in covering almost one tenth of an hectare (a quarter of an acre) and has now climbed to over 14.5m (50ft) high.

Mrs Binny has carried on the traditions of her mother's garden with dedication but has also continued to develop it and additions include the fountain pool in the white garden and the swimming-pool in the valley below the house, as well as many new planting schemes especially on the banks. Throughout the whole garden runs the indefinable individuality that comes from an imaginative and sensitive owner having been closely and consistently involved, not only in each decision, large or small, but also in carrying it through.

The Lammas
Mr and Mrs G.V. Sherren

Hyam
Mr and Mrs Douglas Anderson

Usually open together in summer for RC and again for NGS   At Minchinhampton, 8km (5 miles) SE of Stroud.

THE LAMMAS has a comprehensive 2.8ha (7 acre) garden with many fine mature trees including a splendid Variegated Sycamore, a Copper Beech, Horse Chestnuts and three Wellingtonias. The beautiful bow-fronted Georgian house has an ancient tithe-barn alongside and commands magnificent views over the Avening Valley. Borders flanking the view contain a wide range of shrubs and herbaceous plants. In addition there is a water garden, a rose garden, a swimming-pool and a charming paved courtyard on the north side with a raised central bed and tall climbing roses on the walls. The 0.4ha (1 acre) kitchen garden with its extensive greenhouses is kept in immaculate order and the whole garden is full of pleasure and interest. HYAM shares the glorious view across Gatcombe woods over an apron of parkland. This is separated from the garden by a low wall and fine wrought-iron gates. The garden has a sunken rose garden, herbaceous borders, lavender hedges, sweet peas, dahlias and an unusual 'landscaped' vegetable garden with flowers and vegetables effectively mixed. Together these two gardens make an excellent afternoon out.

Lasborough Manor
Major and Mrs C.A. Fisher

House and garden open for NGS by appointment. 8km (5 miles) W of Tetbury. Garden with herbaceous border and shrubs around beautiful Cotswold Manor of 1609.

The Level
Mr and Mrs R.H.H. Taylor

At Pillowell, 5.6km (3½ miles) N of Lydney via B4234 turning right just before the level crossing. Open for NGS and GS in summer and by appointment all year. Informal garden of 1ha (2½ acres) made since 1975 on site of two slag heaps: Steep westerly side of Forest of Dean, at 60m (200ft). Lime-free shale from surface coal workings, pH 5 to 6.5, with springs. Rainfall 813mm (31in.). Maintained entirely by the owners. Many unusual plants for sale.

Gardens excite a variety of emotions but rarely is the abiding impression one of utter astonishment. One can think of great gardens like Hidcote, for example, which were created thus in response to the limitations of a difficult site, but it is impossible to imagine anything more challenging than was Mr and Mrs Taylor's garden in 1975. Small-scale private coal mining has been carried on in the Forest of Dean since Roman times and even now a few of the 'Free Miners of the Hundred of St Briavels' still operate in small partnerships. The effect has been to give the inhabitants an independence of outlook and the area a special character of unplanned contrasts not found elsewhere in the country. Small slag heaps abound and on a pair of these Mr and Mrs Taylor chose to make their garden.

Although there is no real topsoil and only the remains of discarded mining paraphernalia amongst the shaly waste, even this has been turned to advantage. The coombe in which the garden is situated runs westwards to provide pleasant views with shelter from the east and north and the Severn Estuary has a moderating effect on the climate. The extreme irregularity of the terrain creates a series of separate microclimates, including springs and boggy parts, which are being fully exploited. The problems of lack of topsoil and of gardening help, for the garden has been made and maintained entirely by the owners, is largely solved by the use of pulverized tree bark and sawdust, obtained locally in bulk and used as a mulch to conserve moisture and reduce weeding. Peat and balanced fertilizer are used liberally when planting and, on the lime-free base, fertility improves as organic matter accumulates.

The energy and enthusiasm of the owners is clear from the remarkable rate at which the garden has developed. In the few years since 1975 the whole area has been planted with over 2,000 separate species, many of them unusual or even rare and each recorded with its source and other details in a card index. The collection includes over 90 forms of *Hebe* and many rare old roses, and planting and replanting continues apace. Few gardeners are conscientious enough to keep such good records and the Taylors will no doubt reap the rewards of their thoroughness.

The garden is essentially personal but Mr and Mrs Taylor have a refreshingly open-minded approach, never hidebound by tradition. Their evident success is due to their willingness to experiment and to make changes in pursuit of their ideal, and already some areas have been replanted.

The drive is bordered by old roses, eucalyptus, *Leptospermum* spp., underplanted with various spurges, including the fine *Euphorbia stricta* and the Summer Hyacinth, *Galtonia candicans*. Barberries are prominent especially the glaucous *B. approximata* and *B.* 'Gold Ring' looking better here than I have ever seen it. In front of the house is a large island limestone-scree bed full of the choicest dwarf plants, acid at one end to accommodate Gentians. The house has the only walls in the garden and they are well used to shelter the tender *Olearia stellulata* and *Coronilla valentina* among climbing roses.

Behind the house a new water garden has been made to take advantage of the natural springs with dwarf rhododendron and *Meconopsis* species around. Beyond, an old orchard with the local Cider Apples and 'Blaisdon Red' plums supports old climbing roses like 'Mrs Honey Dyson'.

The heather garden is a major feature and as well as the best of *Calluna*, *Daboecia* and *Erica*, there are dwarf brooms and conifers, with birches for height, the extra whiteness of *B. jacquemontii* conspicuous among several species. A wet area makes an ideal site for willows with the rosemary-leaved *Salix eleagnos* and perhaps the best of the pussy willows *S. gracilistyla*, along with the prostrate, silver *S. repens argentea*.

Dividing the garden is a steep-sided ravine in which a stream runs for most of the year but is apt to flood occasionally. The banks are well clothed with a variety of flowering cherries and rowans, strong-growing shrubs like Golden Elder and willows underplanted with low spreaders such as *Rubus tricolor*. The cool moistness below is in splendid contrast to the hot banks and allows a whole new range of plants to be grown. Here is a well-chosen selection including the more usual species of *Cornus*, *Rodgersia*, *Ligularia* and *Macleaya* together with the less common like *Senecio smithii*, *Mimulus ringens*, *Euphorbia mellifera* and *Cyperus vegetus*.

There is a great deal more to see on the sunny banks above including a vast range of old shrub roses, some of which were rescued from oblivion by Mr Arthur Wyatt who gave them to Mr and Mrs Taylor. There is a rock garden bank and new orchard-like area with ornamental *Sorbus* and *Malus*. The whole garden is intensively planted with all manner of treasures: *Olearia*, *Cytisus*, *Genista*, *Cistus*, *Abutilon*, *Potentilla*, *Kniphofia*, *Euphorbia* — each seems to be a speciality. There is nothing for it but to see it for yourself and come away inspired to try to do almost as well.

Little Barrow

Sir Charles and Lady Mander

Open for NGS in spring and summer. Half-way between Stow-on-the-Wold and Moreton-in-Marsh. Medium-sized with sunken garden, spring flowers, lawns, roses, herbaceous borders and yew hedges, vegetable and fruit garden.

Little Orchard

Miss Hilda Druckler

Open for NGS early summer. In centre of Moreton-in-Marsh. Medium-sized with old orchard, herbaceous borders and small pools.

Lydney Park

The Viscountess Bledisloe

0.8km (½ mile) W of Lydney on N side of A48 Gloucester-Chepstow Road. Normally open on Sundays and some Thursdays late April to early June and again in October, sometimes for GS but for full arrangements see HHCG 4ha (10 acre) informal garden of rhododendrons and other trees and shrubs in woodland setting; 0.8ha (2 acre) formal garden around 1875 house; deer park and site of Roman Camp. On light, lime-free soil over sandstone. Altitude 46-76m (150-250ft). Rainfall 858mm (34in.). Maintained by a head gardener and one assistant plus some part-time help. A good guide book to the Garden and Roman Camp is available.

When in 1875 the Rev. William Hiley Bathurst decided to build a new house he rejected the low-lying seventeenth-century site near the main road in favour of a part of the lovely, undulating park facing south and commanding a broad panoramic view over the Severn estuary, a prospect still impressive but affected by industrial development on the fringe of Lydney. Fine old oaks, Sweet Chestnuts and beeches already formed the bones of the park. In a valley beyond the house is a grove of superb London Planes whose growth has benefitted from a running stream near their roots. These seem certainly to predate the Rev. William Hiley but despite their size are probably not more than 180 years old.

The handsome Victorian house was provided with a wide gravel platform and two more terraces falling away to the south in front of it.

The present planting dates mainly from the time Lord and Lady Bledisloe came to live at Lydney Park in 1950 and they have made good use of the mild and sunny, but windswept, site. In front of the house a line of *Chamaecyparis lawsoniana* 'Kilmacurragh', the best of the fastigiate Lawson's Cypresses, frame the view and the house walls are well used to accommodate the exotic evergreen *Magnolia grandiflora,* wisteria, Wintersweet and *Abelia* spp. There are two fountain pools, both designed by Lord Bledisloe, one at the western end with some stone figures at the edge and the other at the eastern end overhung by the double gean cherry and surrounded with paving and many of the deservedly popular foliage plants of today: Cotton Lavender, potentillas, hostas and *Berberis thunbergii* 'Atropurpurea Nana', with Pfitzer Juniper and the crisp white flowers of rose 'Iceberg'. The terraces below are sheltered by *Cotoneaster lacteus,* the perfect choice where an evergreen late-fruiting hedge is required. Further east, surprisingly for this exposed position, is a collection of *Magnolia* spp. with even the large-leaved *M. obovata* and the comparitively tender *M.* × *veitchii* as well as forms of *M.* × *soulangiana,* all thriving and vigorous. The vast Copper Beech was planted by the late Lord Bledisloe's mother around 1910.

The main horticultural riches lie a short distance from the house in a wooded valley through which runs a stream. The mildness of the estuary combined with shelter and acid soil create the ideal spot for rhododendrons and other choice shrubs and trees. Every advantage has been taken of the conditions to create both a colourful spring spectacle and a fine collection of *Rhododendron* species and many of the more modern cultivars. These are given lightness and variety by the inclusion of maples, conifers, magnolias and other trees and shrubs, all arranged around a series of lakes constructed since 1957.

Near the entrance gate a fiery mixture of Knaphill and Exbury Azaleas with *Pieris forrestii* 'Flame of the Forest' overlooks a small pool which is surrounded by evergreen azaleas, the diminutive *R. impeditum, R. yakushimanum* with its silvery undersides, contrasted with *Bergenia* spp., Japanese Maples and *Chamaecyparis lawsoniana* 'Stewartii'. Further north up the valley, overlooked by a delicate open gazebo on the west side, are huge clumps of hardy hybrids like *R.* 'John Waterer' and *R.* 'Blue Peter', splendidly in scale with the valley as a whole. Fine young trees of the Weeping Silver Lime, Tulip Tree, Swamp Cypress, Dawn Redwood, *Liquidambar styraciflua* and *Oxydendrum arboreum* have been planted with primulas and the giant *Gunnera manicata* between. Crowning the top of the valley and reflected in three large lakes are two stupendous clumps of *Rhododendron* 'Cynthia', in their season the mass of colour overwhelming all.

The west bank is threaded with sawdust paths, both practical and attractive, and planted with a vast collection of choice species and cultivars many of which are labelled and described in the guide book. At the northern end are recently-planted large groups of *R. sutchuenense, R. calophytum,* and hybrids like 'Hawk Crest', 'Lodger's White', 'Tortoiseshell Champagne', 'Avalanche' and the summer-flowering 'Polar Bear' with *Eucalyptus coccifera, Pieris* spp. and *Halesia carolina.* Further south the 20 year old specimens have joined up to give a series of enclosed walks between camellias, *Corylopsis* spp., magnolias, especially *M. wilsonii,* and *Crinodendron hookeranum* with all sorts of rhododendrons including the more tender 'Penjerrick', 'Cornish Cross' and 'Tally Ho' mixed with the hardier hybrids like 'Naomi', 'Betty Wormald', 'Britannia' and 'White Swan'. Leading up into steep but sheltered woodland there is an impressive group of the big-leaved species such as *RR. macabeanum, sinogrande, mollyanum* and *rex* where they can be seen from above for their flowers and below for the various colours and textures of the undersides of their enormous leaves. All in all a rhododendrologist's dream.

Lyegrove House
The Dowager Countess of Westmorland

2.4km (1½m) E of Old Sodbury, 3.2km (2m) SW of Badminton on B4040. Open once a year for NGS Walled and formal garden of 3.2ha (8 acres) within seventeenth-century garden enclosures; house altered in early eighteenth-century and again in 1927 by G.H. Kitchin, who also designed the walled garden layout. Situated at 167m (550ft) in south Cotswolds on well-drained heavy soil over limestone. Rainfall 838mm (33in.). Maintained by one full-time and one part-time gardener.

Since gardens take time to mature and they have constantly to be developed, the role of the owner is, of course, crucial. The great landscapes of the late eighteenth-century were only possible because the designs of Kent, Brown and Repton were accepted and understood by enlightened owners who were able to develop those schemes sympathetically and consistently over several generations. The time-scale with flower gardens is shorter but the principle of continuity and a sustained approach to upkeep is equally important.

Like Rodmarton Manor, Lyegrove was made in the period between the wars using the principle of collaboration between architect, who laid out the outline of stonework, gates and buildings, and inspired artist-plantsman, who clothed and furnished the scheme. This was the partnership followed with such success by Sir Edwin Lutyens and Gertrude Jekyll.

Since 1927, when G.H. Kitchin was employed to alter the house and to design the chief outlines of the first walled garden with the lily pool, Lyegrove has been developed and tended by Lady Westmorland. This continuity is wholly apparent in the highly refined maturity of the planting which has softened and enriched the architectural lines of the garden. The seeming inevitability of the outcome gives rise to a deep sense of tranquillity and repose — indispensable qualities for gardens.

The house is approached from the south along a typically seventeenth-century axial avenue of limes, beeches and chestnuts leading to a forecourt in front of the house, where the low walls are covered with 'Albertine' and 'Alberic Barbier' roses.

The garden to the west occupies the enclosures of the seventeenth-century house with a simple yew-hedged sunken lawn surrounded by a raised walk. Beyond is a 'wilderness' of tall beeches, the fringe of which is full of snowdrops and naturalized daffodils. Along the south side of lawn and wilderness the terrace walk extends, Jacobean style, to a broad space, where there might once have been a mount, giving wide views out to the south and west. A castellated folly, one of the ventilation shafts of the Badminton railway tunnel, catches the eye. North of the lawn, enormous old sycamores shelter a bold group of the ornamental rhubarb *Rheum palmatum* and more bulbs.

The walled garden lies south-east of the house and is approached across the forecourt and past a sheltered south-facing terrace full of valerian, overlooking a lawn where many shrub roses grow.

An imposing gateway with ball-headed finials leads into the square north walled garden. Yew hedges have been planted to enclose axial paths, so dividing the area and separating each quarter from the central sunken lily pool. Double borders of purple sage, roses, aubrietias, violas and *Myosotis*, with the perennial nasturtium *Tropaeolum polyphyllum* growing into the hedges, lead to the steps into the sunken garden where the paving is home for more red valerian, flag irises, thrift, thyme, *Veronica teucrium* and *Campanula pilosa*. Dwarf, flowering shrubs, foxgloves, penstemons and *Galtonia candicans* fill the borders around. At right angles is the main axis through the garden from Kitchin's fine neo-classical gateway in the centre of the northern boundary wall into the southern section where an avenue of the ancient double form of the Sour Cherry, *Prunus cerasus* 'Rhexii', leads to a Bath-stone summerhouse at the far end.

In each quarter of the north walled garden a scatter of old apple trees in grass, supplemented by cherries and thorns, provides a more intimate scale for the perimeter borders. At either side of Kitchin's gate particularly successful borders of light summery colours face south; delphiniums, lilies, paeonies, poppies and fuchsias are supplemented by silver *Cineraria maritima* and *Stachys lanata* and backed by fragrant *Viburnum* spp., *Abutilon*

Lyegrove House. The gateway and main outlines of the north walled garden were designed by G.H. Kitchen.   *Country Life*

vitifolium, and old roses with climbing roses, *Solanum crispum* and vines on the wall.

The contrasting Spring Garden to the south was made by Lady Westmorland after Kitchin had finished at Lyegrove. It consists of two oblong sunken lawns either side of the main axis surrounded by low walls against which a fascinating variety of shrubs, ground cover plants and bulbs grow. Here are magnolias, especially forms of *M. × soulangiana*; flowering cherries; shrub roses such as *R. × cantabrigensis, R. moyesii*, 'Nevada', 'Penelope' and 'Frühlingsgold'; *Hydrangea villosa* and *Kolkwitzia amabilis*. Underneath are hellebores, hostas and the forget-me-not flowers of *Brunnera macrophylla*; a seemingly simple, but in reality a consummately accomplished, piece of labour-saving planting, where there is always much to enjoy.

Returning towards the house the Blue Borders either side of the spring garden gateway catch the eye with their delphiniums, a striking combination of herbaceous plants in dark blue, white and silver, edged with catmint.

Misarden Park

Wing Commander Huntley Sinclair

At E end of Miserden village, 12km (7½m) NE of Stroud. Garden of 4ha (10 acres) surrounding large Elizabethan manor house with a wing added by Sir Edwin Lutyens. Formal herbaceous and vegetable gardens, rock garden and spring bulbs. Open for NGS and RC ; see also HHCG On well-drained calcareous soil overlying Cotswold limestone. Situated high in the central Cotswolds at 197-229m (650-750ft), with spectacular views. Rainfall locally high at 914mm (36in.). Maintained at a good standard by a head gardener and two assistants.

Some gardens are the personal expression of an individual, the work of a lifetime; others have longer pedigrees. The garden at Misarden Park has the timeless quality of a typically English garden that over many years has absorbed a variety of additions and changes that have subsequently been welded successfully into a whole. Despite the ancient origins of the garden, its over-riding character comes from the period between the wars and is a product of Mrs Huntly Sinclair's ideas combined with the solid craftsmanship of the time.

Through tall Horse Chestnuts and limes, the drive, edged curiously with Westmorland limestone, affords spectacular views into the Golden Valley. On either side are groups of Winter Aconites and snowdrops with Victorian daffodils and Martagon Lilies massed in the grass for later effect.

The north forecourt is bounded by yew hedges, perinwinkle and St John's Wort and given dignity by an old lime and some enormous yews, one of which is swathed in autumn colour from the vigorous, large-leaved vine, *Vitis coignetiae*. To the house there clings a climbing hydrangea with the Mexican Orange, *Choisya ternata*, buttressing the walls.

The spacious south terrace is expertly set with random rectangular York paving laid to replace gravel by Mrs Huntly Sinclair in the 1930s and bounded by topiary shapes of yew and box. Sir Edwin Lutyens' east wing contains a loggia overhung with wistaria and nearby a pair of Irish Junipers frame the view to the east where Scots Pines, Atlas Cedars, Silver Firs and Incense Cedars, *Calocedrus (Libocedrus) decurrens*, rise from the low ground. The steps and gravel terraces are also the work of Sir Edwin, who rebuilt the east wing in 1920 after a fire. This succession of smaller terraces contains a magnificent *Magnolia* × *soulangiana* near the house and ledges of Dutch Lavender. Steps lead down to masses of the Mexican Orange and eventually to the small pinetum which, with limes and Horse Chestnuts, shelters the garden from the north-east. Close to the house on this side is a rock bank with a Lutyens-like arrangement of mushroom-shaped hornbeams over campanulas, primulas, aubrietia, pinks and cyclamens. Sir Edwin was also involved in the layout of the north forecourt.

Leading back to the main lawn south of the terrace, along the line of a former drive, are double herbaceous borders containing the unusual white Willow Herb and then a series of unique and finely-detailed grass steps flanked with Irish Junipers, possibly another of Lutyens' innovations. From the lawn there are superb views over a neat yew hedge into the valley and through gates along a beech avenue, a feature created by Mrs Huntly Sinclair in 1936 to mark the coming-of-age of her elder son, Michael.

West of the main lawn and set above the valley and park is an extensive area of pleasure grounds mostly created between the wars. The layout is informal on the south-facing steep bank and more formal at the top, where parallel paths and cedars surround grass tennis-courts and lead to the grand gates of the twentieth-century kitchen garden. Here are masses of naturalized daffodils and splendid trees, walnuts, chestnuts and an enormous Indian Bean Tree, *Catalpa bignonioides*. The bank below affords an ideal site for an extensive rock garden with two pools and a cascade, auriculas, *Primula denticulata*, *Skimmia* and naturalized Grape Hyacinths and Day Lilies. All around are specimen trees of all kinds including flowering cherries; the balsam-scented *Populus trichocarpa*; the Blue Atlantic Cedar and the Deodar Cedar; and *Cercidiphyllum japonicum* for autumn colour.

The Kip engraving of 1712 shows the terraced walled garden west of the house much as it is today, with the main axis from the house dividing it

lengthwise. Here in the sixteenth and seventeenth centuries would have been places for vegetable gardens, orchards and garden knots. Now the central path is a late-Victorian topiary walk of clipped yew hedges topped with domes, leading to a seat from which a fine view back towards the house can be enjoyed. The two sides of the walk are further subdivided to form four large quarters. On the north side is a rose garden and a quadrant of kitchen garden used by the staff. On the south side both quarters are taken up with broad herbaceous borders flanking a wide grass path with climbing roses on pergola poles. These borders at their best in early September when big drifts of tall yellow rudbeckias and light-blue *Aster acris* are flowering.

There is much to be seen but do not miss the ancient sycamore (once no doubt a seedling left in the garden wall) whose roots have become exposed as they clambered over and through the stone. Still clinging together for mutual support, stones and roots make a beautiful combination of pattern and texture, a memorial perhaps to a neglectful gardener for leaving it to grow but also to a succession of discriminating owners for allowing it to continue.

Newlands

H. Hey Esq.

Open sometimes for NGS and local charities. In Stow-on-the-Wold.

Certain styles of gardening are instantly recognizable and Waterers' between-the-wars style is one of these. It was a development of the Edwardian style of Sir Edwin Lutyens, and was often adapted to the smaller garden. Although it suffered perhaps from repetition, it was always characterized by a quiet dignity and by logic. There is a feeling of permanence born of solid craftsmanship and a restful atmosphere resulting from good proportion and practical detailing.

At Newlands, full advantage has been taken of an excellent site looking out far over the Cotswolds towards Broadway. The warm, steep slope to the south-west has been used to create a variety of terraces and the views out from each of them have been cleverly framed in a variety of ways to give variety to the scene.

From the forecourt, enclosed by shrubs, the garden opens out over a large level lawn with the other terraces falling away beside the house. Each of these terraces has a different treatment. A rose garden is linked by steps up to the dining-room bay where *Viola cornuta* romps unhindered in a narrow border. At the other end a stone urn between clipped golden yews is silhouetted against the horizon. Here are hybrid tea roses in the beds and climbing roses on the walls with that long-flowering, half-tender perennial *Erigeron glaucus* enjoying the warm spot.

The lowest and largest terrace has a central, sunken lily pool surrounded by tubs of Agapanthus and lavender. A fine octagonal gazebo standing in one corner contains fascinating 1890 terracotta copies of Florentine friezes. Below the house double herbaceous borders lead downhill to a seat.

North Cerney Gardens

Open for NGS in summer. 6.4km (4 miles) N of Cirencester. The gardens of one Queen Anne and two Georgian houses in beautiful village with a well-known thirteenth-century Church.

THE OLD RECTORY has a small, newly-planted garden; NORTH CERNEY MANOR has a larger, established garden and a well-worked vegetable garden. Largest of all is CERNEY HOUSE with its park-like setting above the village.

Here there are fine trees: beeches, Horse Chestnuts, limes, sycamores, Atlas Cedar and Grey Poplar. The former owner liked the combination of purple and golden foliage and assembled many shrubs and trees. The garden is in the process of being replanned by the new owners.

Notgrove and Leygore Gardens

Two gardens open for RC in spring. THE GLEBE HOUSE *is a steep cottage-garden in Notgrove near the Church and* LEYGORE MANOR *is a once-extensive garden with two fine Weeping Silver Limes.*

Oaklands
(County of Avon)

Open for NGS in spring. At Almondsbury, 11.2km (7 miles) N of Bristol. Formerly owned by the Hiatt Baker family who planted many rare trees, shrubs and plants. Now the 4.8ha (12 acre) garden is tended by one gardener. Fine display of spring bulbs and flowers.

Owlpen Manor
Mr and Mrs C. Mander

Open by prior written appointment, see HHCG   1.6km (1 mile) E of Uley, 9.6km (6 miles) W of Nailsworth. Historic group of Cotswold stone buildings, including a beautiful Tudor manor house and formal terraced garden reconstructed in sympathy with the period.

Painswick Gardens

Three gardens open for RC in spring. 4.8km (3 miles) N of Stroud. Fine views, trees and shrubs and herbaceous plants are to be seen and you can bring your swimming-costume for a swim in the pool, weather permitting.

Painswick House
Baroncino Nicholas de Piro

See HHCG, 4.8km (3 miles) N of Stroud. Fine Palladian house with garden.

Poulton House
Air Vice-Marshal and Mrs I.R. Campbell

Open for RC, late spring. 8.8km (5½ miles) E of Cirencester. Small Cotswold garden with roses, shrubs, herbaceous borders and vegetables.

Rodmarton Manor
Major and Mrs Anthony Biddulph

At Rodmarton, 9.6km (6 miles) SW of Cirencester and 6.4km (4 miles) NE of Tetbury, N of A433 Cirencester-Tetbury road. Open three or four times in summer for NGS, GS, RC and occasionally for other causes. Extensive garden of 2.8ha (7 acres) contemporary with Hidcote and similar in style; around important Cotswold stone house and Chapel completed in 1926 by Ernest Barnsley and furnished by the Cotswold Craftsmen. Situated at 152m (500ft) with views over gently rolling countryside on thin alkaline soil over limestone. Rainfall 864mm (34ins.). Well maintained by the owners and the equivalent of two full-time gardeners.

With its high ideals of the dignity of craftsmanship combined with traditional design arising out of the use of local materials, the Cotswold Movement was mainly associated with houses, where the architecture could be integrated with the design of furnishings and fittings to make a rounded whole. Rodmarton Manor by Ernest and Sidney Barnsley and Ernest Gimson is a final flowering of this great tradition begun as the Arts and Crafts Movement by William Morris before the turn of the century. Although rarely associated with gardens, the principles of the Arts and Crafts Movement are those which have in fact guided the development of many of the great gardens made since the First World War.

Ernest Barnsley certainly designed the main outlines of the original garden at Rodmarton. He was influenced no doubt by his former employer, John D. Sedding, and by the ideas of Reginald Blomfield who wrote *The Formal Garden in England*. This respect for tradition and formality resulted in a firmly architectural layout and a total affinity between house and garden. But other names appear on the plaque in the forecourt. There was Alfred Wright, who made the garden buildings and other stonework; then William Scrubey, the first head gardener and no doubt it was he and the Hon. Claud Biddulph, for whom the house was built, who decided upon the original planting in the Long Garden, Barnsley's main contribution. After wartime neglect and since 1954, the present owners have developed the garden with sensitivity in that seemingly casual and distinctly English style between the strictly geometrical and the natural, and given the planting a little more freedom and informality than before. The result is a fascinating framework of outdoor 'rooms' linked to the house by strong vistas and 'furnished' with that elusive combination of imagination and discipline that distinguishes the twentieth-century English garden. Although it owes rather more to the house, the outcome compares with those other syntheses of architectural layout and artist-plantsman's skill at Hidcote Manor, Crathes Castle and Sissinghurst Castle.

The garden is entered from the decidedly architectural semicircle of the forecourt, with its once-pleached limes and staddle stones, through a door in the high stone wall and past the Chapel into the Leisure Garden. This was a tennis-court and was developed by the present owners in a pattern of large square beds around a central urn, all set in stone paving and enclosed by a slightly raised shrub border and stone walls. With no grass, the beds of roses and other long-flowering subjects like *Potentilla* 'Arbuscula' and roses underplanted with ground covers are labour-saving. 'Rosemary Rose' combines well with purple Bugle, 'Iceberg' with purple violas, 'Tip Top' with double daisies, and lanky 'Queen Elizabeth' with Japanese Anemones and *Alchemilla mollis*. The shrub borders beyond are in colour schemes: gold in one, silver in another. There is a fine combination of pineapple-scented *Cytisus battandieri* with Globe Artichokes and *Senecio* 'Sunshine', and another happy association of *Abutilon vitifolium* with the Butterfly Bush, *Kolkwitzia amabilis*. The last-remaining of many pleached limes encloses a small winter garden well placed south-west at the corner of the house and leads to the main south front past the 'Troughery', a witty mixture of topiary with planted stone troughs perched on staddle stones.

The south terrace extends the length of the house, with roses and choice and tender plants against the wall. The whole wide area is paved and enclosed at the sides by topiary-topped yew hedges and enormous mushroom-shaped Portugal Laurels which give foreground to an unspoilt view towards Kemble and far on to the Berkshire Downs. Within the hedges are 'Barnsley' seats and tubs of *Agapanthus* while two smaller enclosures have bright tubs and vases of geraniums. Apart from the Portugal Laurels,

Above: Westbury Court. Maynard Colchester's seventeenth-century formal water garden survived miraculously for two and a half centuries and has been restored by the National Trust using plants introduced to this country before 1700.

Below: Sezincote. The pool and rock outcrops are said to be the work of Humphry Repton. In the background is a fine specimen of the Weeping Hornbeam and in the left foreground is one of the flowering dogwoods *Cornus kousa*.

Magnolia wilsonii. This June-flowering tree grows in a number of gardens, including Lydney Park.

Above: Rodmarton Manor. The Long Garden. Twin borders, planted according to the principles of Gertrude Jekyll lead to Ernest Barnsley's summerhouse. *Country Life*

Below: Snowshill Manor. The Armillary Court with its columnar gilded sundial in Charles Wade's terraced garden. *Country Life*

this whole area is a creation of the present owners.

Steps descend beyond the terrace to a lower path that begins the main axis through the west part of the garden. Here in front of the terrace are borders of mainly white flowers varying into pink and light blue with silver foliage. The walk extends westward and into a contrasting area shaded by a Mulberry and a Weeping Ash and hemmed in by camellias where Mrs Biddulph has assembled a collection of hostas and snowdrops. A series of enclaves open to the south.

The first is the 'Cherry Orchard', a pleasing mixture of flowering cherries and maples with big shrub roses growing in grass among masses of daffodils. With contrasting regularity a tennis-court comes next, surrounded by borders of Flag Irises, and then a swimming-pool and pavilion set in grass with a superb specimen of the Weeping Silver Lime at the far end. Beyond a hard tennis-court is a dark 'cathedral aisle' of once pleached hornbeams surrounded by hollies and vigorous ground covers which compels the eye to a gothic window at the end and the dazzling view beyond.

Apart from a large, walled garden, well stocked with fruits, vegetables and cut flowers, the other main feature, and possibly the most successful, is the Long Garden. Ernest Barnsley's delightful summerhouse, bedecked with orange-peel clematis, *C. orientalis,* and the tiny pink rosebuds of 'Bloomfield Abundance', creates a distinguished focal point for twin borders contained between the long wall of the kitchen garden and a high yew hedge screening and tennis-courts. The wide, mixed borders framed in lichen-clad paths of stone are planted in the Gertrude Jekyll manner with enormous shrub roses such as 'Nevada', 'Felicia' and *R. rubrifolia* to form the structure. Irises, masterworts, phloxes, Day Lilies, delphiniums, hardy fuchsias and *Phlomis fruticosa* create a profusion of flowers among the telling patterns and textures of New Zealand Flax, *Phormium tenax,* Cardoon, and *macleaya cordata,* the Plume Poppy. Enjoying the warmth of the wall is a mixture of roses like 'New Dawn', 'Veilchenblau' and the more recent 'Handel' with the free-growing *Eccremocarpus scaber;* there is even the tender *Fremontodendron californicum* and that paragon of self-clinging, fragrant-flowered climbers, *Trachelospermum asiaticum.*

Rushbury House
Lt. Col and Mrs C.J. Sidgwick

Open for NGS in summer. 4km (2½m) W of Winchcombe. Medium-sized with shrubs and flowers; farmyard animals and horses. Lovely views and historic 1582 house.

St Francis, Lammas Park
Mr and Mrs Falconer

---

*Open for NGS in summer and by appointment. At Minchinhampton, 4.8km (3 miles) SE of
Stroud. Medium-sized garden made in a mature park around a modern stone house.*

There are fine old beeches and many ornamental tree species have been
added in the informal park area. The south side, where the gardening is
most intensive, is terraced and there is a superb view over the old
Minchinhampton vineyard to Gatcombe woods and the Avening valley.
The borders are filled with an enormous range of unusual plants with the
emphasis on reputedly tender subjects, silver foliage and climbing and
shrub roses. There is an attractive garden house with a fascinating series of
finely manicured trough gardens and bonsai trees.

Sezincote
Mr and Mrs David Peake

---

*Near Bourton-on-the-Hill, 2.4km (1½ miles) W of Moreton-in-Marsh; S of A44 Broadway to
Moreton-in-Marsh road; E of A424 Stow-on-the-Wold to Broadway road. For opening arrangements see HHCG; also open for NGS Part formal but largely informal water garden of 4ha
(10 acres) with Indian features, Orangery and Repton Park. Unique Indian-style house (not open)
by S.P. Cockerell and Thomas Daniell. Situated on an easterly slope at 183-123m (600-700ft) near
the source of the River Evenlode; fine views. Heavy alkaline soil over Cotswold limestone. Rainfall
762mm (30in.) Two gardeners.*

Even the most single-minded garden visitor could not avoid being
captivated by the first glimpse of this astonishing house with its onion-
shaped copper dome and elaborate Mogul Indian decoration. It was built
in 1805 for Sir Charles Cockerell (who had made a fortune in the East
India Company) by his architect brother, Samuel Pepys Cockerell, and
with the assistance of the Indian expert, Thomas Daniell, who also
designed some of the garden features. The house is said to have inspired
the Brighton Pavilion, which was built in 1815, after the Prince Regent
had visited Sezincote in 1807. The house and the setting are truly picturesque both in inspiration and intention. Humphry Repton was consulted
on the siting of the house, which he placed high against the hill overlooking his gleaming lake and the hazy Evenlode valley. He also designed
the park and his superb Cedars remain to frame the view back to the house

from the garden.

The formal garden, south of the house, is enclosed by the curving Orangery, perhaps the most romantically beautiful greenhouse corridor in Britain. It was built, and has recently been rebuilt, in pale almond-white stone in contrast to the deeper-coloured stone chosen for the house itself, tinted orange to give the authentic Indian effect. The elaborate Indian carving of the Orangery shows Daniell's influence at its most convincing, the whole delicious confection ending in a domed pavilion. The formal garden is divided foursquare with a raised fountain pool as its centre-piece. The main axis from the house consists of a long canal pool of recent construction, inspired by Graham Thomas, as is much of the planting in the garden. The canal contains water lilies and is flanked by slim Irish Yews leading to steps on the opposite bank and an elegant little pavilion in the Indian style designed by the former owner, Sir Cyril Kleinwort. The bank is planted with the cream-variegated Dogwood, *Cornus alba* 'Elegantissima', and the golden Westfelton Yew contrasted against the purple foliage of Copper Beech, dark yews and silver willows.

North of the house is a lawn with another vast Copper Beech and an enormous bronze bell as an ornament. A Purple Filbert echoes the beech and there are many variegated shrubs, hollies, dogwoods and *Kerria japonica* to lighten the effect.

The main part of the garden is further north, following the line of a stream and shallow valley through the park and sheltered by towering limes and beeches with yews as understorey. The drive crosses it by a bridge, designed by Thomas Daniell, with sturdy cast-iron Brahmin bulls decorating the balustrade. This is a splendid vantage-point but only part of the water garden can be seen, enough to tempt but not to bore.

Above the bridge at the head of the valley the scene is most strongly Indian. The round Temple Pool with its curious umbrella-shaped fountain lies in front of a Coade stone figure of Souriya in an Indian shrine. Around the pool are a series of small grottoes containing enormous shells, surmounted by borders superbly planted for bold foliage effects with green and variegated *Aralia elata*, silver *Senecio* 'Sunshine', grey *Lonicera korolkowii*, purple *Cotinus coggygria*, Plume Poppy and the big leathery leaves of *Bergenia crassifolia*. Nearby is an old, twisted Judas Tree and several other small trees for spring and autumn effect: *Malus floribunda*, *Prunus sargentiana* and *Parrotia persica*. In July a yew thickly hung with rose 'Kiftsgate' and 'Pauls' Himalayan Musk' is a spectacular sight.

The stream descends through rocks to a second pond where the planting is equally varied and well considered. The giant grass *Miscanthus sacchariflorus* looks well with *Rodgersia* and a mass of *Hosta sieboldiana* contrasts with the fine texture of a purple, cut-leaved Japanese Maple. Nearby is the unusual weeping form of the White Mulberry planted like many of the other young trees, by Lady Kleinwort, and the rare bamboo *Chusquea couleou*. The sound of water, which enlivens any garden, comes from two waterfalls half-hidden among waterside planting. Near the bridge is a superb group of the giant *Hydrangea sargentiana* flourishing in a cool and shady corner and the Varnish Tree, *Rhus verniciflua* — source of the original Japanese lacquer.

The bridge is cunningly designed so that there is a watery pavilion underneath with stepping-stones and a stone seat, and it also forms a frame for views of the lower garden. Below is the third pond, ruled from the centre by a three-headed serpent fountain and surrounded by summer-flowering *Primula florindae* and Rose of Sharon with the bold leaves of *Vitis coignetiae* on the bridge as background. A memorable piece of planting for spring effect consists of the Weeping Cherry, *Prunus subhirtella* 'Pendula Rubra' surrounded by a mass of that aristocrat of primroses, 'Garriade Guinevere'.

The stream gushes on past a profusion of irises, *Hydrangea involucrata* 'Hortensis', spiraeas, Day Lilies, musks and Solomon's Seal, with a fine flowering dogwood, *Cornus kousa,* nearby. Now the scene loses its Indian influence and becomes truly English. The splendid rock outcrops by the fourth pool are said to have been placed by Humphry Repton and the magnificent Lebanon Cedars are certainly his. The informal planting around this pool continues in the finest tradition of the English garden style. The influence of Graham Thomas is evident from the bold and free arrangement of purple *Cotinus coggygria*, with *Hydrangea villosa* and 'White Wave' contrasted with the big leaves of *Peltiphyllum* and *Rodgersia* species. Beyond is what must be the finest specimen of the Weeping Hornbeam, *Carpinus betulus* 'Pendula', to be seen in these islands, a superbly graceful tree of medium size which fits more easily into the garden scene than the more extreme weepers, some of which can be a little grotesque, especially when young.

The streamside planting continues with the emphasis as elsewhere on strong foliage effect, becoming subtly larger and more generous in scale as the spaces broaden. There is purple New Zealand Flax, bamboo and Weeping Silver Pear teamed with *Acanthus mollis* and Gardener's Garters; Plume Poppy with *Hosta sieboldiana, Iris ochraurea* and *Rodgersia aesculifolia*; and many more.

The garden finishes convincingly with the largest pond of all, its juniper-planted island connected by a plank bridge of an unusual articulated zigzag design, another of Graham Thomas' ideas. Here is another feast of fine waterside planting with several interesting trees including the contorted willow *Salix matsudana* 'Tortuosa' and a Weeping Pagoda Tree, *Sophora japonica* 'Pendula'.

The whole adds up to a rich slice of English gardening at its best, a synthesis of Georgian design and Victorian trees topped up with modern planting of rare sensitivity and exuberance.

Sheldon Nurseries
The Williams Family

Open for GS late spring. 5.6km (3½ miles) W of Cheltenham on Tewkesbury Road. Small garden attached to a tomato and cucumber nursery with 10.4ha (26 acres) of plums and vegetables.

Sherborne House
The Beshara Trust

Open for RC in summer. 4.6km (3 miles) E of Northleach, off A40. Extensive lawns and parkland; kitchen garden.

Snowshill Manor
The National Trust

In Snowshill village, 4.8km (3 miles) S of Broadway. For opening arrangements see HHCG and NT; also open occasionally for NGS Terraced garden of 0.8ha (2 acres) developed from a design by M.H. Baillie Scott, in the Hidcote manner, by Charles Wade, who also made a museum in the Tudor Manor House. On a steep westerly slope at 228m (750ft) with unspoilt views into the valley; well-drained alkaline soil over Cotswold limestone. Rainfall 675mm (26in.). One gardener.

With its warm-coloured local stone 'Snozzle' is typical of all that is so much admired in Cotswold manor houses. It is easy to understand how in 1919 Charles Paget Wade, the architect and antiquarian, was attracted by its Tudor origins and its seventeenth and eighteenth-century additions, also by its ancient dovecote, its unspoilt views and its position, set then on the edge of a village not yet touched by the bustle of tourism.

Charles Wade had shown an interest in gardening long before he began to convert the ruinous cattleyard at Snowshill into a garden. In 1907 he had won second prize in a garden design competition organized by *The Studio* magazine and when he came to Snowshill he incorporated many of

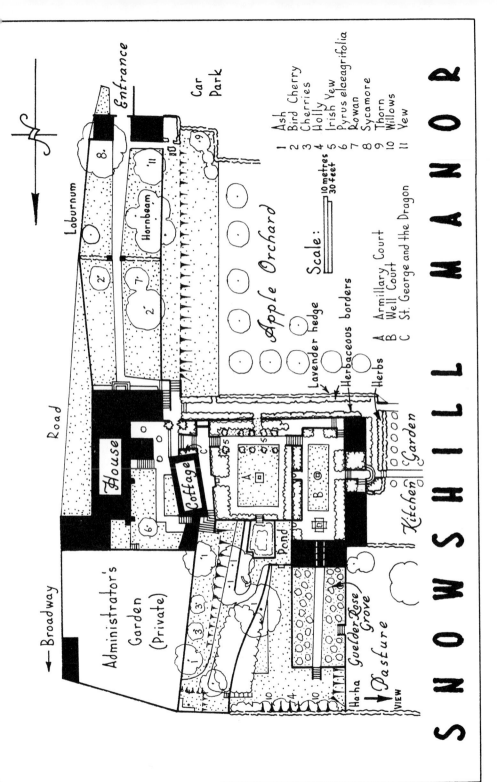

SNOWSHILL MANOR

Entrance

Car Park

Laburnum

Road

Broadway

House

Cottage

Administrator's
Garden
(Private)

Guelder-Rose Grove

Ha-ha

Pasture

VIEW

Apple Orchard

Lavender hedge

Herbaceous borders

Herbs

Kitchen Garden

Pond

Scale:
10 metres
30 feet

1   Ash
2   Bird Cherry
3   Cherries
4   Holly
5   Irish Yew
6   Pyrus elaeagrifolia
7   Rowan
8   Sycamore
9   Thorn
10 Willows
11 Yew

A   Armillary Court
B   Well Court
C   St. George and the Dragon

the features — flagged walks, enclosed courts, dovecote and double borders — into his new garden. A recently discovered plan indicates conclusively that the main layout of the central core of the garden — the Armillary Court and the Well Garden — was developed from a 1920 design by M.H. Baillie Scott, an architect whose work Wade greatly admired. Although he used Baillie Scott's basic concept Wade simplified it, omitting some of its rather fussy paths to its considerable benefit. He also extended it and added new features linked closely to the house and to the central scheme, until he arrived at the satisfying progression of linked spaces that comprises Snowshill today. Few English gardens have been created entirely from an original master plan and Snowshill is not the exception.

Although there is no evidence that Charles Wade knew Major Lawrence Johnston or even that he visited Hidcote, there are obvious similarities of style in the firmness of the architectural style and the soft profusion of the planting; also the strong overall unity of design despite the sudden changes of mood.

Broadly, the garden can be said to be a variation of the compartmentalized Hidcote style, with an interconnecting pattern of outdoor rooms, here becoming a fascinating series of terraces, steps and ramps, each partly concealed from the next by walls and arches and by the steep fall of the ground. Mr. Wade was an artist-craftsman in the great Cotswold tradition of William Morris, Ernest Gimson and the Barnsley brothers. His absolute belief in the rustic ideal and his interests in heraldry, mediaevalism and astrology were expressed in a variety of surprise features which give an intensely individual, even eccentric, quality almost as much to the garden as to the house.

Charles Wade transformed his 'wilderness of chaos', a nettle-covered slope, into an intriguing pattern of enclosures, richly ornamented and profusely planted in the deceptively casual, so-called cottage-garden style. The first priority was to build dry-stone terrace walls in the traditional Cotswold style, in Charles Wade's words 'to lose the feeling it gave of being about to slide into the depths of the vale'. Like all great designers he turned necessity to his advantage in the variety and interest he created in the walls, steps and paving and in the spaces they enclose.

Although he seems to have collected almost everything else, he never pursued a collector's interest in plants, preferring to use flowers as an artist uses paints to create the effect intended. In conjunction with the deep honey-coloured north Cotswold stone he preferred blues, mauves and purples with light yellows and creams for contrast. He painted the woodwork, seats and tubs a particular shade of powdery dark blue with a touch of turquoise, now known as 'Wade Blue' and retained by the National Trust.

The garden is entered through an area overhung with trees and dark with evergreens, yews, laurels and mahonias, where there are spring bulbs in the grass and Autumn Crocuses in September. All this is meant to emphasize the open brilliance and the trim smoothness of the garden beyond Mr Wade's stone gate piers. The high stone wall to the village street is festooned with *Cotoneaster microphyllus*, through which grows *Clematis viticella* 'Abundance', and at its foot grow blue muscari, *Salvia patens* and the little *Ceratostigma plumbaginoides* with a few ornamental grasses in the dry soil. The autumn-flowering *Cyclamen hederifolium* (*neapolitanum*) also grows in profusion here both against the wall and under the old Bird Cherry on the lawn while ceanothuses and lavenders against the hot south front of the house add to the predominant theme of blues and purples.

Steps descend past spring-flowering *Clematis montana* and *C. macropetala*, white and blue respectively, to a long terraced bank of smooth green grass above the rough, sheep-grazed orchard. At the end of this restful stretch of unbroken lawn the Trust has restored Charles Wade's original intention of a seat as a focal point. Downhill between the orchard and an old garden wall are double borders, always colourful with an unsophisticated mixture of hardy plants, lavenders and clumps of purple sage, with *Solanum crispum* and clematises of the Viticella group clambering through old espalier fruit trees on the walls.

Through an arch the dramatic figure of St George slaying the Dragon compels attention, especially if the clock behind happens to be striking. These painted figures are set high among 'Brant' vines overlooking a little paved area with steps where tubs of standard fuchsias, heliotropes and Lemon Verbena are grown. Here begins the main axis from the west door which continues down successive flights of steps and between an avenue of clipped Irish Yews right down into the Well Court and to the late-medieval dovecote beyond.

The first main terrace, where the main battalion of Irish Yews is stationed, is called the Armillary Court, a plain grass rectangle with a gilded sundial on a tall stone column as its centrepiece. Roses as shrubs and climbers are the main theme of the planting but they are always fronted with lavender or mixed informally with other plants rather than used alone. Mr Wade tamed a once muddy spring that rises here to spout water from a bronze mask on the wall into a tank, a feature which recurs in another guise in the Well Court below. He was evidently highly conscious of sound in the garden for as well as trickling water and a striking clock-bell he had windbells in the Elder Grove.

The best view of the Well Court below is from a raised terrace at its southern end where the pattern can be seen. A Venetian well-head placed centrally in the lawn is balanced by a square sunken pool in the paved sitting-place at the far end. The pool has Wade-blue boxes containing *Juniperus communis* 'Compressa' to mark its corners and reflects the little Madonna shrine which projects dormer-like from the roof of the former cow-byre behind.

In contrast to the Armillary Court, the Well Court is enclosed, save for a vista down through gates to the herb and vegetable gardens and an intriguing glimpse northwards through the cow-byre to the Elder Grove beyond. The borders are profuse with colour from an intimate mixture of bulbs, plants, shrubs and climbers. At the southern end is a shady seat-niche set among summer-flowering *Schizophragma integrifolium* and the rampant, blue-flowered *Clematis × jouiniana*, with hostas in the border in front.

The transition from the bright and flowery Well Court through the dark barn to the Elder Grove is an example of Charles Wade's genius for creating variety and interest from the manipulation of contrasts — sun and shade, hard and soft, light and dark, fine texture and coarse, simple and complex. The elders, which collapsed in the icy winter of 1963 have now been replaced by bushes of the Guelder Rose to make a similar high canopy with white flowers in spring and branches of shiny translucent fruits in late summer, under which Martagon Lilies, squills and Ladies' Smock grow and where the grass is a carpet of blue Speedwell in spring.

Coming out of the green shade at the end an open view over a ha-ha into the unspoilt valley is all the more effective because of the contrast. Back toward the Armillary Court is a deep trout-pool once the quay for a model village that occupied the slope nearby. Among the tall ash trees that are a feature of Snowshill are more walks and informal areas containing a variety of vigorous shrubs and young trees, with bulbs in the longer grass. From a high vantage-point at the top one can sit and admire the view and contemplate the ingenuity of the complex maze of paths and garden 'rooms' that make up this little garden masterpiece, surely one of the outstanding small gardens owned by the National Trust.

Southrop Gardens

Three gardens open for NGS in spring. 2.4km (1½ miles) N of Lechlade. The gardens contain a great deal of variety and interest including waterside planting by the River Leach, fine trees, shrubs and hedges, and spring bulbs. John Keble was Curate here.

Springfield Barn

Mr and Mrs J. Woods

Open for NGS in early summer. At Upton Cheyney, Bitton. 8km (5 miles) NW of Bath.
Garden of about 0.4ha (1 acre) started in 1960 and now containing several hundred species all
planted by the present owners.

Stancombe Park

Mr and Mrs B.S. Barlow

Half-way between Dursley and Wotton-under-Edge on east side of B4060. Open one weekend for
NGS Garden of largely modern planting near the house and separate Victorian folly garden.
Situated at 60-91m (200-300ft.) above a valley; views to the south-east. Free-draining soil over
Cotswold limestone. Rainfall 838mm (33in.). Maintained by a single-handed full-time gardener.

Gardens sometimes fall into two parts but rarely as decisively as at
Stancombe Park. Near the house is a piece of flower-gardening in the
modern country-house style as pleasant as you could wish for and from
the house there is a simply stunning view over parkland towards Wotton-
under-Edge. The so-called 'Folly Garden', out of sight of the house, is
entirely another matter; here is a genuine period-piece, eccentrically
original and yet typical of its time.

The house is well sited at the head of a valley hard on the park; there is
little garden here and none is needed for the outlook is idyllic. Save for a
terrace the Herefords come almost to the house wall. As the house is
approached so the view into the valley over the curving park wall unfolds.
The bank along the drive has been planted to a modern theme using plants
with bold foliage — rues, spurges, hellebores, *Crambe cordifolia*, as well as
many with silver leaves. On top of the bank is a Gazebo, covered with a
'New Dawn' rose, which enjoys to the full the lovely view across the
valley.

The main pleasure-garden occupies high ground above a bank south of
the house where a large centrally-placed urn provides a focal point set in a
circle of close-planted 'Profusion' crabs. Although sheltered from the east
and from the west by mature oaks, Sweet Chestnuts and Lebanon Cedars,
the major part of the layout is recent with York stone steps flanked by
Irish Yews and silver foliage leading up to double herbaceous borders
framed by ropes of rambler roses supported on posts. On the lawn are

several promising young trees such as cherries, thorns and Japanese and Norway Maples.

The double borders lead to the tennis-courts which are cleverly screened by *Thuya plicata* and a border of silver foliage — Silver Pear, *Senecio* 'Sunshine' and *Ballota pseudodictamnus* blended with the purple-leaved Smoke Bush, *Rosa rubrifolia,* rose 'Dortmund' and the Butterfly Bush, *Kolkwitzia amabilis.*

In the far north-west corner is a separate area, railed off with an elegant white fence, where pleached limes lead to a splendid seat, surrounded by stone cherubs. All around are old shrub roses, buddleias, paeonies and Day Lilies.

A path under towering cedars skirts the edge of the valley with the garden above and the park below. The walk is never dull, here shady, there open, and gives a series of lovely views into the valley and of an obelisk in the distance; then the lake comes into view with a pretty Chinese Bridge leading to an island with silver willows.

Now the path descends more steeply into an ominous wood beset with laurels, the approach to the folly garden. First comes a trickling spring channelled into a stone fount and thence into a series of charming little stone rills. Hereafter the garden becomes a mysterious and bewildering succession of well-staged surprises, far better experienced than described. The result is a miniature caricature of the Stourhead landscape; the changes of mood are melodramatic and the changes of scale are grotesque. The story goes that it was made by a former owner, a certain clergyman, as a refuge from his wife. Far from the house and near the road, it was a convenient place to meet his illicit lover! Whatever it was to him and to her, it remains today as full of excitement and amusement as ever.

Stanton Gardens

A number of small gardens open for NGS in early summer. Near Broadway.

Stanway House

Lord Wemyss' Trust

Open for G S in spring and summer. At Stanway, 5.6km (3½ miles) NE of Winchcombe. 8ha (20 acres) with lawns, bulbs and trees. Important Tudor house with remarkable gatehouse of 1630 and splendid fourteenth-century tithe-barn.

Stowell Park

The Lord and Lady Vestey

Open for NGS in late spring and for R.C. in summer. 3.2km (2 miles) SW of Northleach. Large garden with spacious formal terraces giving magnificent views south over the upper Coln Valley.

The garden is meticulously maintained with colourful flowering plants on the upper terraces; swimming-pool and tennis-court lower down. On one side is a fine seventeenth-century dovecote and columbarium with attractive double herbaceous borders leading up to it. The house is approached through wrought-iron gates and handsome stone-built gazebos set diagonally on either side. These and the terrace walls were presumably the work of Sir John Belcher who enlarged the Elizabethan house toward the end of the last century and gave it its present appearance. There is an unusually large and comprehensive kitchen garden with peach and vine houses as well as other glasshouses; everything in immaculate order.

Sudeley Castle

Lady Ashcombe

At Winchcombe, 9.7km (6 miles) NE of Cheltenham, signposted in town from A46. For opening arrangements see HHCG ; normally daily from early March to late October. Mainly Victorian garden of about 4ha (10 acres) around fifteenth-century, and later, Castle (restored in nineteenth-century) and Church. Situated at 91m (300ft.) in the sheltered Winchcombe valley on well-drained, heavy alkaline loam over Cotswold limestone. Rainfall 686mm (27in.). Maintained by three gardeners full-time.

In 1837 John and William Dent, the well-known glove makers of

Worcester, bought the Castle and estate of Sudeley and with their brother, Reverend Benjamin Dent, they restored the fifteenth-, sixteenth- and seventeenth-century structure. They added to the house and repaired the Church of St Mary while other parts such as the banqueting-hall with its huge oriel window were preserved in their picturesque ruined state. By 1855 all three brothers had died and their nephew, John Coucher Dent, inherited. He married Emma Brocklehurst of the celebrated Cheshire family. Emma Dent made the restoration, furnishing and preservation of Sudeley Castle her life's work and an exhibition of mementoes from her collection is on show in the Castle. The garden layout dates from her time and there can be no doubt that she was deeply involved in its design and planting.

With her passionate interest in history she respected precedent in the garden as much as in the house. The enclosed Jacobean garden to the east, now called the Queen's Garden, was restored together with the balustraded terrace walk which surrouds it, and the precincts of St. Mary's Church. From the terrace walk and from the windows of the banqueting-house Katherine Parr might have looked over 'diverse knots': Renaissance patterns made of dwarf box, lavender and rosemary, filled with coloured earths and gravels. Emma Dent's highly effective layout was sympathetic to the original but, like most Victorian schemes, was simpler in pattern to allow for much more complex planting and the ubiquitous tender bedding plants of the time. Now the formal garden is in the process of being re-planned and planted to a less labour-intensive scheme. The fountain and balustraded lily pond in the centre seems to have been a later addition.

This type of gardening relies for its effect upon crisp edges and a trim-ness which is elusive with today's labour costs. As well as having great domed pairs of clipped yews along the main axis, the Queen's Garden is flanked on either side by intriguing walks enclosed by broad yew hedges punctuated with openings. In contrast the surrounding terrace-walk gives open views across the well-kept park with its oaks and Horse Chestnuts to the Cotswold hills on either side.

The approach to St. Mary's Church from the house has a genuinely Victorian character with broad yew hedges giving way in front of the west door to a circular bed, where wallflowers followed by summer bedding-plants give a splash of colour. Around the Church and along the terrace-walk are golden and Irish Yews in a variety of eccentric shapes and close to the east window is a fine Lebanon Cedar. Beyond the Church an old stone wall forms the northern boundary of what must have been the enclosed Jacobean garden. Here, advantage has been taken of a sheltered south-facing site to create a mixed border where sun-loving shrubs such as *Ceanothus*, including the summer flower *C.* 'Gloire de Versailles' and the excellent *C. impressus*, scarlet *Phygelius capensis*, potentillas, brooms and

Hebe and *Cistus* spp. thrive. In a warm corner is *Hoheria sexstylosa*. The border is crammed with interest and variety, including many excellent hardy plants such as rose 'Nevada', *Coryopsis* spp., *Elaeagnus pungens* 'Maculata', buddleias and heathers all competing for space.

In the courtyards enclosed by the Castle, advantage has been taken of the walls and shelter to plant climbers and other wall shrubs. The northern 'outer' courtyard has an early-Victorian fountain pool with a raised edge as its centrepiece in an oval of grass. The south-facing wall is luxuriant with wistaria and *Magnolia grandiflora* while on the west-facing wall there is a splendid climbing *Hydrangea petiolaris*. Good use has been made of the ruin of the banqueting-hall, which is decorated with climbing roses, by the creation of a paved sitting-area covered with valerian with good Victorian seats in a niched yew hedge nearby. Do not miss the vast Trumpet Vine, *Campsis radicans*, smothering the low corridor which houses the Emma Dent collection. Further south by the dungeon tower is a marvellous old mulberry split into several sections, each of which has layered to form separate trees.

North and west of the Castle the garden consists of an informal and more extensive transition to the park. It is clear that Emma Dent must have liked limes for they are the predominant trees, filling the air with their subtle fragrance in June. The future has been well provided for with plenty of young trees — planes, Atlas Cedar, and Sweet Chestnuts — eventually to succeed the older trees, which include two venerable old walnuts on daffodil-covered mounds near the north front. Naturalized daffodils are colourful everywhere in April together with the less bold but more unusual drifts of blue *Anemone blanda* and *Anemone apennina*.

The moat pond, used for waterfowl, is surrounded by some fine cedars and is partially enclosed by a line of Weeping Silver Pears, contrasting sharply with alternate Irish Yews.

On returning to the car park, the garden surrounding the ruins of the former tithe-barn provides a pleasant and relaxing incident. Here a large rectangular lily pool creates reflections and a tranquil atmosphere, helped by flanking hedges of yew and groups of the horizontally-branched Japanese Cherry 'Shirotae'. The planting has been carefully chosen to harmonize and complement the ruin and maintenance is appropriately relaxed. Strong climbers such as Wistaria, *Clematis montana*, rose 'Albertine' and the thornless *Rosa banksiae lutea* ramble over the structure and bold-leafed shrubs and plants show up well against the stone. *Hydrangea villosa* and the tender *Mahonia lomariifolia* shelter in the roofless interior while outside *Romneya coulteri*, *Choisya ternata* and the pungent *Clerodendrum bungei* are contrasted with splendid groups of *Kniphofia caulescens*. In the mortar grow wallflowers, arabis and aubrietia to give the final touch to a romantic place.

Sudeley Lodge
Mr and Mrs K.J. Wilson

Open for N G S in summer. 2.4km (1½ miles) SE of Winchcombe. Medium-sized garden in lovely setting with lawns, borders, stone walls and greenhouses. There is even a swimming-pool for garden visitors to use!

Talbot End House
See Bradley Court

Upper Slaughter Manor House
Eric Turrell Esq

Open Friday afternoons; see H H C G 4km (2½ miles) W of Stow-on-the-Wold. Part fifteenth- and mainly sixteenth-century Cotswold Manor with later additions. Built on sloping ground with an extensive terraced garden.

Vine House
Professor and Mrs T.F. Hewer

At Henbury, N side of Bristol, near Salutation Inn. O.8ha (2 acre) informal garden behind house of local stone, entirely enclosed except to NW. Open for N G S , G S and others frequently. Sheltered site at 46m (150ft), mainly on slight slope to the east but also with a steep scarp down to Hazel Brook on the NW boundary. Well-drained alkaline soil over rocky conglomerate. Rainfall 813mm (32in.). Owners and one part-time gardener.

From a wilderness in 1945, Professor and Mrs Hewer have made a fascinating garden of enormous variety and imagination. Although construction involved engineering works of daunting magnitude this garden is no impersonal product of the landscape contractor. With the help of Mr Edward Lowe, other friends and their gardener, Mr George Taylor, the Hewers did the work themselves. Their aim was to create an informal garden in the tradition of the south Gloucestershire gardens of Canon Ellacombe of Bitton, one of the great garden writers of the late nineteenth-century, and Mrs Hewer's father, Hiatt Baker. The extent of their achievement is here to see. The subtle balance of the main vista at the back of the house recalls that at Trewithen in Cornwall, although of course the scale and the plants are different. A satisfying informal garden of this kind is difficult to achieve and even more difficult to sustain at its peak. It requires the knowledge of a plantsman and the critical eye of an artist, combined with the ability to be both flexible and ruthless at the proper times. The garden at Vine House is not only satisfying still but also increasingly interesting; it is full of good plants, accurately labelled, with many trees just beginning to mature.

Quite properly the garden now gives no hint of the struggles that brought it into being. Initial clearance of trees and scrub revealed an old Mulberry which remains, but sadly one enormous English Elm by the stream has succumbed to disease. The vegetable garden, which was made at an early stage, has the effect of narrowing the main area near the house by dividing it longitudinally. This increases its apparent length but creates a hard line and a sharp corner, both of which have been skilfully concealed by south-facing borders of trees and shrubs where *Genista aetnensis* is prominent among flowering cherries, Rowans, *Osmanthus* 'Burkwoodii' and *Elaeagnus* × *ebbingei* with *Escallonia* 'Edinensis' coming forward to form 'stage wings'.

The opposite side is balanced by March-flowering cherry *Prunus* × *yedoensis* and Weeping Silver Pear in a large border of Tree Paeonies and ground covers, which screen the path. Occupying a key position near the house is a splendid specimen of the horizontally-branching *Malus sargentii*.

A pigeon-house in the SE corner near the entrance overlooks an intimate corner of raised beds of dwarf shrubs. The path runs informally near the southern boundary wall which is screened by a great variety of shrubs and small trees underplanted with shade-tolerant carpeting plants such as *Tellima grandiflora*, forms of the Deadnettle, *Lamium maculatum*, ferns and Solomon's Seal.

The lawn opens out into an arboretum where the old Mulberry and a fine *Magnolia kobus* grow. Further on are a variety of trees growing as specimens: a group of conifers, a fine young Handkerchief Tree, Japanese Cherries, magnolias, a superb *Cornus controversa* and that unbelievably white-stemmed birch *Betula papyrifera*. There are groups of shrubs too and especially notable is the vast *Aesculus parviflora*.

The path leads back to the vegetable garden with tempting glimpses down a steep bank to Hazel Brook. West of the kitchen garden is a small summerhouse and a formal arrangement of double herbaceous borders with paeonies and irises. Nearby, a long pond begins the water garden constructed by Professor Hewer to run diagonally down the steep slope to Hazel Brook, almost at right angles to the natural fall. To create a seemingly natural coombe necessitated excavations on a mighty scale and the construction of a 2.4m (8ft) concrete wall to hold the bank and to stop the whole thing slipping sideways down the hill. The design and the execution is of such quality that none of this is apparent. The detailing of the little cascades and especially the edges of the artificial stream, which can make or break a feature of this kind, is highly effective and the steep bank below is entirely screened with a mass of hazel and yew to support the illusion. As with everywhere in the garden, no opportunity to include exciting plants has been missed and here there are all kinds of streamside subjects: Siberian Irises, primulas, hostas and musks near the top, and big drifts of *Gunnera manicata*, Royal and Shuttlecock Ferns and *Rodgersia* spp., among willows in the boggy area at the bottom.

The rest of the garden occupies the remainder of the steep bank to Hazel Brook, with many interesting trees including a 18.3m (60ft) *Metasequoia glyptostroboides*. In the far corner a magnificent group of the felty-leaved *Hydrangea sargentiana*, undoubtedly the best in the whole region, catches the eye and leads to the cleverest illusion of all. In the deep shade of two yews a cliff of natural stone, perhaps the quarry for the house, seems to trickle with water to make a perfect habitat for *Ramonda myconi*, one of many plants introduced into the garden from the wild by Professor Hewer. In reality the 'spring' is bogus. Cleverly concealed by Climbing Hydrangea is a pipe supplied from the well to make damp areas for more primulas and Shuttlecock Ferns. Under the yews are masses of hardy cyclamen, *C. hederifolium* from Italy, *C. europaeum* and *C. repandum* from Yugoslavia.

As well as being a great personal triumph by the owners this is above all a garden for plantsmen.

Westbury Court
The National Trust

On the eastern edge of Westbury-on-Severn, on the A48 Gloucester-Chepstow road 14.4km (9 miles) south-west of Gloucester. For opening arrangements see N T and H H C G ; normally every day except Mondays and Tuesdays, May to September. Formal water garden of 1.6ha (4 acres) with Pavilion and Gazebo. Low-lying site close to the River Severn at 9m (30ft) on heavy alkaline alluvial soil. Rainfall 686mm (27in.). One gardener with some part-time help. Good guidebook.

In 1694 Maynard Colchester inherited the estate of Westbury Court from his grandfather, Richard, and during the next decade, before Kip's engraving of 1705, the major part of the garden was made. Since then the

WESTBURY COURT

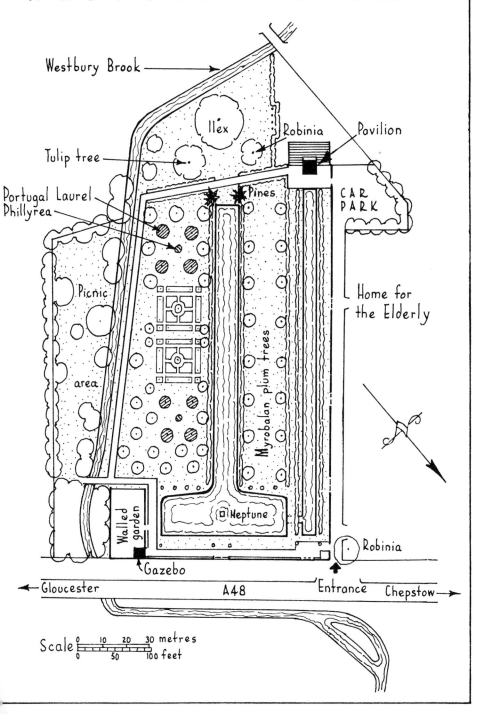

Westbury Brook

Tulip tree

Portugal Laurel
Phillyrea

Ilex

Robinia

Pavilion

Pines

CAR
PARK

Picnic

area

Myrobalan plum trees

Home for
the Elderly

Walled garden

Neptune

Gazebo

Robinia

← Gloucester

A48

Entrance

Chepstow →

Scale

0 10 20 30 metres

0   50   100 feet

house has been demolished and rebuilt three times and the site and its immediate curtilage is now an old people's home. But remarkably the main part of the garden, lying to the east, has remained largely unaltered for 250 years. It has now been restored by the National Trust as far as possible according to Maynard Colchester's meticulous account book, which confirms the accuracy of Kip's engraving.

The extensive use of water was common in gardens of the time but the result at Westbury differed from contemporary designs by London and Wise. The neighbouring Boevey family at Flaxley had Dutch connections and certainly the design of the summerhouse with its great height combined with the low-lying site, the canals, the intricate topiary, the sense of enclosure and independence from the house and above all the horticultural emphasis, resulted in a garden more Dutch than French in character.

The brook which originally ran close to the house was diverted progressively further to the east. Its water was used first to make a long canal and a fountain in front of a garden pavilion and later to make a T-shaped canal further east to enclose the kitchen garden. Each canal is bordered by yew hedges to emphasize the repeated parallels.

Bulbs of many kinds were planted as well as shrubs, especially evergreens for clipping into shapes. But the main emphasis was on useful plants; fruit trees were trained on the walls and an orchard of plums (still common in the neighbourhood) surrounded the extensive vegetable garden. There were fish and eels to be had from the canals.

Many of the apples, pears and plums have now been replanted, using a selection of varieties grown before c.1700 and trained formally as espaliers against the walls. The borders are now full again with the tulips, irises, crocuses, hyacinths and narcissus of the time, accompanied by a great variety of other plants, all chosen from those introduced before the eighteenth-century.

A small, walled garden — with its adjacent Gazebo thought to have been built between 1715 and 1745 — has been used to make a little formal flower garden with arbours to house a collection of contemporary plants. The design of the original parterre near the house has been re-created nearby, surrounded by a pattern of trees of kinds that might have been grown at the time.

Since it was acquired in 1967, and thanks to gifts from various sources, the National Trust has been able to restore the garden from its former derelict state. Its layout is much simplified compared with the original because of the need for economy in labour but as it matures it will no doubt recapture much of the dignified orderliness of the early eighteenth-century garden. Maynard Colchester, after all, enjoyed the help of more than one gardener as well as several 'weederwomen' recruited from the village.

Westend House

Keith Steadman Esq.

At Westend, near Wickwar, 6.4km (4 miles) N of Chipping Sodbury; 550m (about 600yds) down lane from Wickwar to Rangeworthy and Cromhall. Garden and adjacent nursery open by appointment and for NGS and GS Large and varied collection of shrubs and trees informally planted in 1.2ha (3 acre) garden; apart from 4 or 5 trees entirely planted since 1950. At around 60m (200ft) on gentle westerly slope. Deep loamy soil. Rainfall 813mm (32in.). Catalogue available. Garden and nursery maintained by the owner.

The main area of the garden, which lies to the north of the house, drops away to the west, and on a hot summer's day one goes down the slope into an oasis of cool refreshing green. Generous plantings of trees and shrubs are arranged informally to display their best qualities and to create a series of restful spaces where the lush grass adds to the effect. Here is a distinctive and original garden, set out for minimum maintenance, in which the pleasure of foliage and form, stem colour and fruit, are of greater importance in the year-round effect than the more ephemeral flowers. In true eighteenth-century fashion the boundaries are concealed to make the modest area seem larger and the winding paths provide mystery and surprise.

Incredibly, a specimen of the hybrid Wing Nut, *Pterocarya* × *rehderana*, planted only in 1960, is already 16.5m (50ft) high, and is displaying its multitudes of hanging tassles of pale lime-green winged fruits. This plantsman's paradise is full of the rare and the unusual; dogwoods like *Cornus controversa* 'Variegata', *C. mas* 'Variegata' as well as the red-stemmed kinds; summer-flowering *Aesculus parviflora*; flowering privets like *Ligustrum lucidum*, *L. delavayanum* and the finest of them all *L. quihoui*; a young Weeping Silver Lime, *Tilia petiolaris*; the broad-leaved Foxglove Tree, *Paulownia tomentosa;* a splendid group of silver birches; many hollies; and providing a focal point is an attractive gazebo made from the ironwork of an old Georgian verandah.

The way leads on downhill through a mysterious tunnel of green until suddenly it opens again into the pond garden, a corner of the neighbouring field enclosed and planted by Mr. Steadman when his desire for plants outgrew the space available. Here is a collection of willows; there are thirty or more species and cultivars in the garden, including two of the finest in flower *Salix* × *meyerana* and one of its parents *S. pentandra*, the Bay Willow, so called because of its aromatic leaves. Nearby is perhaps the choicest of all flowering ashes *Fraxinus mariesii*.

On ground just west of the house is a small, walled garden overlooked by a terrace decorated by a fine *Magnolia grandiflora* and some handsome Victorian garden seats. A narrow lawn is fringed with skilfully arranged, mostly evergreen, shrub borders so dense that no weed could thrive; *Escallonia iveyi, Osmanthus × burkwoodii, Viburnum davidii, Hypericum* 'Hidcote', *Spartium junceum*, the tender *Elaeagnus macrophylla* and many more. This leads through hedges to a small, paved rose garden enlivened in late summer with *Galtonia candicans* and *Campanula lactiflora*; then back along a secret path by a south wall sheltering a fig, various clematis and tender shrubs like *Raphiolepis umbellata* and *Mahonia lomariifolia*, then towards the house past a fountain of the glaucous-leaved rose 'Wickwar' — a natural seedling which arrived in the garden.

Here is a garden of dignity and great beauty. It relies for its considerable effect on the owner's discriminating selection of plants and on his ability to use them with understanding to their best advantage. In its unpretentious way the garden of Westend House is having a considerable and an entirely beneficial influence on other gardens, not only of the immediate vicinity but also further afield.

Westonbirt Arboretum
The Forestry Commission

At Westonbirt, 5.6km (3½ miles) SW of Tetbury, N side of the A433 road to Bath. Main Arboretum of 46.5ha (116 acres) and Silk Wood of 77ha (190 acres) plus 24ha (80 acres) under development; more in reserve; planted by the Holford family. Open every day, see HHCG. At 122-137mm (400-450ft) on southern Cotswold country of low relief. Largely clay loams over limestone but with an area of deep, lime-free, sandy loam. Rainfall 889mm (35in.). Excellent reception building and interpretive displays and guidebooks available.

In quality and quantity no nation in the world has arboreta to match those in Britain. The romantic travels of the great plant hunters of the nineteenth and early-twentieth-centuries — Douglas, Lobb, Fortune, Wilson, Forrest, Kingdon Ward and others — were sponsored by landowning families who had the enthusiasm and the expertise as well as the means to create extensive collections of exotic new species. Novelties poured in, first from North America and then from Japan and the Chinese continent. Many owners were content with the excitement of growing species never before seen in these islands, planting a stream of novelties that seemed unending, but they mostly thought little of arrangement and grouping. Westonbirt is pre-eminent not only for its collection but also for its arrangement.

Robert Holford began in 1829 and planting has continued subsequently without a break; from 1870 under his son, Sir George Holford, then from 1926 with the fourth Earl of Morley, and then since 1956 under the Forestry Commission. That Robert Holford was a man of remarkable vision is clear both from the overall layout of the Arboretum and from the testimony of his brilliant tree groupings, now evident in their maturity but which he could have seen only in his mind's eye. He arranged the Arboretum as an extension to the pleasure-grounds of Westonbirt House (q.v), where he lived. The main rides form radial vistas across the sunken road from the house and entrance gates, a connection that sadly has been lost in recent years. A tribute to the quality of the planting is that, despite the separation from its focal point and historical purpose, the Arboretum retains its appeal not only to the dedicated dendrologist but also to the many thousands who pay to visit each year. Robert Holford was particularly attracted by the north-western American conifers such as the Douglas Fir and the Wellingtonias; some at Westonbirt are among the tallest in the country. He had an unerring sense of scale rare in his contemporaries and Mitchell Drive especially shows how he had the courage and discipline to leave large spaces for the enjoyment of large trees. Both he and his son, Sir George Holford, must have had a highly-developed appreciation of form and texture as well as colour in trees, a talent that has given the Arboretum qualities which can be appreciated whatever the time of year. The changing seasons superimpose their own patterns on the infinite variety of shape and colour that make up the collection. There is always something of interest and beauty — leaf, steam and bark effects as well as the colour and fragrance of flowers and fruits.

The most popular visiting time is in the autumn and Westonbirt is famous for its colour at this time and especially for its glades of Japanese Maples. The original glade was a highly successful example by Sir George Holford of planting for effect, a walk bordered by a vast array of forms of *Acer palmatum*, given unity by the succession of tree boles among which they were planted. The new glade is wider to accommodate more visitors and is fast becoming even more spectacular, if less cohesive. But there is autumn colour everywhere; as well as all kinds of maples there are many *Cercidiphyllum japonicum*, *Liquidambar styraciflua* and *Parrotia persica*.

The *Rhododendron* collection is also attributed to Sir George Holford and is situated mainly in the Circular Drive area where the soil is acid, sandy loam. The Arboretum is far from being merely a collection of trees and the range of shrubs of all kinds is almost as wide and extensive as the conifers and broad-leaved trees. Many of these were added by the fourth Earl of Morley who continued to plant trees and to diversify the collection, assisted by his Curator, Mr W.J. Mitchell, and Mr Bruce Jackson who recorded the collection and obtained many of the new species. Since

Circular Drive
Sarill Glade

Office

Waste Gate

Visitor Centre, Cafe
and Lavatories

Corsican Pine

The Waste

Maples

American
Oaks

Undeveloped

Poplars

European
Oaks

Oak and Hazel coppice

Maples

Experimental
area

Map

Broad

Maples
Poplars Elms & Walnuts
Hickories
Beech
Elms

Elms

Leyland
Cypress

Conifers

S

Hornbeam & Ash
Beech

Maples, Limes

Drive

Willesley Drive Byams

Rhododend

Hemlocks

Poplars

Nothofagus
procera

Maples

Pines

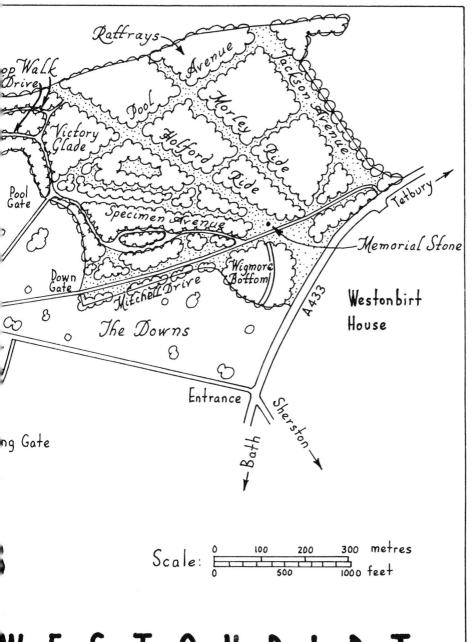

WESTONBIRT
ARBORETUM

then the Forestry Commission has continued energetically to expand and supplement the plantings and to create new collections such as the cherries. The enormous task of cataloguing is daunting but vital and the listed collection now stands at over 10,500 specimens.

Undoubtedly the best hike at Westonbirt is around Silk Wood, which is situated beyond the valley west of the car park. Sir George Holford planted the main walks and here another wonderful collection of mature trees — notably limes, hickories, walnuts, oaks and Southern Beeches — are to be seen. The undeveloped areas of Silk Wood provide much needed space for development and experiment.

In recent years the Forestry Commission has catered increasingly for the visitor through new reception and exhibition facilities, improved publications and an expanded educational programme.

The problems of conserving an arboretum of the botanical complexity and the scenic quality of Westonbirt are legion. Competition for space as trees grow necessitates the taking of firm decisions before important specimens are spoilt. Constant replanting is required to maintain a proper balance of ages of all important species. Most difficult of all is the need to maintain the right proportion of open space essential to the enjoyment of trees and shrubs.

Westonbirt House

Westonbirt School Ltd

At Westonbirt opposite the Arboretum, 4.8km (3 miles) S of Tetbury on A433 road from Tetbury to Bath and Bristol. Formal garden, informal plantings of trees and shrubs and park, once linked to the Arboretum, around large 1870 house by Lewis Vulliamy, now a girls' school. Situated on heavy but mostly well-drained, neutral soil at 122m (400ft). Rainfall 889mm (35in.). Maintained by a Head Gardener and two assistants. Open for NGS and others.

R.S. Holford's great Arboretum, now owned by the Forestry Commission, is rightly much visited and highly regarded both for the remarkable collection he and his successors assembled and for the imaginative arrangement of its trees. But the garden around his house, although more varied and more typical of the best of its age, is less well known. The ambitious scale of its layout, the variety of its features, the consistent quality of its masonry and the mature excellence of its planting confirm the garden as an important example of the high Victorian period.

The monumental neo-Elizabethan style of the house is carried through to all formal parts of the garden where the same hard brown stonework,

Westonbirt House. Part of the extensive formal flower garden and one of
the elaborate pavilions.

still in a marvellous state of preservation, has been worked with great skill
to form massively intricate terrace walls, fountains and gazebos. The
heavy grandeur of the house is emphasized on the garden front by the way
it rises from a simple broad grass terrace facing south enclosed by a
balustrade framing a stepped central vista down three further terraces to a
stone fountain pool. Each of the east-west terraces varies in character,
those at the top being more open and terminated westwards by the little
church and the lower terraces being enclosed with fine specimen trees
including both Deodar and Atlas Cedars, the rare Sumach *Rhus chinensis*,
False Acacias, an enormous *Parrotia persica,* a tall old Madrona, *Arbutus
menziesii* and an Hungarian Oak, *Quercus frainetto.*

The broad central terrace extends eastwards to form the main cross axis
of the garden with fine views into the park and pairs of specimen trees
and shrubs: Golden Yews, Sumachs and the unusual weeping form of
Copper Beech. The shrubs thicken on either side to emphasize a well-
planned surprise opening into the formal Italian Garden, cunningly
arranged so that its ground level is at eye level. This focuses attention first
on the splendid fountain where water gushes from a circular pool at the
top via stone dragons on either side into an apron-shaped lily pool;
secondly on a view across the formal garden to the delicate conservatory
set centrally in the far wall, its symmetry now sadly spoilt by the insen-
sitive siting of a modern classroom looming up alongside. The terrace
walk continues eastwards to finish at another surprise: a sunken garden
surrounded by Japanese Maples with a statue of Mercury set in a circular
pool. Overlooking this to terminate the vista is an ornate stone seat
covered by an elaborate arbour constructed in such a way as to provide a
platform on top giving views back along the terrace walk and out into the
park.

Turning back a little way, the formal Italian Garden is entered by way
of heavy shell gates leading to a gravel terrace along the north side set
between two enormous and impressive gazebos linked by a high wall
surmounted by a series of stone finials. The warm wall supports a variety
of climbers including the large-leaved *Actinidia kolomikta,* summer
flowering *Ceanothus* 'Gloire de Versailles', *Garrya elliptica,* Wintersweet
and the purple-leaved Teinturier Grape. A central opening in the wall
reveals that finest of Victorian garden innovations, the conservatory
complete with camellias. The terrace overlooks a complex layout of stone-
edged beds set in grass arranged around an enormous stone urn and
backed with Irish Yews and a long herbaceous border. The beds are still
well maintained and colourful with a traditional Victorian bedding scheme
in summer. Off to the west the remains of a fine iron rose pergola and a
rather overgrown tufa rockery and grotto provide a touch of mystery.

West of the house a path curves past the church to a large undulating area contrasting in style with the firm terraces and architectural shapes of the rest of the garden. Here there is a Venetian well-head and splendid trees: Black Walnut, Judas Tree, late-flowering *Ligustrum lucidum* and a mature group of Scots Pines drifting into the valley. A glimpse of the lake encourages further exploration past the Theatre and magnificent groups of Golden Yew. Robert Holford's planting around the lake is an outstanding example of the dynamic composition of a wide range of trees and shrubs for landscape effect; the contrasting shapes and greens of Pfitzer Junipers, Weeping Hollies, Westfelton Yews and White Mulberry being used to advantage.

A view back to the house leads through massive rock outcrops with bamboos and maples to complete the tour of this plantsman's paradise arranged with great skill and originality to a strong and disciplined plan.

Willersey House

Colonel and Mrs P. Arkwright

Open for the Council for the Protection of Rural England and again for NGS in spring and summer. At Willersey, 2.4km (1½ miles) N of Broadway. Old Cotswold house, formerly a farmhouse and enlarged in 1912 by A.N. Prentice. Lovely views. Flowering shrubs and bulbs, especially masses of daffodils, are a feature in spring. For July there are flowering shrubs, herbaceous borders and a rose garden.

Windy Ridge

C.J. Williams Esq

Open for NGS in summer. 4.8km (3 miles) NW of Stow-on-the-Wold, on E side of A424 road. Garden of 1.2ha (3 acres) packed with interest and excitement, all immaculately maintained.

Developed since 1951 with a series of terraces on an exposed site facing east, now sheltered by many young trees, especially conifers. A great variety of shrubs and plants and a whole host of features have been assembled around the house. The terraces nearest the house are the most colourful with bedding plants, roses, including big beds of the multi-coloured 'Masquerade', and pools, set in a complex of lawns and patterns of paving and cobbles. A brick-built moongate leads to a croquet-lawn and shrub roses. Elsewhere are a swimming-pool and folly; thatched-roof loose boxes and garages; greenhouses and kitchen garden and the whole garden can be floodlit. There is variety of ornaments, statuary and urns, a fountain and a little summerhouse made to resemble a dovecote. The effect is colourful and stimulating and it is as well to arrive early on open days because the garden is very popular and should not be missed.

Winson Mill Farm
Mrs Robert Henriques

Open for NGS and again for RC in summer. At Winson, 11.2km (7 miles) NE of Cirencester. Charming riverside flower garden in the idyllic setting of the Coln valley. Unpretentious and effective arrangement of shrubs and trees; spacious lawns and trees, roses, and fine old Victorian cast-iron seats.

Witcombe Park
Mrs W.W. Hicks Beach

Open for NGS in summer. At Great Witcombe, 6.4km (4 miles) E of Gloucester. Medium-sized with roses, flowering shrubs and a sunk garden. Set in beautiful Cotswold scenery.

Withington Gardens

Several gardens in one of the most lovely of all Cotswold villages. Open for NGS in early summer. 4.8km (3 miles) S of Andoversford.

Wormington Grange
Lt Col M.J. Evetts and The Hon. Mrs Evetts

Open for GS in early summer. 6.4km (4 miles) W of Broadway. Regency house with lovely views; roses and trees, and small enclosed gardens.

Yew Tree Cottage

Brigadier and Mrs H. Shuker and Miss P. Strange

At Ampney St Mary, 0.8km (½ mile) N of A417 Cirencester to Fairford road turn at Red Lion Inn, Ampney St Peter. Cottage-style and alpine garden of about 0.4ha (1 acre) and small nursery around old Cotswold stone cottage. Situated in open, fairly level country at 107m (350ft) heavy alkaline soil over Cotswold limestone. Rainfall 810mm (32in.). Maintained by the owners. Open for NGS and others.

There are many charming cottage gardens in the Cotswolds area but none where the variety of interest and the standard of cultivation is better than at Yew Tree Cottage. To see beautiful plants well nurtured is an inspiration that can be frustrating if there is no immediate source of supply but here the visitor can buy from an excellent stock of reasonably-priced, pot-grown alpines and dwarf perennials, a facility that only those who visit Cirencester market on Fridays can share.

For those to whom the miniature and the intricate in plant life is their pleasure, this is the garden to visit. From the moment of entering the garden the owners' attention to detail becomes apparent; a caring atmosphere extends to visitors as well as to plants. Past the summerhouse and by the immaculate little kitchen garden there are stone troughs set out on the gravel containing finely-worked tiny landscapes of tufa with choice alpines like *Rhodohypoxis, Phyteuma* and *Saxifraga* 'Tumbling Waters' grown to perfection.

Just behind the house pride of place is given to a well-arranged rock garden of weathered Cotswold Jurassic limestone arising imperceptibly out of a scree of matching limestone chippings, which also forms the drive. Against the biblical prediction, many a seedling has found a home and thriven in the stony ground, quite apart from the neat alpine cushions that have been encouraged to overflow. Among the rocks is a framework of shrubby potentillas, dwarf lilac and purple barberry; golden juniper and other dwarf conifers including *Picea glauca albertiana* 'Conica', *Cistus* × *corbariensis* and other sunlovers. These build up to larger shrubs and climbers in the shade behind the house: *Garrya elliptica, Hedera colchica* 'Variegata', hypericums and Variegated Snowberry. The variety of alpines is remarkable for so small an area; all kinds of saxifrages, pinks, geraniums and violas have responded to the evident loving care that they receive, and great pads of the enormous houseleek, *Sempervivum* 'Commander Hay', are a star turn. There is even a little moist area and pond surrounded by Kingcups, Musk and Plaintan Lilies with Bowles' Golden Grass sprinkled around.

In the little orchard nearby the dappled shade provides ideal homes for hardy cyclamen, spring bulbs fritillaries and *Trillium* species among a variety of shade-loving ground covers including the pretty, but unstable, variegated *Brunnera macrophylla*, the continuous flowering *Viola cornuta* and its white form, and the invaluable evergreen *Euphorbia robbiae*. All these are tucked between a selection of trees and shrubs like the pineapple-scented *Cytisus battandieri*, purple *Cotinus coggygria*, *Rosa moyesii* and the greeny-gold *Philadelphus coronarius* 'Aureus', chosen for their long period of interest.

Separated by a wall and the house itself is an entirely separate area facing east on to the lane. The little lawn, surrounded by well-stocked borders, has a more typically cottage character with shrub roses of the Rugosa and Hybrid Musk kinds, and with 'Nevada' and the dusky *R. rubrifolia*, among cherries, dogwoods, hollies, buddleias, clematises, *Senecio* 'Sunshine' and *Viburnum carlesii*. But closer inspection reveals the same skill at making every inch pay its way by intensive underplanting with low-growing perennials. Also here is the spectacular climbing *Tropaeolum speciosum* which wreathes the shrubs with its scarlet flowers in summer.

All this complicated plantsmanship is offset cleverly near the house where a little paved area is given over to a few well-shaped large shrubs, among which the Pfitzer Juniper is prominent.

The Gardens of Somerset
and
South Avon

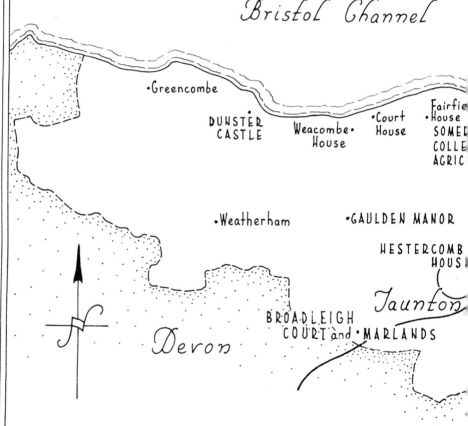

The Gardens of
SOMERSET AND
SOUTH AVON

Bristol Channel

•Greencombe

Fairfie[
•House

•Court
House

DUNSTER
CASTLE

Weacombe•
House

SOMEl
COLLE
AGRIC

•Weatherham

•GAULDEN MANOR

HESTERCOMB
HOUS

BROADLEIGH
COURT and •MARLANDS

Jaunton

Devon

Scale:

| 0 | 5 | 10 | 15 | 20 | 25 kilometres |

| 0 | 5 | 10 | 15 miles |

Brackenwood
Nurseries

DON COURT·

Rayne Thatch·
and University
Botanic Garden

Bristol

Avon *Bath*

CLAVERTON
MANOR and
·ORCHARD
HOUSE

Rainbow Wood and
CROWE HALL
PRIOR PARK

·Parish's House
Tinsbury

Old·
Rectory
Beckington

ORCHARDLEIGH·
PARK
·MILTON LODGE·Oakhill Park
·Bishops Palace
Wells·

·BABYCHAM GARDENS
·Southill House
·Westholme House
·Pitton Manor Vinyard

·Wootton House

·Redlynch Park

HADSPEN HOUSE·
·LYTES CARY
·Bratton Farm House
·Yarlington House

·STOWELL HILL

AST LAMBROOK
MANOR·
RINGTON·
COURT
·Stapleton Manor
·TINTINHULL HOUSE
·MONTACUTE HOUSE
·Brympton d'Evercy
·Little Norton Mill Nursery
·Scotts Nurseries

Dorset

WAYFORD·
MANOR·
·Clapton Court

M5

The Babycham Gardens

Showerings Ltd

In Kilver Street, Shepton Mallet, behind Showerings Mill. Open for NGS usually one day per year in June. Factory garden of 2.8ha (7 acres) with rock garden, lake, waterfall and formal rose garden. Situated at 106m (350ft) in a sheltered site on slightly acid, peaty soil. Rainfall 1,143mm (40in.). Maintained by a horticulturist and three assistant gardeners.

In the surroundings of factories, horticultural opportunities are so often missed that it comes as something of a shock, as well as a pleasure, to discover what can be done when an enlightened company gives priority to providing beautiful surroundings for its employees and puts the work into the hands of expert craftsmen. Although the Mill has the advantages of maturity and of course there is plenty of water, the site is far from ideal, being dominated by an enormous railway viaduct on one side and the inevitable paraphernalia of industry on the other. Yet here is an immaculate garden boasting a standard of upkeep so high by today's standards as to be unique.

The garden in its present form is relatively new, having been developed since 1959, and lacks large trees except on the town side beyond the lake where a large lime, Horse Chestnuts and a Weeping Willow screen the backs of houses. However, this one shortcoming is entirely recompensed by the extraordinary variety and quality that has been packed into such a small area.

The high ground on the north side is dominated by a rock garden in a setting of rhododendrons. Its design was based on an award-winning design at the Chelsea Flower Show in the early 1950s and so meticulous is its upkeep that it could be there still! Expertly built by Gavin Jones Ltd, it shows all the best qualities of the subtle craft of rock garden construction, the peak of which has now sadly passed. A gushing, recirculated stream bubbles from pool to pool over a cunning variety of rocky outcrops and waterfalls into the lake. The planting is varied, comprehensively labelled and thrives in the fertile, peaty soil thanks to the care and attention to detail of those in charge. Among a wide range of rock garden plants there are many dwarf conifers, heathers, Rock Roses, thrifts and dwarf phloxes. *Iberis sempervirens, Genista lydia*, and especially *Incarvillea delavayi* are outstanding, as are many of the stream and lakeside groups of *Hosta, Iris* and *Astilbe*.

Also on the high ground is a shrub garden surrounding immaculate lawns, each edge manicured to perfection. The borders contain colourful small trees such as Red May, *Prunus* 'Amanogawa' and *Amelanchier laevis*, and a selection of flowering shrubs including *Viburnum plicatum* 'Mariesii' and *V. farreri*, *Berberis darwinii* and *B.* × *stenophylla*, *Escallonia*, and *Hibiscus syriacus* grown to perfection — all underplanted with early bulbs and lilies to give beauty and interest throughout the year.

Contrasting with all this informality is a strictly geometric rose garden set in York stone paving and a lawn of golf-green quality. Here there are long beds of hybrid tea roses bursting with health and vigour, and standard roses in a central bed of 'Fragrant Cloud'. The apsidal-shaped end of this garden points to the confluence of two waterfalls, one from the rock garden and the other from the lake, the water eventually finding its way into the former mill stream.

Every part of the limited space is fully used to give refreshment and delight to workers and visitors. There is a putting-green and a further variety of shrubs beyond the railway viaduct, and a shady walk around the lake where there are mallards and muscovies; the sound of water is everywhere.

Barrington Court
The National Trust

In Barrington, 4.8km (3 miles) NE of Ilminster. For opening arrangements see HHCG and NT; also open for NGS Mainly formal garden of 3.6ha (9 acres) laid out in 1920s with the help of Gertrude Jekyll. Important sixteenth-century house, restored after 1920 by Colonel A.A. Lyle and the architects Forbes and Tate, who also converted the seventeenth-century stable block and designed the whole group of estate buildings. Situated in low-lying, gently rolling country at less than 30m (100ft) on heavy alkaline soil. Rainfall 762mm (30in.). Head gardener and three assistants.

There has been a house at Barrington Court since mediaeval times. The present Ham stone house with all its rich Gothic and Renaissance detail is thought to have been built, not by Henry Daubeney as earlier evidence suggested, but by William Clifton who bought the estate in 1552. If there is doubt about the exact date of the house, there is no doubt about the garden because there was none to speak of until after the First World War. After the Clifton family the house belonged for a time to Thomas Phelips of nearby Montacute House and then in the middle of the seventeenth-century to William Strode, who built the stable block that bears his name. After the Strode family had sold Barrington in the eighteenth century the place had a chequered history, frequently changing hands until, largely through the generosity of Miss J.L. Woodward, it was acquired by the National Trust in 1907, one of the first of its great houses.

The house was in a sad state but fortunately in 1920 Colonel A.A. Lyle became the National Trust's tenant. With the help of the architects Forbes and Tate he immediately set about restoring and rehabilitating what had become a mere shell, using panelling and fittings he had collected. He employed the same architects to convert the Strode stable block into a dwelling house and to build a complete set of farm and estate buildings, roads and tenants' houses. With the Strode block and its walled curtilage and ox-pens, these buildings form the framework of the garden. The architects designed the buildings and cottages in traditional style to blend with the house and tied the whole design together with two impressive avenues of Horse Chestnut, one leading to the house and the other coming in at right-angles.

Forbes' original plan was for about four hectares (ten acres) of elaborate garden within virtually the whole of the area enclosed by what is called 'the Moat'. It is not a moat in the usual sense but more a swift-flowing shallow stream which nevertheless adds a great deal of charm and interest to the garden. Forbes planned a complex layout with yew hedges covering the south front of the Court and an 'Elizabethan Garden' in what is now the orchard. Colonel Lyle and the National Trust wisely decided on a simpler scheme especially near the Court where nothing was to be allowed to detract from the grandeur of the architecture.

Colonel Lyle asked Gertrude Jekyll to design the planting, so establish-ing the classic combination of architect and artist-plantsman which has so frequently been successful in the creation of great English gardens. Miss Jekyll, by then getting on in years and with failing sight, took Forbes' plans and worked on them, ruling the orchard out of the garden scheme altogether, which reduced the area considerably. The broad herbaceous border facing south across the orchard was the first border to be planted but it was not designed by Miss Jekyll, having been made before she began at Barrington Court. It is within the walled gardens that Gertrude Jekyll left her distinctive mark and her plans still exist in the Beatrix Farrand Collection in the University of Berkeley, California, USA.

The Lily Garden occupies the area immediately north of the converted Strode stable block. As so often happens in English country house

Above: Barrington Court. Although not precisely as Gertrude Jekyll planned it, the garden has been maintained in sympathy with her ideas.

Below: Hestercombe. The Plat with the pergola beyond.　　*Somerset County Council*

gardens, it is a compromise on the original plan, which would have involved much excavation. It is a feature of the garden at Barrington that the details have been gradually amended and developed over the years, particularly by Sir Ian Lyle who succeeded Colonel Lyle as tenant until 1978, when A.I.A. Lyle Esq., took over the tenancy on the death of Sir Ian. If not exactly to her plan, the Lily Garden is much in Miss Jekyll's style with raised beds of azaleas (not hydrangeas and crinums as she planned) in imported lime-free soil either side of the oblong lily pool. Behind are narrow brick paths in a basket-weave pattern and wide borders of mixed flowers and shrubs against the walls. Where Miss Jekyll suggested yuccas in the raised corner beds, now there are equally effective crinums.

Although the plans are said to have been made in something of a hurry, Miss Jekyll took great care with her mixtures of flowering shrubs, perennials and annuals, all worked into characteristically subtle colour schemes. She was also eminently practical and had biscuit tins of soil taken from various parts of the garden and sent to her so that she could choose the plants accordingly. Most of the plants came from nurserymen, including Scotts of Merriott for hedge plants, Gauntletts of Chiddingfold for flowering shrubs, Notcutts of Woodbridge for lilacs and Cants of Colchester for roses. She supplied some of the herbaceous plants herself while the rest came from Allgroves of Langley.

The late Mrs Lyle, in her account of the garden written in 1925, says that the 'Rose Garden' was made that year with a box hedge to enclose it. There used to be roses in the present Iris Garden but they have given way to lavenders and purple clematises. The Flag Irises, now a valuable historic collection of between-the-wars cultivars, have been maintained, traditionally separated by patches of petunias, heliotropes and clary. Now the Rose Garden is accommodated in a square, walled enclosure with a statue forming the centre of a circular design.

The long colour border near the ox-pens is separated from the Iris Garden by a spreading box hedge and enclosed by more of Miss Jekyll's patterned brick paths. Originally a border for cut flowers, the present colour scheme was begun by Mrs. Lyle in 1960. In Jekyll-style it grades from yellow through orange and the hotter colours to cool colours, mauves and blues at the far end.

The big, walled kitchen garden is laid out in traditional style, divided into quarters by paths. Old, beautifully trained espalier fruit trees and borders of perennial flowers line the paths, and vegetables and soft fruits still fill the plots, with more trained fruit trees on the walls. Few kitchen gardens of the old style remain productive, and small wonder with the rapidly increasing costs of hand labour.

In recent years Sir Ian Lyle had made new informal plantings of trees and shrubs in wide variety on the east side. Thanks to the continuous generosity of the Lyle family and the steadfast purpose of the National Trust we can still enjoy this lovely garden, made by the combined talents of Mr Forbes and Miss Jekyll, not forgetting the family who had developed and nurtured it.

The Bishop's Palace, Wells

Lord Bishop of Bath and Wells and Mrs Bickersteth

Open with other gardens in Wells for NGS and Wells Cathedral Preservation Fund, three times in late spring. The Bishop's Palace has a 2.8ha (7 acre) moated garden with fine mature trees and newly-planted Jubilee arboretum, wild fowl, and fine views of the Cathedral and countryside. MILTON LODGE (see separate entry) is open in conjunction. The others are small town gardens but contain much well-considered planting and a variety of interest.

Brackenwood Nurseries

John Maycock Esq

Open for NGS and GS frequently. In Nore Road, Portishead; on coast road to Clevedon. 1.6ha (4 acre) woodland garden on steeply sloping site overlooking the Bristol Channel with fine views. Adjacent to nurseries.

Rhododendrons, azaleas, species of *Pieris*, *Embothrium*, and other lime-hating woodland plants thrive in the mild climate, given shelter. Waterfowl and ornamental lily pools; pheasants and parakeets.

Bratton Farm House

Mr and Mrs A.J. Brock

Open for NGS in early summer. At Bratton Seymour, 4.8km (3 miles) N of Wincanton. 0.8ha (2 acre) enclosed garden with various features and interesting plants.

Broadleigh Court
See Marlands

Brympton d'Evercy
Charles E.B. Clive-Ponsonby-Fane Esq

For opening arrangements see HHCG; also open for NGS 3.2km (2 miles) W of Yeovil. 4ha (10 acres) around superb group of Ham stone buildings; Tudor mansion house with late seventeenth-century south front.

The garden retains its seventeenth-century form as illustrated in the Knyff engraving, with forecourt, south terrace and bowling-green but there is now a lake beyond. The garden is in the process of being reinstated by Judy Clive-Ponsonby-Fane and there are already herbaceous and shrub beds and extensive lawns. Many shrub roses have been planted. An extensive and productive vineyard is a feature of particular interest and wine can be bought.

Clapton Court
Capt. S.J. Loder

Open for NGS in spring and early summer. 4.8km (3 miles) S of Crewkerne. 3.2ha (8 acre) garden laid out in 1950 in beautiful park-like surroundings with many fine mature trees; 1 ha (2½ acre) arboretum. There is a terraced garden, rhododendrons and azaleas, a rose garden, a water garden and a rockery.

Claverton Manor
The American Museum in Britain

At Claverton, 6km (3¾ mls) SE of Bath via the Warminster Road (A36) and Claverton village. For opening arrangements see HHCG; usually daily except Mondays. Mainly informal garden of 6 ha (15 acres) around classical Georgian house in Bath stone by Jeffrey Wyattville. On well-drained alkaline soil over limestone on steep slopes to the south and east. At 122m (400ft) with fine views of the Limpley Stoke valley and the Avon below. Rainfall 787mm (31in.). Head Gardener, Mr Holson, and two other gardeners, directed by Mr Ian McCullum.

The great joy of Claverton Manor is its superb position with glorious views over the wooded Limpley Stoke valley, surely one of the finest unspoilt valleys so close to a city anywhere in these islands. Beside it the garden has difficulty in competing but it contains much of interest, including some features introduced since the house became the American Museum. The Museum was founded in 1961 by Dallas Pratt and the late John Judkyn to foster the arts and to further Anglo-American understanding.

Apart from the view, the other major asset is the fine framework of mature trees, many of the eighteenth century. Amid limestone outcrops beeches, limes and Holm Oaks line the drive and make a park-like setting, while fine cedars grace the lawns. Extending the lines of the house is a tall screen wall topped with a balustrade behind which are old climbing roses such as 'Alister Stella Gray' and 'Mme Alfred Carrière', with tubs of clipped bay trees and a fine white eighteenth-century-style garden seat, one of several in the garden.

The openness of the sunny east side is a total contrast, as is the juxta-position of the little herb garden against the vast scale of the surroundings. This box-hedged formal feature, given by the Garden Club of Southampton, Long Island, is well stocked and contains several unusual herbs including Poke Root, *Phytolacca decandra* and Skullcap, *Scutellaria latifolia*.

The south terrace is furnished tastefully with terracotta pots filled with mixed summer flowers and silver foliage. Nearby, the high wall facing east has a pattern of repeated Irish Yews and ceanothuses and a beautiful border of mixed roses, shrubs, bulbs and herbaceous plants providing a succession of colour in front. This attractive corner was designed by Mr Lanning Roper who gave a good deal of help soon after the Museum was set up.

On the slope south of the house is an interesting Indian-style summer-house and beyond, down steps, a cool grotto with a lion's head dribbling

water onto tufa, all overhung with evergreen and planted around with
moisture-loving *Rodgersia* spp., Plume Poppies and ferns. This looks
down a line of flowering cherries with more steps and flanking urns
leading to a grass terrace. Here are shrub roses, especially rugosas, and the
slope below is being planted as an arboretum of American trees, ferns and
shrubs, and as an orchard by Mr Paul Miles. At the end of a grass walk a
fine curving seat shows up well in front of old roses and purple cotinus.
Above, a magnificent cedar towers against the sky and a stone staircase
with flanking borders of irises and handsome carved stone urns at the top
leads back to the house.

The west end of the grass terrace leads through a gate to steps overlooking a replica of part of the rose and flower gardens at George
Washington's old home, Mount Vernon, on the Potomac river. The great
man had obtained plants and seeds (and even his farm manager) from
Somerset and followed Batty Langley's *New Principles of Gardening*
(London, 1728) in the layout of his garden. Now, by a curious coin-
cidence, the outcome has returned thanks to the generosity of the Colonial
Dames of America and the work of Mr Ian Mylles. Although it is never
easy successfully to recreate a garden, lock, stock and barrel, in entirely
different surroundings, the work has been done with great care and the
result is impressive.

Clevedon Court
The National Trust

On the E side of Clevedon N of B3130 Bristol road and near the M5. For opening see
HHCG and NT Garden of 3.2ha (8 acres) with eighteenth-century terraces around a
fourteenth-century Manor incorporating a twelfth-century tower and thirteenth-century Hall.
Situated on a south-facing slope above 30m (100ft); overlooking low-lying Nailsea Moor; light
alkaline soil. Rainfall 813mm (32in.). One full-time gardener.

The garden at Clevedon Court, like many an English garden with ancient
beginnings, has developed gradually over the centuries in response to the
varying needs of its owners and the taste of the day. The present garden is
entirely the work of the Elton family who owned the house from 1709
until in 1961 it came by Treasury transfer to the National Trust with an
endowment from Sir Arthur Elton Bt. The Trust is lucky to have Lady
Elton, who still works long hours in the garden, to guide the work and to
add her personal touch.

In *Wall and Water Gardens* (1901), Gertrude Jekyll recognized the quality of this garden but was scathing about the planting. She wrote: 'The planting at the base of the lowest wall seems in these more horticulturally enlightened days to be quite indefensible. The foot of one of the noblest ranges of terrace walls in England is too good to be given over to the most commonplace forms of bedding . . .'. She was reacting to Victorian splendour in the form of a seemingly endless series of prim little beds set square against the wall, a scheme that had been praised lavishly in *Country Life* only a couple of years earlier: 'Clevedon Court, in the general character of the terraces, is scarcely excelled in England . . .'. Here was a watershed of garden history, for Miss Jekyll has had her way, and not only at Clevedon Court.

The original terraces were made early in the 1700s before the Octagon, which was added later in the eighteenth-century, when they were extended further west. This charming gazebo is the focal point of the middle terrace and indeed of the whole garden. Like the terraces at Powis Castle, which are contemporary, those at Clevedon were made to take the fullest advantage of the sun, mainly no doubt for the production of fruits and vegetables and to provide a sheltered place to walk and sit. Enjoying as they do the mild coastal climate, the terraces at Clevedon Court are exceptionally favoured and would have been equally suitable for peaches, apricots and figs as for the tender shrubs and climbers of today.

A bird's-eye view of the house, painted by an unknown artist about 1740, shows fruit trees pleached against the pink brick wall of the lower terrace. Court Hill, once The Little Warren, was dramatically bald, but the beginning of tree planting is in evidence.

Throughout the eighteenth-century the first Scots Pines were steadily augmented by sycamore, beech and the now naturalized Holm Oaks which create the present exotic, Mediterranean-type background. Early in the nineteenth century this phase of planting came to an end. By 1840, 'old' Lady Elton, wife of the fifth baronet, adapted the principles of Humphry Repton to transform Court Hill and indeed the whole garden for she was a notable landscape gardener. Romantic and picturesque paths were designed and vistas revealed, including views of the house and the moors beyond.

In the valley near the house the open soil and high water-table favour trees of a different kind. There are groves of False Acacia and a mighty London Plane by the drive where masses of daffodils grow. Nearby, a shapely Indian Bean Tree flowers profusely in summer and an old mulberry is still fruitful, though described as 'ancient' in 1819. The view west from the house is one of the glories of Clevedon Court. The lawn emerges into a long meadow framed by hanging woods on the right and craggy Monterey Pines towering over yews on the left, and Rickman's Christ Church enhances the whole scene as if it were an eighteenth-century folly.

The lawns slope up towards the terraces past a large Holm Oak with the Octagon to catch the eye. Victorian photographs show the area directly behind the house set out as an elaborate parterre, first planned in 1857 and removed a century later. The symmetry of pool and paths is now reflected in pairs of hollies and the glaucous *Cupressus arizonica* while bushes of Rugosa roses and a luxuriant *Rosa brunonii* recall its earlier status as a rose garden. Against the warm wall behind are Pomegranates, white crinums, Arum Lilies and ceanothuses. Magnolias are a feature of this terrace slope and one vast Yulan has joined forces with a spread-eagled Irish Yew and a large specimen of the variegated Cornelian Cherry to create a shady gove where ferns, species of *Skimmia* and *Mahonia*, including *japonica* and *acanthifolia*, thrive alongside *Viburnum davidii* with its conspicuous turquoise-blue fruits.

There is a myrtle close enough to the steps to touch on the way up and the unique combination of flowers and foliage of *Fuchsia magellanica* 'Versicolor' cascades from the terrace above.

The Octagon is placed at the very heart of the garden, commanding views down the main terrace, known as the Pretty Terrace, and out across country now sadly marred by the M5 motorway. In early summer the warm bank below the terrace is a mass of the so-called Creeping Blue Blossom, *Ceanothus thyrsiflorus* 'Repens', here a rampant spreading shrub.

Over the years the terrace planting has been gradually changed, consciously or not, to something that might have appealed to Gertrude Jekyll. It is now filled with a fascinating selection of shrubs and plants which enjoy the warmth and tolerate the sea breezes. Most memorable of a spring visit is a magnificent old *Photinia serrulata*, its leaves opening bright coppery-red, with the aristocratic *Mahonia lomariifolia* nearby; also the deep rosy-purple goblets of *Magnolia* × *soulangiana* 'Lennei' and the fragrant *Drimys winteri*. But there is beauty and interest here at all seasons and especially in summer when the tender *Buddleia colvilei* is dripping with crimson and several species of *Hoheria* and *Abelia* and *Magnolia grandiflora* 'Exmouth' are blossoming white. Despite the alkaline soil *Eucryphia* 'Nymansay' puts on a good summer display and the border contains lovely white agapanthuses and Japanese Anemones and large clumps of the spectacularly exotic *Canna iridiflora* with its large banana-like leaves. In front of the summerhouse at the other end of Pretty Terrace is a row of the showy fuchsia 'Mrs Popple', their roots shaded by the retaining wall. Through a gateway behind the summerhouse is a sun-drenched bank of purple and blue hebes and silver foliage plants with a purple vine for contrast.

The top terrace is known as the Esmond Terrace because part of *Henry Esmond* was written here by William Makepeace Thackeray. Here the emphasis is strongly on evergreens with a preponderance of free-fruiting Strawberry Trees which, with Laurustinus, have naturalized on the fringe of the ilex woodland. With Judas Trees, the European Dwarf Palm and Yuccas growing where the rock is not far below the surface, the impression is strongly Mediterranean and exotic.

Clevedon Court is not for the lover of spectacular displays of flowers but rather for those who appreciate subtle colours and sensitive foliage effects. It is a garden for the plantsman who likes to see beautiful plants cared for lovingly. Above all it is a great example of the English garden tradition, a garden that bears the imprint of successive generations of a single family that has occupied it for nearly 300 years. It is this evidence of continuity that makes British gardens unique.

Court House
Colonel and Mrs Walter Luttrell

Open for NGS in spring. At East Quantoxhead, 19.2km (12 miles) W of Bridgwater, 1.2ha (3 acres); shrubs, roses and some herbaceous around Tudor house. Fine views.

Crowe Hall
John Barratt Esq.

At Widcombe, 1.6km (1 mile) E of Bath, S up Widcombe Hill off A36 road near White Hart public house. Terraced garden of 2.4ha (6 acres) on steep SW slope at around 76m (250 ft). Fine classical house of Bath stone (not open). Open for NGS Well-drained alkaline soil over limestone. Rainfall 787mm (31in.). Owners and equivalent of one gardener full-time and another half-time.

Although Widcombe is contiguous with the City of Bath, Crowe Hall has what must rank among the finest views in Britain, for it looks directly up to Prior Park with Lancelot Brown's landscape in the foreground. With this unique backdrop on one side and the City of Bath spread out on another, it could hardly be an ordinary garden, and its layout and content make it the more notable.

The house was perched high on the steep south-westerly slope and given a broad terrace only by the construction of massive stone walls. The former owners were the Tugwell family and it was they who created the main framework of the garden in the last century. Evidently they planted the yews, now vast and draped with Russian Vine and *Clematis armandii*, below the high terrace wall. The result is a shady yew walk below and a valuable shelter for the terrace above. On the south side of the house the comfortable sun room with its *trompe l'oeil* opens out on to a narrow, paved terrace where valerian and the little daisy-like *Erigeron mucronatus* grow and magnolias and wisterias embellish the golden stone walls. Beyond this, as foreground to the view of Prior Park, is a sunken lawn with a pool made by the previous owners, the Maconochies; Sir Sydney Barratt added the fountain. A raised walk backed by a yew hedge along the east has been provided now with elegant iron seats and leads to a little statue and a fine Japanese Maple on a mound.

At the end of the lawn, water trickles from a magnificent rock outcrop surmounted by Pfitzer Junipers giving a hint of what lies beyond. Winding steps descend steeply into the Tugwell rock garden, now romantically overgrown into a dark and secret tunnel. Strewn about with ferns and overlooked by an ivy-clad grotto, the scene is perfectly picturesque in the manner of the Rev. William Gilpin. A succession of little streams and pools follow the path under arches of bamboo to the beginning of the yew walk, where a large urn makes a splendid focal point.

Around the existing framework of trees and terraces and since 1961, a completely new garden has been superimposed by Sir Sydney and Lady Barratt and latterly by their son, the present owner. Almost all the roses, bulbs, flowering trees and shrubs and the lawns are their creation, especially on the terraces below the house, which would formerly have been the productive areas for fruit, vegetables and cut flowers. Although difficult to work, the warm slopes would have been ideal for early vegetables and have now been successfully adapted for an enormous variety of flowering trees and shrubs. Among the established fruit trees are masses of spring bulbs. Japanese Cherries, birches, maples, and old shrub roses are prominent and near the road is an elegantly slim young Weeping Beech. Much more mature are a pair of rugged old mulberries near the steps leading back to the house.

An unusual and striking feature of the garden is the impressive array of flowers on display in baskets and tubs. Above the house Neptune presides over a little pool and commands a rock bank thickly clad with heathers, dwarf conifers and Spanish Gorse, *Genista hispanica*. Beyond, a wide sweep of grass stretches up the hill to an old-established beech wood, making an amphitheatre backed by trees of many kinds ranging from Japanese Cherries and Crabs to Atlas Cedars and tall limes. All this and a vast array of shrubs, which look especially well in autumn, has been planted by the Barratts.

In less than twenty years an English garden has been created in a

Right above: Crowe Hall, Bath. View over the formal sunken garden to the classical façade of Prior Park, top right. *Iris Hardwick*

Right bottom: Prior Park, Bath. The reciprocal view, with Crowe Hall visible in the middle distance. With its Palladian bridge this is one of Lancelot 'Capability' Brown's most famous landscape views. *Iris Hardwick*

magnificent Italianate setting among Victorian essays in the Picturesque.
Here is another successful example of the English gardening talent for
adapting the old to blend happily with the new.

Dunster Castle
The National Trust

---

*In Dunster, 3.2km (2 miles) SE of Minehead on S side of A396 Taunton road. For opening
arrangements see HHCG and NT 6ha (15 acres) of garden and woodland occupying the
Castle slopes at 15-45m (50-150ft). Castle dating from thirteenth-century, remodelled by Salvin
in nineteenth-century; with magnificent views. On near-neutral soil over shillock, thin on the hill,
deeper in the valley. Rainfall 1,016mm (40in.); exceptionally mild on the steep south-east slopes.
Three gardeners.*

From the Taunton road the first sight of Dunster Castle, perched high on
its Tor, is so irresistibly romantic that it would be a magnet to visitors
even if there were no house or garden to see. Its conical hill rises
dramatically out of the water meadows of the River Avill where once was
seashore, now a mile or more away. But Dunster is more than merely
picturesque, the grounds provide an extraordinary variety of conditions
and a wide disparity of gardening.

The strategic position of the hill has ensured its occupation for over a
thousand years but while defence was the main consideration little in the
way of gardening can have been possible. It is recorded that early in the
eighteenth-century the site of the Keep at the summit of the hill was level-
led to make a bowling green and the little octagonal summerhouse, which
still exists, is shown clearly in Buck's view of the Castle dated 1733.
Today the Keep is well worth the climb to enjoy some of the finest
panoramic views to be had from any vantage point in the land. Recently
the lawn has been restored in an elliptical shape and the space between it
and the perimeter path planted with shrubs tolerant of the dry soil and
breezy position, myrtles, brooms, Sun Roses, hebes etc., to supplement
the Mexican Oranges, variegated pittosporums and griselinias, *Feijoa
sellowana* and others planted by the Luttrell family.

Even in the early eighteenth-century the lower slopes were thickly
wooded but Buck's engraving shows a formal arrangement of trees higher
up and the southern slopes may well have been used as a vineyard, no
doubt very successfully. By 1830 the mount is described by James Savage
as 'covered with ever-greens, flowering shrubs, and trees to its top, where
there is a bowling green encircled by a wall, skirted with Laurustinus and

other shrubs . . .'. Winter-flowering Laurustinus was one of the earliest evergreen shrubs introduced into this country and it has naturalized strongly through the woods by means of its blue-black seeds. Savage may as well have been referring to Rose of Sharon, Lesser Periwinkle, Spurge Laurel, Common Laurel and Mock Orange which have also taken charge of the stony and unstable woodland slopes.

The precipitous terrain has always caused difficulties for the occupants and erosion and subsidence is still a problem on the miles of paths and drives. The present drive is the third, the others having been converted to footpaths because of their steepness. The difficulty of access and the shifting surface have limited woodland management to such an extent over the years that it has been necessary for the National Trust to undertake — in the interests of visitors' safety and at considerable cost — a comprehensive programme of felling and replanting. It will be several years before the garden woodlands of Holm Oaks, Field Maples and beeches are fully restored, with yews, hollies, laurels and *Griselinia littoralis* underneath for screening and shelter, but the worst stage is now over. One exciting prospect is a wood of Strawberry Trees, *Arbutus unedo*, on the southern slopes, where over 100 have been planted.

Besides the recently-planted Keep, gardening at Dunster is concentrated in three areas, each with contrasting conditions of soil and aspect because of their position and orientation.

The first area to be seen by any visitor is that situated between the car park and the Castle where the steep slope has been planted with hydrangeas and groups of the columnar Mediterranean Cypress, *Cupressus sempervirens*, to frame the first glimpse of the Castle. Opposite the stables, now a shop, are handsome wrought-iron gates leading to a path, which was constructed as an alternative to the impossibly steep original drive through the thirteenth-century gateway. On this cool and shady north-east orientation the character of the planting is firmly Victorian with *Leycesteria formosa*, hydrangeas and Spotted and Cherry Laurels underplanted with ferns. In recent years *Senecio* 'Sunshine' (*S. laxifolis*), a highly successful ground cover here, has been planted in large drifts together with choice shrubs like *Embothrium coccineum* and *Crinodendron hookeranum* as specimens. Yews predominate but just inside the gates there is a fine old Cork Oak and the Turkey Oak. Where dangerous trees have been removed, space has been made not only for future replacements for the framework of trees but also for a group of *Hoheria* 'Glory of Amlwch' for quicker effect.

The path winds upwards past a new planting of Tamarisks and vines to the southern and perhaps the most remarkable of the garden areas. The close proximity of the sea and the steep sunny aspect, combined with shelter from the prevailing winds, provide a microclimate that is more Mediterranean than English. The sharp drainage and the warmth reflected from the stone walls make it possible to grow plants normally only found under glass. Here are *Correa backhousiana*, an Olive, Cabbage Trees and groves of Mimosa spreading freely by suckers, with the hardier *Colletia armata*, yuccas, Tree Paeonies and *Magnolia grandiflora* to add to the exotic effect. Ground cover is provided by *Libertia ixioides* which produces its attractive white flowers in early summer. The more formal terrace above is equally favoured and here there are Chusan Palms, a bank covered with *Beschorneria yuccioides, Coronilla glauca* and the European Dwarf Palm, *Chamaerops humilis*. Against the wall grows *Mandevilla suavolens*, and the borders are edged with *Echeveria glauca*; even the Shrimp Plant, *Beloperone guttata* manages to survive outside here with a little winter protection. In a sheltered recess, past the newly restored Conservatory, is the famous lemon which has grown and fruited here for at least 150 years with only the protection of a glazed lean-to shelter. It was described in 1830 by Savage who admired the ingenuity of the 'moveable shed' which protected it.

The last of the four gardened areas is a complete contrast, being situated adjacent to the River Avill that flows fast along the foot of the hill. With moist soil and humid atmosphere a variety of conifers have grown well and in their shelter and shade thrive hydrangeas, bamboos. Tree Ferns and species of *Rhododendron, Pieris, Corylopsis* and *Cornus*. New Zealand Flax, gunneras and watsonias provide contrasting foliage textures and a *Celastrus orbiculatus* climbs to a prodigious height up one of the trees. The walk leads to Castle Mill, now restored, past a most beautiful pack-horse bridge incorporating a rocky cascade, built consciously as a picturesque feature in the late eighteenth-century by Henry Fownes Luttrell. Near the mill, and quite self-contained, is one area of planting untouched by the upheavals of recent years, comprising amongst other things hydrangeas, magnolias, a fine Handkerchief Tree and *Cornus nuttallii*.

East Lambrook Manor

Mr and Mrs F.H. Boyd-Carpenter

At East Lambrook, 3.2km (2 miles) N of South Petherton on the B3165 Martock road, 6.4km (4 miles) N of A303 between Yeovil and Ilminster. For daily opening arrangements see HHCG; also open for GS in summer. Margery Fish's cottage garden of about 0.4ha (1 acre) around fifteenth-century house with sixteenth-century additions (also open) and Malthouse. Situated in fairly level, low-lying country at 30m (100ft) without views; heavy clay soil. Rainfall 760mm (30in.). Tenants (sister and brother-in-law of Margery Fish) plus two full-time and six part-time workers run nursery and garden. Many unusual plants for sale.

The garden at East Lambrook Manor was made after 1938 by Mrs Margery Fish, helped at first by her husband, Walter. She continued the work alone after he died until her own death in 1969. In the development of gardening in the second half of the twentieth-century no garden has yet had a greater effect and no garden writer has had a more profound influence. Although like many she did not take to gardening until middle age and knew little when she began, Mrs Fish learned quickly, not by the preconceived conventional wisdom of the textbook but by her own acute observation and searching enquiry. The result was an originality born of an already discerning and cultivated intelligence applied to new problems, and a freshness of approach arising out of her personal experience in garden-making.

Her avowed aim was to make 'a typical cottage garden' but the result was much more than that. In the tradition of Gertrude Jekyll she evolved an unselfconscious style less sophisticated than Hidcote and entirely in sympathy with the old Ham stone house around which it was made. Its charm was based not upon grand gestures and strong architectural lines but on a finely-observed understanding of the visual qualities of plants, in combination with one another and in conjunction with lawns, paving, buildings and walls. Starting from the house the garden was made gradually by trial and error and, like most gardens, constantly adjusted and remade as skill and experience were gained. In no measure should it belittle Mrs Fish as a garden-maker to recognize the influence of her husband, Walter, who died before she wrote her first book *We Made a Garden*, which was to have been called *Gardening with Walter*. Few great gardens have been made by a single individual acting alone, or for that matter by a committee, but there is something about garden-making that seems to be stimulated by two people testing their often contrasting views on one another.

Mr Fish, it seems, was responsible for some of the decisively firm lines of drives, lawns, paths and hedges, and Mrs Fish acknowledged that he taught her much of the rudiments of gardening in the early stages. But, above all, the outstanding quality of the garden was due to her ability to choose plants and to arrange them as much for textural effect of foliage and form as for colour and flowers. Her planting had that richness and freedom that comes from a concern for the welfare of each plant and from the ability to notice and use the happy accidental effect. By using a variety of weed-smothering perennial plants, in carefully-chosen combinations, she showed how to make a garden full of interest and to maintain it with a minimum of labour — everyone's post-war problem.

To have created such a garden was achievement enough but perhaps it would not have become a mecca for gardeners had it not been for her books. The first, now a classic, was published in 1956 soon after she first opened her garden. Until her death thirteen years later she held the undisputed position of Leading Lady of gardening, not only here but also in many other parts of the world. Even when quite elderly she retained her enormous energy for writing, lecturing and for conducting her copious correspondence, as well as for gardening. She wrote in a practical way of her successes and failures; communicating her deep understanding of plants with wit and enthusiasm in a way that is still an inspiration to the beginner and to the most experienced gardener alike.

The garden remains largely as described in her books with its intimate and complex planting. The hot south front with its valerian on the roadside wall and roses on the house is where the paved garden was made, now filled with thymes, pinks, creeping mints, *Raoulia australis*, *Campanula carpatica* and other carpeters with the little daisy *Erigeron mucronatus* seeding around.

I like to think of the little enclosure by the house, hedged with Mrs Fish's beloved *Lonicera nitida*, as a tentative early effort before summoning confidence to tackle bigger jobs. This sunny spot is used for a mixture of silvery plants including the form of Wormwood called 'Lambrook Silver', pinks, spurges, *Anthemis cupaniana* and other tender daisies.

Behind the house and bounded by the road, the Malthouse and the orchard is the main lawn. The big variegated sycamore, one of only a few original trees on the site, has now been joined by Norway and Silver Maples, cherries and a Weeping Willow to enclose the area and make Margery Fish's book *Gardening in the Shade* even more valuable here than in her day. Near the house a mass of Angelica lolls over the hedge and the simple uncluttered lawn acts as an admirable foil to the complexity of the stone-edged borders and the rock garden beside the drive. Every wall is fully used for climbers and wall shrubs with roses, clematises, ceanothuses, wisteria and a fig on the Malthouse.

Stepping up between house and Malthouse is the terraced garden, one of

Mrs Fish's major projects of the early years. The repeated clipped cones of *Chamaecyparis lawsoniana* 'Fletcheri' in pairs along the path and the pattern of parallel terraces and narrow paths give firmness and order to a rich tapestry of complex planting now becoming perceptibly more crowded and shaded as the shrubs and trees develop. Here is a place in which to loiter and enjoy the many beautiful plants.

Behind the Malthouse is the 'primrose ditch' where a former stream, now only damp, has been transformed into a small ravine and given spectacular planting for foliage effect with big clumps of sword-like *Phormium tenax* contrasted with the parasol-shaped leaves of *Peltiphyllum peltatum*, bergenias, Bog Arum and ferns.

Gardens are never static, and intimately personal gardens like East Lambrook Manor are fragile and inevitably ephemeral to some degree. Margery Fish wrote that 'firmness in all aspects is a most important quality when gardening' and the quality of ruthlessness is needed even more in those who aim to conserve gardens than those who make them. Shrubs and trees that seemed right when small become crowded and rank as the vital spaces between them disappear. Borders need to be reworked and invasive plants checked. Gardens, especially of this kind, need frequent variations on the theme in order to keep them lively and fresh. The present owners have gallantly undertaken this difficult task so that we can continue to visit and to learn.

Fairfield House
Sir Michael and Lady Gass

Open for NGS in spring. 1.6km (1 mile) W of Stogursley, 16km (11 miles) NW of Bridgwater. Woodland garden with bulbs and shrubs.

Gaulden Manor

Mr and Mrs James LeGendre Starkie

1.6km (1 mile) from Tolland Church, 14.5km (9 miles) NW of Taunton via A358 Minehead
road. Informal garden of 1.2ha (3 acres) around small manor house dating back to twelfth-century.
House and garden open, see HHCG ; also for NGS in late spring. Well-drained neutral soil
over red sandstone in a little combe with a stream, at 106m (350ft). Rainfall 838mm (33in.).
Maintained by the owners with the help of one young man one day a week. Leaflet sets out
owners' philosophy of a series of small gardens.

Seemingly lost in the winding lanes of the Somerset countryside in the
valley between the Brendon Hills and the Quantocks is this charming
manor house, modest in size but full of historic interest. There is an unsophisticated, almost rustic, quality about the surroundings which is a
refreshing change from the better-known but often over-organized stately
homes. The country sounds and smells of a running stream and farm
animals are not yet drowned by those of the motor car and the cash
register!

A low wall and an arch covered with a sprawling 'New Dawn' rose
mixed with 'Hagley Hybrid' clematis marks the beginning of the appropriately simple courtyard enclosed by the west front of the house, a
pantiled woodshed and other outbuildings, on one of which the big-leaved
variegated ivy, *Hedera colchica* 'Dentata Variegata' is scrambling. Facing
south is a pleasing mixture of modern shrubs with purple cotinus, Gallica
and other roses and lavender.

Through a sandstone arch by the stacked wood there is a rose garden
overlooking the valley but the main feature of the garden is the stream
garden which lies south-east of the house. The stream comes from a lake,
formerly a fish pond when Gaulden was owned by the monks of Taunton
Priory. The lake has an island and a shady walk right round for the
adventurous. The garden banks are planted with Day Lilies, ferns and
Primula florindae; a fine Weeping Silver Pear leans over and vast Black
Italian Poplars revel in the moisture.

From the lake the stream runs between old hazelnuts and the banks are
thick with irises, primulas and *Alchemilla mollis*. The valley below the dam
has been exploited with great success as a bog garden with a variety of
moisture-loving plants, the bold leaves of *Peltiphyllum peltatum*, *Rheum
palmatum*, *Hosta* spp. and *Gunnera manicata* contrasting with Shuttlecock
Ferns, Day Lilies and *Aruncus dioicus*. Primulas are a special feature and
June is the time to come when *P. florindae*, *P. japonica* and *P. pulverulenta*
are all at their best.

Further down the valley is an attractive formal herb garden and plants can be obtained at the house. But the garden is still developing and some interesting new plantings have been made on the lawns. There are shrub roses grouped in colours and other shrubs with trees for the future including Tulip Tree, False Acacia, Copper Beech and walnut as well as flowering trees like *Magnolia sinensis* and *Cercis siliquastrum*, the Judas Tree.

Greencombe
Miss Joan Loraine

Open for NGS in spring. 0.8km (½ mile) W of Porlock. Fine woodland garden overlooking Porlock Bay; lovely views. Camellias, rhododendrons, azaleas and other lime-haters grow well in the mild climate.

Hadspen House
Mr and Mrs Paul Hobhouse and Trustees of the late Sir Arthur Hobhouse

3.2km (2 miles) SE of Castle Cary on A371 Wincanton road. 2.4ha (6 acre) Edwardian garden set in parkland around eighteenth-century stone house (not open). For opening arrangements see HHCG, also open for NGS. Well-drained, slightly alkaline soil over limestone on sheltered south slope, at 122m (400ft). Rainfall 762mm (30in.). Mrs Hobhouse and one gardener, plus seasonal help. Good range of unusual plants for sale.

The unique feature of British gardens is the sense of continuity that they convey. It is not unusual, as at Hadspen House, for a family to have enjoyed unbroken ownership of house and estate for two hundred years, each generation making its contribution according to its own ideals and needs, sometimes caring and sometimes neglecting. Taking on such a garden presents special problems and opportunities because the owner has a responsibility not only for the legacy of the past but also to future generations.

When Mr Paul Hobhouse and his wife, Penelope, moved into the family home in 1967 they took on a garden neglected for thirty years. Every sort of pernicious weed was established and much needed to be done. Mrs Hobhouse tackled the job with determination. While she dug and cleared she also read and learned, wisely waiting until the weeds were really gone before planting. By then the books of Gertrude Jekyll, Christopher Lloyd, Graham Thomas and others had pointed the way towards solving the dilemma of the day: how to have a large and beautiful garden at minimum net cost.

One solution was the now classic ploy of using broad masses of ground-hugging shrubs with ground covers underneath so that at no time of the year is bare soil exposed. This is planting to reduce work by copying the natural ecology of our hedgerows and woodlands, converting its principles for the garden by using plants of similar function but different appearance. Pursuit of the maximum period of display with the minimum of pruning and spraying, as well as weeding, led Mrs Hobhouse to foliage and texture — effects she has used with a freedom and sensitivity which sets out the garden at Hadspen House as something special.

The other answers were to allow the garden to pay its way by opening it to visitors; also to sell from the nursery plants of the kinds that are becoming more difficult to get as nurserymen's catalogues shrink. In this Mrs Hobhouse had for three years the inestimable help of Mr. Eric Smith, formerly of 'The Plantsmen', who has also carried on his plant breeding work, especially with the genera *Hosta* and *Helleborus*.

Challenges, then, there certainly were but of a kind that many would welcome, given the advantages of a sheltered south slope and a mature, parkland setting. The 'bones' of the garden were good, having been created by Mr Hobhouse's Edwardian grandmother, with borders, banks

and retaining walls containing many unusual subjects, now mature. Most valuable of all is the framework of trees, fine old beeches, Holm Oaks and Horse Chestnuts near the house, a splendid group of Scots Pines and many mature exotics in the garden. Sadly all the many elms have gone but many other trees remain in the park.

By gardening standards, in no time Mrs Hobhouse has given life to the 'bones' and clothed all in riches unimaginable only ten years ago.

The house faces SW into the park over a ha-ha and the garden front is SE where a loggia of classical style, complete with marble statues, projects to create a sheltered corner where unusual tender plants in a motley of interesting containers find homes. The warm stone walls support *Magnolia* × *soulangiana*, the showy new *Abutilon* × *suntense* and Pomegranate.

A large sloping lawn dominated by that superb group of Scots Pines is separated from the park by a grass walk enclosed by double shrub borders set below the original ha-ha wall. Evidently the redoubtable Edwardian lady filched this piece from the park and planted the splendid Horse Chestnut and Variegated Sycamore, a recurring tree in the garden. Mrs Hobhouse has planted thickly *Viburnum tomentosum* teamed with purple *Cotinus coggygria* and underplanted with herbaceous geraniums, and *Hydrangea villosa, Osmanthus delavayi*, Mexican Orange, Scotch and other shrub roses, with *Alchemilla mollis* and *Tellima grandiflora* for ground cover. A young Oriental Plane and a *Pterocarya fraxinifolia* give a choice of trees for the future.

Rather than continue toward the tennis-court it is better to turn north to the Fountain Garden, another Edwardian creation, consisting of curved walls forming concentric terraces facing south and overlooking a pretty cherub fountain in a round pond. The whole area has been brilliantly planted for foliage effect, ranging from forms of *Rheum, Rodgersia, Hosta, Astilbe* and *Osmunda* in the moist lower part of the dell to *Euphorbia wulfenii, Phlomis italica, Vitis coignetiae* and *Alchemilla mollis* in the sunny upper terraces. Above all is a magnificent *Cornus controversa* 'Variegata', its tabular shape echoing that of the Fountain Garden itself.

Eastwards is a long meadow garden bordered on either side by mown grass paths and broad shrub borders, with trees behind. The long grass is full of wild flowers, orchids and Corncrake as well as bulbs, but also unfortunately Marestail. The borders show Mrs Hobhouse's planting at its best: broad sweeping masses of golden foliage from Dogwood, Weigela and *Physocarpus opulifolius* set against Copper Beech, Weeping Silver Pear, *Hydrangea villosa, Eucalyptus* and *Olearia* spp., all underplanted with *Brunnera macrophylla*, Plantain Lilies and many other ground covers. Behind, some of the big Himalayan roses and *Clematis montana* scramble around on the older trees. In one part a charming statue of a young girl has been complemented by the contrasting textures of *Phormium tenax,*

Rodgersia, Olearia, Silver Willow and bamboo.

At the highest and steepest part of the garden, dramatic new developments are taking place. The area is backed by tall trees and enclosed on the north and west sides by walls and on the east by the walled kitchen garden. In the centre is an oblong pond with steep sides, originally the reservoir for the house, now converted as a lily pool. The high ground around has already been intensively developed with a collection of sun-loving shrubs and tender climbers against the walls, including *Drimys winteri, Clianthus puniceus* and *Nandina domestica.* Near a thatched cottage on the west side are large borders filled with shrub roses interspersed with variegated and silver foliage and flowers giving lightness and contrast, while in a sunny corner near the nursery is a striking combination of silver foliage plants, *Bupleurum fruticosum,* variegated New Zealand Flax and *Eryngium amethystinum* seeding itself into the gravel everywhere.

Now the whole south side of the pool has been lowered to make a semicircular paved garden in contrast to the steepness of the climber–clad opposite bank. The whole forms a great horticultural amphitheatre and an exciting climax to the garden. Not that it finishes here, or ever will be finished, because no garden ever can be. There are new treasures from Australasia in the walled kitchen garden and even the damp and sheltered woodland slopes beyond are being penetrated and planted.

Hestercombe

Somerset County Council (Fire Brigade Headquarters)

At Cheddon Fitzpaine, 3.2km (2 miles) NE of Taunton on a by-road from the A361. Recently restored formal terraced garden of 0.5ha (1¼ acres), 1.2ha (3 acres) in all, designed by Sir Edwin Lutyens and Gertrude Jekyll south of a mainly Victorian house by Henry Hall, now adapted as Fire Brigade Headquarters. Open by appointment and usually on Thursday afternoons in summer. On light, alkaline fertile soil at 76m (250ft) on south-facing lower slopes of the Quantocks overlooking Taunton Dene. Rainfall 762mm (30in.). Two gardeners. Since 1973 the garden has been in process of restoration by the County Council. Map-guide available.

In the late eighteenth century Hestercombe was the home of Copleston Warre Bampfylde, a notable landscape gardener, architect and illustrator of books. As a friend of Henry Hoare of Stourhead, he was in the vanguard of the English Landscape movement and his drawings and paintings of that garden, which no doubt he influenced, are a remarkable early record. At Stourhead is a painting of the cascade at Hestercombe where Bampfylde remade the coombe in about 1770 in the fashion of an

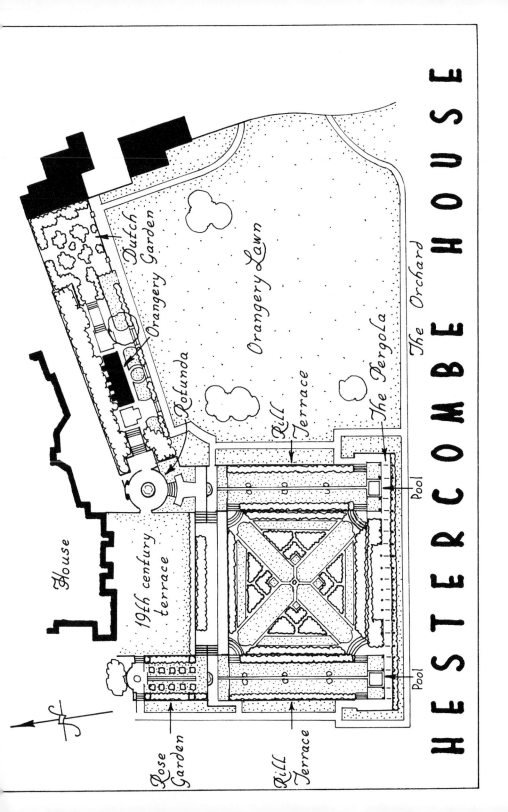

HESTERCOMBE HOUSE

House

19th century terrace

Rose Garden

Rill Terrace

Pool

Pool

The Pergola

The Orchard

Rill Terrace

Orangery Lawn

Rotunda

Orangery Garden

Dutch Garden

idyllic landscape, making ponds, cascades and arcadian walks among newly-planted trees. He made a doric temple and summerhouse in the form of a witches' cave which inspired the Vicar of Blagdon to write:
'O'er Bamfylde's woods by various nature graced,
A witch presides, but then that witch is taste'.
Taste of a different kind returned to the garden in 1904 when Viscount Portman commissioned Sir Edwin Lutyens and Gertrude Jekyll to make a new garden. Not only did it prove to be one of the best products of this successful partnership but it has also survived intact. Lord Portman had bought the eighteenth-century house and altered it between 1874 and 1877 and now he wanted an orangery and a flower garden below the broad terrace on the south side.

Great gardens often result from the combination of two great talents working together; there are so many dimensions to gardening that few individuals can combine them all. So it was with Lutyens and Jekyll: the architect creating the structure, manipulating the spaces and levels and providing the rich architectural detail of walls, paving and steps; the artist-gardener interpreting the design in planting of a subtlety and elegance never seen before.

The heart of the garden is The Plat at the lowest level — a huge square with a diagonal pattern of beds, grass and paving designed to be seen with the vale of Taunton Deane and the Blackdown Hills beyond. The Plat is enclosed on either side by raised terrace walks along which water is channelled to give cohesion to the layout. On the side furthest from the house a substantial pergola surmounts the third walk to give a sense of enclosure and at the same time windows to the view beyond.

The big and simply planted, nineteenth-century terrace below the house leads down in total contrast to the arbour and rose garden. Here is a shady half-sphere covered with Wych Elm looking on to small rose beds with 'Little White Pet' and *R. gallica officinalis* and allowing a glimpse of country beyond the enclosing balustrade. Giving shelter either side are high beds of Centifolia roses. Here begins the rill, running down a central stone channel to the Rill Terrace below.

From the rose garden, steps lead to the lower terrace where drifts of silver foliage — Jerusalem Sage, lavenders, Snow-in-Summer and Cotton Lavender — mix with the whites, mauves and blues of Mexican Orange, Rosemary, *Echinops ritro* and Catmint and tumble over the wall to the plat below.

The west Rill Terrace when completely restored, will begin with a wall fountain in the concave niche where a circular pool catches the sun to reflect dancing patterns on the stone. The musk-filled rill forms a spine to the grass terrace with borders of old roses, *Clerodendrum bungei*, delphiniums and verbascums with London Pride and all kind of 'lilies' —

Day, Plantain and the real Madonna kind. As with the matching Rill Terrace east of the plat the stone rill leads to a pool near the pergola and a view of the grazing cattle beyond.

The pergola forms a clear boundary and the sharp drop beyond emphasizes the contrast between park and garden. Like much of the stonework in the garden the heavy columns are made of the local rough limestone and support substantial sawn woodwork bearing masses of climbing roses, clematis and vines underplanted with English and Cotton Lavender and Jerusalem Sage.

Steps down to the plat are overhung by a tortuous old wisteria and are a home for the little daisy-flowered *Erigeron mucronatus*. The firm evergreen *Bergenia cordifolia* is used as an edging to pick out the pattern of the beds containing lilies, paeonies, roses and delphiniums and the borders around contain dwarf shrubs and low herbaceous plants spilling over on to the paved edge.

Between the main garden and the Orangery, acting like a ball and socket joint, is the rotunda, a typically simple but effective Lutyens device for linking quite different features. It consists of an outer wall with niches enclosing a pattern of paving in which a simple circular pool should be brimming with water.

One axis leads down steps, in which are set millstones, with lilacs, acanthus and the pink-tipped *Actinidia kolomikta* alongside, to the eastern end of the Orangery. This classically beautiful building of richly-marked Ham stone is set on a terrace adorned with hummocks of *Choisya ternata*, lavender and rosemary. The axis continues through the Orangery to finish at the Dutch garden, a raised plateau of complex paving patterns with beds of 'Cécile Brunner' roses, catmint, lavenders, hostas with the silver *Stachys lanata* as an edging. In contrast to the brilliant but self-conscious formality elsewhere, the Orangery looks out to informal groups of trees and undulating lawns running down to the park.

Little Norton Mill Nursery
Mr and Mrs J. McClintock

Open for NGS in early summer. At Norton sub Hamdon, 7.2km (4½ miles) NE of Crewkerne. Garden of medium size developed since 1969; includes a pond and a variety of interesting shrubs and plants.

Lytes Cary

The National Trust

At Somerton, 3.2km (2 miles) NE of Ilchester; on W side of A37 Fosse Way, Shepton Mallet road; signposted from A303. For opening arrangements see HHCG and NT. Formal garden of 1.2ha (3 acres) around fourteenth- and fifteenth-century manor house and chapel. In gently undulating level country at 61m (200ft) on ill-drained, alkaline clay soil. Rainfall 762mm (30in.). One gardener.

Apart from the undoubted architectural and historical importance of the house, Lytes Cary has strong horticultural connections. In the sixteenth-century the Lyte family were accomplished gardeners and Sir Henry Lyte became famous for his herbal published in 1578, *A Niewe Herball or Historie of Plants*. It was a translation from De l'Écluse's herbal which was in turn the French edition of the *Cruydtboeck* written by the great Flemish physician and botanist Rembert Dodoens. In common with other botanical writers of the day, Dodoens was preoccupied largely with the medicinal value of plants. But Sir Henry Lyte's book was not a mere translation because he added a number of his own observations and the most exciting frontispiece of any sixteenth-century herbal.

Nothing is known of the appearance of the garden in Henry Lyte's day. One can only speculate that, as befitted a small manor house in the sixteenth century, it was primarily a useful garden for the production of fruits, vegetables and herbs. Indeed it is recorded that Henry's son, Thomas, was an accomplished grower of fruits and nuts. Perhaps he supplied plants to furnish the gardens of the great house at Montacute when it was completed late in that century?

The present layout is Edwardian, having been made by Sir Walter Jenner, who gave the property to the National Trust. It comprises a series of outdoor 'rooms' and 'corridors' enclosed by hedges and strung around a formalized orchard. The garden is modest both in design and intention but there is a satisfying unity in the outcome. The garden unfolds in an interesting way because of the variety of its enclosed spaces and its planting, which is restrained and restful. It has been entirely restored and replanted in recent years by the National Trust and its tenants.

Apart from the north front the garden is enclosed and inward-looking, probably in response to the exposed countryside. At present this is as well because elm disease has been a total catastrophe in this part of Somerset where the species once accounted for more than three quarters of the total stock of trees. Some trees of other species remain at Lytes Cary thanks to prudent planting and many more have been put in. But nothing will

Above: Lytes Cary. The long border leading from the house. Beyond the niched hedge on the left is the orchard. *National Trust*

Below: Milton Lodge. Fine views over Wells can be enjoyed from the house and the terraced garden.

replace for the foreseeable future the venerable elms that once towered over the garden.

The first sight of house and garden comes beyond pleached limes that line a short drive to the back of the house. The house is approached through a low-walled forecourt by way of a garden gate and a flagged path, all in the local grey, lichen-covered limestone. The north garden is a dignified formal composition of varied greens: dark, rounded shapes of clipped yew against the pale-green lawns with box hedges against the walls and limes above. Looking back from the house, the vista of yew topiary continues between the ball-topped gate piers and across a ha-ha to a fine old dovecote set some way out into the field, truly a view to savour.

The enclosed garden is reached through an old wooden gate in the side wall, straight into the most flowery part. Against the wall a long border leads off to the left, full of colour in summer. Together with much more of the garden it was redesigned by Graham Thomas some years ago and it now contains a profuse mixture of roses, shrubs and flowering plants with clematises on the wall. In the Jekyll tradition, he made a separate section at the end for white and silver plants. The yew hedge opposite has a series of clipped buttresses making alcoves enclosing small, stone vases set on curiously disproportionate stone columns.

Steps at the end lead to a terrace, an obligatory feature in sixteenth-century gardens, edged with *Hypericum calycinum* and regularly-spaced Irish Yews. It overlooks the orchard, now strewn with naturalized daffodils and planted for decorative effect with diagonal avenues of crab apples and fruit trees, leading to a central sundial. Weeping Ash trees have been planted at the corners which will eventually form shady and intriguing arbours at the places of entry.

At the end of the terrace a handsome stone seat overlooks a long yew-hedged alley leading to a circular pool, also the focal point of the main axis from the house. Here are statues of Flora and Diana and a hornbeam tunnel leading to a little shady secret garden enclosed by a circle of *Mahonia* 'Undulata' and *Weigela florida* 'Variegata'.

Thence back to the main lawn in front of the house through another enclosure with stone seats on either side. On the house a Passion Flower, a double yellow Banksian Rose and a myrtle grow, and under the windows is a narrow border containing varieties of plants which might have been grown by Sir Henry Lyte in the sixteenth-century.

Marlands
Mr and Mrs Peter Etherton

At Sampford Arundel, 4.8km (3 miles) west of Wellington, 1.6km (1 mile) south of the A38 Wellington-Exeter road turning at the sign to White Ball. Open for NGS in spring usually in conjunction with Broadleigh Court. Woodland garden of 5ha (12 acres) around late eighteenth-century and early nineteenth-century house. Low-lying sheltered situation at 91m (300ft); open view south up to the Blackdown Hills. Light, lime-free peaty loam with a high water-table and running streams. Rainfall 762mm (30in.). Owners and one gardener, Mr Nicholas Bunn.

Despite the close proximity of the railway, there is a marvellous sense of rural seclusion and peace at Marlands. Perhaps it stems from the mature trees and the sound of running water or the way the lawn seems to run unbroken to the south, across the ha-ha, into the tranquil pastures beyond. Whatever the reason, it possesses qualities ideal for garden making and it is not surprising that successive owners have become enthused.

Marlands was owned from 1942 to 1965 by the Rev. and Mrs A.R.K. Wells and they and their son, Mr J.J. Wells, MP seem to have been gardeners of some skill. It was they who developed the woodland garden and laid out the features to be seen today. They bestowed many choice plants and made a plantsman's garden in the woodland dampness east of the house. Between 1965 and 1974 Mr John Gibson owned the property and he added a number of plants and converted the tennis-court into an alpine garden, now overgrown. After his departure the standard of upkeep declined for a while but the new owners, Mr and Mrs Peter Etherton, have been enthusiastically restoring and reclaiming with sensible caution and proper advice.

The woodland garden provides a variety of habitat and a fascinating progression from the more open areas near the house to deeper shade near the river. A pond near the house, bordered with musk and kingcups has been dredged recently to accommodate fat rainbow trout but the yellow spathes of the Bog Arum, *Lysichitum americanum*, still appear in spring. Nearby is a south-facing rock bank which provides ideal conditions for the purple-podded *Decaisnea fargesii*, *Desfontainea spinosa*, with its little orange trumpets, *Staphylea colchica*, *Stranvaesia davidiana* and *Viburnum tomentosum* 'Mariesii' densely planted and fighting for light.

The moist soil and warm, sheltered climate have resulted in lush growth and further down a little stream and its banks have been skilfully used to make a water garden in a glade with an ideal balance of light and shade. Here there are choice trees like *Cercidiphyllum japonicum* and the Snowdrop Tree, *Halesia carolina*, surrounded with drifts of primulas including *P.*

helodoxa and *P. japonica*, species of *Camassia*, *Eremurus*, *Hosta*, *Rheum* and *Acanthus*, all rich and exotic. The effect continues into shadier areas nearer the river with rhododendrons, *Mahonia* 'Charity' and hydrangeas surrounded by splendid groups of the Shuttlecock Fern, *Matteuccia struthiopteris*, *Smilacina racemosa*, *Hosta fortunei*, *Peltiphyllum peltatum* and *Rodgersia aesculifolia* — a *tour de force* in planting for foliage contrast.

Of smaller size but more intensively planted is BROADLEIGH COURT (Mr and Mrs R.D. Kathro). It is situated near Marlands and is usually open in conjunction with it. It is a very well planted garden of 1.6ha (4 acres) with a large rock garden and a great variety of spring bulbs. There are also rhododendrons, azaleas and other flowering shrubs. The short account given to this garden compared with Marlands is only for want of space. A visit to one makes the other almost obligatory for they are close and complementary.

Milton Lodge
Mr and Mrs David C. Tudway Quilter

On north side of Wells, north of A39 on Old Bristol Road. Terraced garden of 2ha (5 acres) below rambling Mendip stone Georgian house of great charm. Garden open for NGS in late June and early July. Separate Coombe of 3.5ha (9 acres) open on Sundays throughout the season. Good quality alkaline soil on Mendip limestone. On steep slope facing SSE with fine views of Wells and the Vale of Avalon at 91-122m (300-400ft). Rainfall 864mm (34in.). One full-time and one half-time gardener.

Start with a breathtaking view from sun-drenched terraces and add time-honoured stone walls and dignified yew hedges and you have the basis for beauty regardless of season. But Milton Lodge also has great trees and a profusion of well-considered planting too, tumbling around the steps, basking below the walls and profiting from every sheltered corner on this already favoured site.

The house faces a little east of south on high ground on a plain terrace with four Napoleonic cannon pointing at the incomparable view over Wells Cathedral to the unspoilt Somerset farmland beyond. Below this terrace is an arboretum with a fine Maidenhair Tree, a Weeping Ash and two thorns, *Crataegus × lavallei* and *Crataegus prunifolia*, all planted some 70 years ago, to which have been added *Sorbus cashmiriana*, *Acer pseudoplatanus* 'Brilliantissimum', various conifers and shrubs as well as bulbs and vigorous herbaceous plants naturalized beneath the trees. The warm stone walls of the house, carry jasmines, a purple vine, clematises, a ceanothus and 'Golden Showers' roses supported by 'Hidcote' hypericums fuchsias and the silver of *Phlomis fruticosa* and *Senecio* 'Sunshine'. The deep lavender blue of a tall *Abutilon* 'Suntense' looks well against the limestone. East of the house a huge old cedar frames the view and mature beech woodland gives shelter from the north and west.

Like the older trees, the neat yew hedges were planted, with admirable foresight, by the owners' grandfather, Mr Charles Tudway, early in this century. Together with the smooth lawns they provide an ideal foil to the complex planting and give unity to a garden full of variety. A paved path from the house leads through one such hedge and down steep steps where the bold foliage of *Vitis coignetiae* forms the handrail and the equally exotic *Magnolia grandiflora* scents the air with lemon from its huge flowers.

On the path below, *Alchemilla mollis,* a favourite plant here, grows in the stone paving. This broad grass terrace is bordered by flowering shrubs tucked in with ground cover, and 'Frensham' roses are ranged along the low front wall. Opposite, the high retaining wall is richly furnished with tender sun-lovers such as *Abutilon vitifolium*, (both the pale lavender and white constantly recur in the garden), *Feijoa sellowiana*, *Abelia* × *grandiflora* and *Escallonia* 'Iveyi'. Further along a variegated evergreen spindle contrasts with purple cotinus, and *Romneya coulteri* has monopolized a large area. Here also is the Judas Tree revelling in near-Mediterranean conditions and likewise a large mulberry nearby. In one corner, occupying the site of a former greenhouse, is a small formal lily pool set in gravel and surrounded by tubs of agapanthus and an enormous Jerusalem Sage.

Steps lead to a contrasting narrow terrace below, possibly the finest feature of the garden, with a generous border of shrub roses underplanted with geraniums and *Brunnera macrophylla* set against a retaining wall decorated with clematises, ceanothuses, *Garrya elliptica* and the potato-flowered *Solanum crispum autumnale*. This is a glorious midsummer mixture with Rugosas, Hybrid Musks, 'Iceberg', *R. rubrifolia,* the excellent 'Little White Pet' and other roses. The trim lawn and meticulous yew hedge opposite lead the eye to an attractive stone gazebo of 1909 at the end. This also serves as a pavilion for the swimming-pool on the lowest terrace, reached by steps concealed under a vast *Elaeagnus pungens* 'Maculata' and overhung by *Clerodendrum trichotomum.*

The steps and the random rectangular paving around the swimming-pool have been colonized by the delightful little daisy *Erigeron mucronatus,* *Corydalis lutea*, campanulas and pinks all enjoying this sheltered corner of the garden, ideal for a pool. The pavilion is draped with clematises, including the yellow *C. tangutica,* jasmine and rose 'New Dawn', with the favourite abutilons, *Choisya ternata* and the white variegated *Philadelphus coronarius* 'Variegatus' grouped alongside. In front of the stone retaining wall is another highly successful combination with the elegant, clear-blue

Ceanothus 'Cascade' supported by groups of *Senecio* 'Sunshine' and *Phlomis fruticosa*.

Outside the garden near the main road is the Coombe, a 3.5ha (9 acre) arboretum developed originally by the Tudways as an extension to the garden of The Cedars, the 1758 family house, now part of the Cathedral School in Wells. It consists of a mown green valley running southwards, the steep sides furnished with large groups of shrubs set between towering trees, both native and exotic. This is an oasis of tranquillity so close to a town teeming with cars and tourists. The Handkerchief Tree, *Davidia involucrata*, and gloxinia-flowered *Paulownia tomentosa* thrive in the shelter and warmth and an enormous oak tree dominates all.

Mr Tudway Quilter has done much to restore and replant the area and it now contains many promising young maples, rowans, birches and other trees and shrubs to supplement the older plantings of oaks, Atlas Cedar, Weeping Silver Lime, Cut-leaved Beech and silvery White Willows. Paths traverse the steep slopes among wild and naturalized plants and bulbs and at one point there is a glimpse of the Cathedral with which the family, the Coombe and the garden have been so closely involved.

Montacute House
The National Trust

In the village of Montacute, 6.4km (4 miles) W of Yeovil on north side of A3088 road to Crewkerne. For opening arrangements see HHCG and NT Formal garden of 4.8ha (12 acres) around pre-eminent late sixteenth-century house built in a park of 121ha (303 acres) for Sir Edward Phelips. Situated in gently undulating country at 76m (250ft) on heavy alkaline soil. Rainfall 762mm (30in.). Three gardeners.

The name Montacute comes from *Mons Acutus*, the pointed hill nearby, which can be seen from the garden, crowned by its folly tower. This most splendid of Elizabethan houses with all its complex Renaissance detail, pavilions and garden walls, is made from Ham stone, a warm golden limestone quarried from another hill at Stoke sub Hamdon a few miles away. The garden is famous for its exquisite garden pavilions on the east side. Together with the balustraded walls, with their pierced lanterns and pointed finials, they enclose the forecourt, the main drive having been originally through the park from the east. Originally there were gate lodges too and, although these disappeared in the late eighteenth century, the gates remain.

A description of the garden of 1667 from the Phelips papers and a

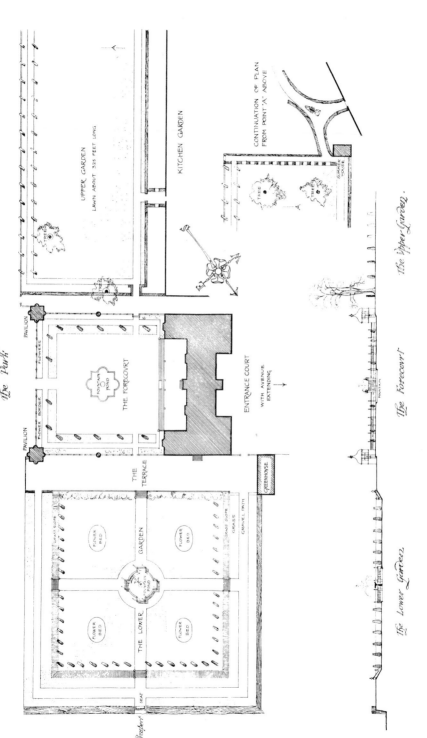

MONTACUTE IN SOMERSETSHIRE.

The Park

The Lower Garden.   *The Forecourt.*   *The Upper Garden.*

Montacute House. Plan of the garden in 1902.
H. Inigo Triggs, *Formal Gardens in England and Scotland*

SCALE OF FEET

survey map of 1774 show that the garden then extended further east 'with several walkes and rowes of trees . . . and a variety of pleasant walkes, Arbours and Coppices full of delight and pleasure'. Then simply a place for carriages and horses to come and go, the east court is now a garden with neatly manicured grass and mixed borders against the walls. The borders are in strong colours with the contrasting foliage textures of Plume Poppies and yuccas and the purple foliage of barberries is repeated at intervals. These borders were originally designed by Phyllis Reiss of nearby Tintinhull House.

Visitors now enter from the village by the south drive, always the back entrance, past a charming gate lodge with its own little garden of catmint, lavender and roses, into the larger of two former walled kitchen gardens, now planted with Norway Maples to shade the parked cars. Near the shop are groups of shrubs including the floriferous *Ceanothus* 'Autumnal Blue', one of the hardiest of the hybrid evergreen types.

The way leads through a gate and a yew hedge into the Cedar Lawn. The yew hedges were planted thus in the sixteenth-century so that gardeners and servants could move discreetly to and fro without being seen. Now the figs on the east-facing wall have been allowed to grow out and low carpeting plants are being planted beneath. The Cedar Lawn has all the timeless simplicity that is the dominating impression at Montacute. Two Spanish Chestnuts of great antiquity are linked to a couple of Cedars, one Atlas and the other Lebanon, by a gravel walk guarded by pairs of Irish Yews. Beyond a low wall is the park. In the eighteenth-century the Cedar Lawn was called 'Pig's Wheatie Orchard', a logical place for fruit trees alongside the kitchen garden and Laundry Court. Beyond the cedars is a small semicircular area enclosed by yew hedges and sheltered by a copse of Scots Pines and Holm Oaks. This layout dates from the late 1960s when an existing group of *Yucca recurvifolia* was balanced by another, with a little pool between. Stone pillars form a colonnade along one side and a seat is set into the yew hedge on the other. Here is a restful place to sit and relax, an appropriate finish to the orderly calm of the Cedar Lawn.

Because of the immense scale of the house, the garden at Montacute does not seem large, but the main axis from the arcaded garden house at the southern end of the Cedar Lawn to the far northern end of the sunken garden is 273m (300yds), enormous by Elizabethan standards. From the Cedar Lawn this axis crosses the path on the south side of the house along which in Elizabethan times horses would have been taken from the fore-court to the stables. It then passes through the forecourt across the great terrace and into the north garden.

The garden north of the house is on the site of the main Elizabethan flower garden and the terrace and raised perimeter walks date from that time. The mount and banqueting-house have long since gone but now

Montacute House. The fine bole of one of the old Sweet Chestnuts in the Cedar Lawn.
Iris Hardwick

there is a classic Orangery dating from the eighteenth-century, full of fuchsias and begonias and festooned with the sweet-scented, white *Jasminum polyanthum*. Against the wall at the back Maidenhair Fern grows on a pyramid of tufa rock kept wet by a trickle of water. The present layout of the north garden dates from the late nineteenth-century when William Phelips, whose wife Ellen was a keen gardener, owned the house. Indeed it was their head gardener, Mr Pridham, who planted most of the garden features to be seen today, including the older trees and the Irish Yews, so popular in formal Victorian gardens. The 44 clipped Irish Yews surrounding the sunken north garden are now contrasted against the round heads and glossy leaves of *Crataegus* × *lavallei* planted in 1964 to replace failing cypresses. A nineteenth-century balustraded lily pond is the centre piece of a dignified formal scheme. Apart from some splendid clumps of shrubs, cotoneasters, senecios and juniper on the terrace, the main horticultural feature is the border of shrub roses underplanted with *Hosta fortunei hyacinthina*. This was first planted by Vita Sackville-West, with help from Graham Thomas, in the late 1940s and their selection includes roses introduced to England before the house was built, like the Red Rose of Lancaster, *R. gallica* 'Officinalis', the White Rose of York, *R. × alba*, as well as old roses of more recent introduction including the China Monthly Rose, *R. chinensis* 'Old Blush', and species like *R. rubrifolia* and *R. moyesii*, Hybrid Musks, Rugosas and Sweet Briars.

When the west front of the house was reconstructed in 1785 the main entrance was moved to this side and a straight drive nearly 400m (¼ mile) long was made to connect it to grand entrance gates on the western side of the village. The west drive is strongly Victorian in character with Ellen Phelips's and Pridham's ubiquitous Irish Yews set against a mixture of exotic evergreens. They also planted an outer avenue of Wellingtonias and a mixture of trees among the evergreens in the foreground which have required considerable thinning in recent years. In 1976 a middle avenue of limes was planted and the foreground shrubs are now being pruned and supplemented.

Although always the least grand of the three approaches to the house the south drive has been for several years the one most used. Here again the trees are a rich legacy of the nineteenth-century. There is a well-shaped Fern-leaved Beech near the Laundry Court, a pair of enormous Golden Yews near the stables and nearby is the tallest recorded specimen in England of *Cupressus macrocarpa*, the Monterey Cypress, and a flourishing young one bears witness to the National Trust's concern for the future. All along the drive are bushes of the Californian Redwood, *Sequoia sempervirens*. Giant trees in nature, these were cut down when Montacute was requisitioned during the Second World War. Now the regrown feathery mounds are kept pruned to be burnished bronze by the cold winds each winter, silent witnesses to another page in the long history of Montacute.

Oakhill Park
W.W. Harper Esq.

See HHCG for opening. At Oakhill, 6.4km (4 miles) N of Shepton Mallet. Mansion house set in 3.2ha (8 acres) of garden with fine trees and a lake. The small estate of 18ha (45 acres) is open as a day out for those interested in models relating to transport and there is a miniature railway from the car park to the house.

The Old Rectory
Mr and Mrs R.V. Showering

Open for NGS in summer. At Beckington, 4.8km (3 miles) N of Frome. Grounds of 3.6ha (9 acres) including paddocks, in which there is a 1.6ha (4 acre) garden of varied interest. Some very old trees, especially a fine Cedar of Lebanon, formal garden, roses, herbaceous borders and shrubs. There are greenhouses with an orchid house and mist-propagation unit. The house is Tudor with Queen Anne and Georgian additions.

Orchard House, Claverton
Rear-Admiral and Mrs Hugh Tracy

At Claverton, 5.4km (3½ miles) from centre of Bath; 1.6km (½ mile) E of American Museum; on W side of A36 road to Frome. Open occasionally for NGS. Plantsman's informal garden of 1ha (2½ acres). At 106m (350ft) on sheltered easterly slope with fine views over unspoilt valley. Near-neutral soil over alkaline clay-marl. Rainfall 787mm (31in.). Small wholesale nursery for herbs and alpines, normally for sale at the American Museum but available at the garden on open days only. Hand list of shrubs and trees. Garden and nursery run by the owners and one gardener.

Some of the gardens most attractive to visitors are those where the plant-ings can be related to their own needs and where they can see what is possible in a comparatively small space. Such is the case at Orchard House where Rear-Admiral and Mrs Tracy have assembled a wide range of interesting plants in an attractive layout. Although large by most standards, a generous slice of the garden is given over to the nursery, full of fascinating plants with culinary and medicinal connections. The garden itself is intimate in scale with plants and features small enough to be realistic to the owner of the usual suburban plot. The effect is unpretentious and informal with collections of herbs, alpines, silver plants and particular genera like *Sedum* and *Hedera*. Good use has been made of ground cover plants.

The garden is divided informally into three main areas, each of different character and several subsidiary parts so that the garden seems far more extensive than it is in reality.

The house is orientated sideways to the lane and looks east over grass terraces supported by stone walls on which Rock Roses and a variety of vigorous alpines grow. Privacy is provided by a high mixed hedge and informal plantings: an old Winter Cherry, *Sorbus hybrida* 'Gibbsii' and *Magnolia* × *soulangiana* in the lawn, and a great variety of trees and shrubs, including *Arundinaria nitida*, Variegated Dogwood, *Cotoneaster henryanus*, a eucalyptus, hollies, cherries, lilacs and conifers all jostle for position in the borders.

Through an intriguing tunnel of shrubs the second area contains perhaps the greatest horticultural riches as well as fine views of the valley beyond. Here is a small pool and the 'old' rock garden, now becoming largely a place for dwarf conifers and other slow-growing shrubs like the diminutive forms of ivy, *Hedera helix* 'Conglomerata' and *H.h.* 'Erecta'. The informal herbaceous borders are a particular success with *Iris ochroleuca*, *Achillea* 'Moonlight', the new peppery-scented *Helichrysum* 'Sulphur Light' and the excellent, prickly *Morina longifolia* prominent. There are many choice shrubs too, like *Cytisus battandieri*, *Pyrus salicifolia*, *Alnus glutinosa* 'Imperialis' and the Golden Elder, frequently chosen as much for foliage as for floral effect.

The sunny tea-terrace at the end of the house is hung with *Vitis coignetiae*, *Muelenbeckia complexa* and clematises and overlooks a small sheltered area where roses, a collection of stonecrops and a number of tender shrubs are grown.

Like all good gardens, that at Orchard House is still developing. Further south the already large collection of herbs is being supplemented and below is a big new rock garden with scree and peat beds. A long dry bank above demonstrates the value of ground cover plants in some variety.

Apart from the immaculate little nursery there are well-kept gardens for vegetables and soft fruits and a little pool garden surrounded by species of *Crambe*, *Ligularia*, *Rodgersia* and *Phormium*.

Orchardleigh Park

Arthur Duckworth Esq.

4.8km (3 miles) N of Frome on E side of A363 Radstock road; through Lodge gates and up long drive. Formal terraced and informal garden of 4ha (10 acres) around Victorian mansion (not open) of 1856 by Thomas Wyatt and set in beautiful and extensive park open to pedestrians and cyclists. Garden open for NGS and GS in spring. On a south slope at 91m (300ft) with glorious views over valley and lake. Soil alkaline, mixed with much heavy clay. Rainfall 991mm (37in.). Three full-time gardeners.

The park is the great glory at Orchardleigh and the long drive through it from the Lodge gates to the house is a pleasure not to be missed. It has all the variety of the English Landscape tradition. Although the elms have gone, there are fine trees, beeches, hornbeams, oaks, sycamores, Horse Chestnuts and Grey Poplars, arranged to provide a succession of open spaces and dense woods, with views out here and there.

The house looks out to the south over a tranquil valley where only birds

disturb the stillness. At the bottom a stream has been dammed to create a vast winding lake, entirely appropriate to the enormous scale of the valley and the distant view south-eastwards, where Oldford is effectively screened by trees. Again oaks, chestnuts and sycamores predominate, with a sprinkling of Grey Poplars to give lightness in summer.

In keeping with the style of the time, the Victorian mansion is set firmly on a level platform with a second terrace below it. Apart from the view, the outstanding feature of the terraces is the quality of the eighteenth-century urns, vases and statuary ranged along them, curiously varied in scale from an intricate low balustrade by the park to enormous urns flanking the steps in pairs at either end. They came from the ancient manor-house that once stood south of the lake. The elaborate roofless shell of the former conservatory, at the corner of the house, has been ingeniously converted into an arbour filled with roses.

The main pleasure-garden lies west of the house with the walled garden beyond. The standard of upkeep has had to be relaxed considerably but there is still much to be seen, principally fine trees and masses of naturalized bulbs in the grass. The layout is in the best traditions of Victorian gardening with winding, gravel walks and a broad grass vista mown to form the backbone. On either side groves of mature specimen trees include conifers of many kinds: Atlas Cedars and Monterey Cypresses, Corsican and Bhutan Pines and the West Himalayan Spruce, *Picea smithiana*. Magnificent Horse Chestnuts, several Fastigiate Oaks, limes and beeches give further variety of colour and texture. Underneath laurels, hollies and yews also remain from the original plantings to give shelter and to support the authentic nineteenth-century atmosphere.

The romantic remains of a Victorian fernery pool and rockery, surrounded by laurels, mark the start of a water-course which seems to be piped under the main vista to reappear in a steep gorge on the other side. Although wild now with the Giant Cartwheel Flower, Polygonum and Stinking Ransomes, the high quality of the rock-work is still apparent and in the spring there are bluebells, primroses and a lovely group of the native Snake's Head Fritillary.

The main vista finishes with a view through yew hedges into the park near an old orchard crammed with daffodils on one side and on the other a formal Italian Garden of radiating beds with a rose pergola. The walled garden nearby, with its pretty pink brick, dates from the time of the old manor house.

Parish's House

B.G.S. Cayzer Esq.

Open for NGS in spring. At Tinsbury, SW of Bath. Medium-sized garden of general interest.

Pilton Manor Vineyard

Nigel de Marsac Godden Esq.

Open for NGS in September. The Manor House, Pilton, 4km (2½ miles) SW of Shepton Mallet. The Manor House and vineyard date back to 1235. Small garden; grounds with stream, weir and waterfall; large chestnuts and fine lime avenue. Rare square-built dovecote.

Prior Park, Bath

Prior Park College

Overlooking Bath on the south side of the city. Not normally open but permission can be obtained by application to the Principal. At 61-76m (200-250ft).

Although open only on special occasions and by previous arrangement, Prior Park has one of the most famous of Lancelot 'Capability' Brown's landscape views. The classical mansion commands a fine panorama of the city and is set above a valley. This shelves steeply down to two lakes linked by Lancelot Brown's Palladian bridge, a perfect eye-catcher, balanced by the borrowed landscape of half-concealed church towers and the city beyond.

Brown worked at Prior Park around 1762 for Ralph Allen who, with his architect, John Wood, had laid out the grounds twenty years earlier in the formal style of the time. Brown 'naturalized' the two straight-sided lakes and where they join concealed the dam by building the Stowe-like bridge. He also converted the woods framing the valley to the balanced informality of 'the modern taste' and no doubt he was responsible for the flowing lines of the gently undulating turf. Unfortunately, some of the specimen trees, so carefully sited by Brown, have now gone and the turf no longer retains its sheep-grazed smoothness.

But we must be thankful for a remarkable survival; for the opportunity to see this superb view, perhaps on a drowsy summer evening when long shadows enliven the foreground and lend emphasis to the sculptured forms of the grass expanse and when the lakes reflect the clear sky.

Rainbow Wood
Major Lock

Open for NGS in spring. At Widcombe Hill, Bath. Trees, wild garden and views over Bath.

Rayne Thatch
Mr and Mrs A. Thompson

Open for NGS in spring. At Leigh Woods, 4km (2½ miles) W of centre of Bristol. Bristol University Botanic Garden 0.7ha (1¾ acres), woodland garden on the edge of Leigh Woods (National Trust). Landscaped pools and rocks.

Redlynch Park
Colonel and Mrs P.L. Pengelly

Open for NGS in early summer. 2.4km (1½ miles) SE of Bruton. Garden with shrubs, trees, roses, water garden and fine views. The house has been converted from a larger mansion and is now a school. It is interesting chiefly for the beautiful 1670 Orangery; also for the dignified layout by Sir Edwin Lutyens at the eastern end of the house, with its paved terraces and steps and handsome summerhouse.

Scotts Nurseries

Open daily with collecting box for GS. At Merriott, 3.2km (2 miles) N of A30 at Crewkerne. Large and interesting nurseries.

Somerset College of Agriculture and Horticulture

Open for NGS and GS in spring. At Cannington, 4.8km (3 miles) NW of Bridgwater.

The old college near the Church was a Benedictine Priory in 1138 and has a fine Tudor W front. Nearby, the ancient sandstone walled gardens now contain modern aluminium glasshouses and tennis-courts but the outer walls remain. Their shelter, combined with the mild coastal climate, enables a remarkable collection of unusual ornamental plants to be grown and the College has taken full advantage by building up collections of genera like *Ceanothus, Phormium, Pittosporum, Eucalyptus, Mahonia, Iris, Fremontia*, etc.; also succulent and tender perennials such as *Agave, Yucca, Acacia, Echium* and South American *Salvia* spp. The ten modern, heated glasshouses contain an exceptionally wide range of both ornamental and economic plants, especially *Passiflora, Datura, Abutilon, Bouganvillea* and insectivorous plants. These are used like the rest for student instruction in connection with courses in Amenity Horticulture, which is a speciality of the College.

The new College buildings on the north side of the main street were completed in 1970 and from the higher ground there are fine views to the Quantocks. The extensive gardens and sports-fields have been laid out imaginatively for landscape effect and for teaching purposes with a large formal bedding area, a rose garden, trials of lawn grasses and sports turf mixtures; ground cover plantings, horticultural science plots and tree and shrub collections. Most plants are labelled. There is a particularly effective area of modern planting for textural and foliage effect near the east entrance with junipers, Sun Roses and Rose of Sharon, contrasted with New Zealand Flax. One astonishing inner courtyard is entirely exotic with a mixture of the silver and glaucous foliage of such plants as *Stachys lanata, Festuca glauca* and *Tanacetum ptarmaciflorum* teamed with the spiky crowns of *Phormium* and *Cordyline* c.v., *Kniphofia caulecens* and even *Beschorneria yuccioides*, with carpets of the tender South African daisy-flowered *Osteospermum, Euryops* and *Felicia* between.

It adds up to one of the largest collections of ornamental plants in SW England. Undoubtedly for the plantsman it is the pick of the educational gardens in the region, if not in the country.

Southill House
Mrs R.B. and Mrs D.R. Horsfield

Open for NGS in summer. At Granmore, 6.4km (4 miles) E of Shepton Mallet. Pond garden, shrubs, walled kitchen garden being developed. Lovely views.

Stapleton Manor
Mr and Mrs G.E.L. Sant

Open for NGS in summer. At Stapleton Oak, 9.6km (6 miles) NW of Yeovil. 0.6ha (1½ acre) garden around scheduled Georgian Ham stone house. Lily pond, roses and shrubs.

Stowell Hill
Lady McCreery

At Stowell, between Templecombe and Charlton Horethorn 6.5km (4m) NE of Sherborne; turn west off A357 0.8km (½ mile) N of Templecombe. Open in spring for NGS and GS ; see HHCG. Part formal, mostly informal garden of about 2ha (5 acres) around substantial house and stables built by Spillers in the early 1920s. Situated on a slight slope to the south at 122m (400ft). Soil: lime-free greensand. Rainfall 914mm (36in.). One gardener, Mr Norman (30 years at Stowell).

Until he died in 1968 it was General McCreery who was the prime mover in gardening at Stowell Hill, but now Lady McCreery has expanded her interest and successfully taken over. Like his mother and his grandmother, General McCreery was a keen and knowledgeable gardener and the garden he largely created around the handsome solid house is testimony to his skill. That Mr Norman now manages alone when he once had two assistants is a sign of the times but it is a tribute to him and to Lady McCreery that so much of interest and beauty has been retained despite the inevitably more relaxed maintenance.

The axial approach to the north front is bordered by daffodils in grass and dignified by splendid old oaks. It passes the extensive stable block with its elegant clock tower and leads to a circle of roses around an hexagonal pool, while under the house are borders of camellias, azaleas and hydrangeas.

The formal garden terraces on the south side can be reached from east of the house, near the extensive kitchen garden, by passing under an enormous old Copper Beech next to a contrasting Blue Atlas Cedar. The house is well sited to make the most of a magnificent view stretching to Bulbarrow Hill, far into Dorset. The sun-soaked terrace is well constructed, Lutyens style, with random rectangular paving and a sheltered loggia. Clipped box balls in pairs provide a pattern and a low stone wall topped with urns gives a sense of enclosure without spoiling the view. The borders contain a pretty mixture of hypericums, irises, fuchsias and penstemons with Welsh Poppies escaping into the paving, while on the house walls a magnolia, a Banksian Rose and a splendid wisteria enjoy the reflected warmth. Separated only by a ha-ha, the grass terrace below would seem to flow on into the meadow beyond but beds of roses and a statue of Mercury intervene. Here there are herbaceous borders against the terrace wall and the ends are effectively enclosed by 'Frau Dagmar Hastrop' roses suggested by Lanning Roper some years ago. On either side of the grass terrace are smaller secret gardens, one with fuchsias bedded around a sundial and the other with a stone seat, raised beds and pansies.

The largest area of the garden extending westwards incorporates an extensive informal garden merging into established trees on the north side and protected by a beech hedge on the other. A broad stretch of lawn leads to bold plantings of azaleas including the evergreen Japanese kinds as well as the deciduous Ghent and Exbury hybrids. Vast groups of hardy hybrid rhododendrons have reached maturity and an enormous 'Pink Pearl' is teamed up with a purple Japanese Maple. Needless to say all this adds up to a riot of colour in May.

Beyond is a water garden, fed from a spring, where although only minimal maintenance can be given, there are many fine maples and conifers to see. Evidence of the excellent growing conditions is the pair of Lebanon Cedars at the end, now 21m (70ft) high 55 years after planting. A woodland walk through many more rhododendrons, especially 'Loderi' forms, leads back to the house. Nearer the house among a group of choice magnolias and maples is undoubtedly the finest specimen at Stowell, the magnificent April-flowering *Magnolia* × *veitchii* rising to 28m (60ft) or more to offer its waxy, pink-flushed goblets to the sky.

TINTINHULL HOUSE

Fountain Garden

Kitchen

Garden

Eucalyptus gunnii

Orchard

Stone trough

Holm Oaks

Seat

Stone seat

Azaleas

Armillary sphere

Pool

Romanesque statue

Clipped Box

Irish Junipers

Tubs

Tubs

Summerhouse

Azalea

Garden

Garden

Seat

Seat

Eagle

Court

Yew

Yew

Magnolias

Cedar

Nursery and glasshouses

Cedar

Lawn

West

Front

Arch

Italian well-head

Magnolias

Tintinhull House

Courtyard

Lavatory

Scale 0   5   10 metres
0   10   20   30 feet

N

Tintinhull House
The National Trust

At Tintinhull, 8km (5 miles) NW of Yeovil, 0.8km (½ mile) S of A303 Ilminster to Ilchester road. For opening arrangements see HHCG and National Trust Opening Arrangements; walled Hidcote-style garden of 0.8ha (2 acres) created by Mrs P.E. Reiss. Fine seventeenth-century house of Ham stone with early eighteenth-century, classical west (garden) facade. Well-worked, heavy alkaline loam; level site at 30m (100ft). Rainfall 762mm (30in.). Tenant and one gardener. Garden leaflet with plan and exhaustive plant lists available.

The garden at Tintinhull is one of the smaller but brighter jewels of the National Trust. Phyllis Reiss and her husband, Captain F.E. Reiss, lived here for 28 years creating and perfecting their masterpiece and in 1953 Mrs Reiss gave it to the National Trust. Gardens cannot continue unchanged but thanks to the excellence of successive tenants and to the continuity of the Trust, the garden still retains much of its personal charm even a generation later.

The dominating Cedar of Lebanon and the two yews north of the house had been planted by an unknown hand long ago and Dr S.J.M. Price, a former owner, built walls and laid out some of the paths early in this century. Apart from these and the pair of Holm Oaks west of the house the canvas was bare. Capt and Mrs Reiss had been much influenced by Lawrence Johnston's work at Hidcote when they lived nearby and the Tintinhull garden, although entirely original in concept and detail, follows that same great English garden tradition. Planting schemes in the Gertrude Jekyll style woven into an intricate and varied pattern of garden spaces is the theme.

Like her friend and neighbour, Margery Fish, Mrs Reiss had a wonderful eye for discovering, and rediscovering, good plants but they each had to fit into her predetermined scheme. This truly artistic ability to use plants as part of the overall pattern, and to see the detail as part of the whole, was her genius and it resulted in a garden of rare tranquillity and restfulness. Not that there is any lack of interest, for the range of plants and the variety of the colour schemes is immense. But so well devised is the progression by which the garden is revealed and so well balanced and varied are the parts, that the outcome cannot be other than a sense of inevitability and repose.

The main vista west of the house is a classic of garden composition, both when seen from the house and more especially when seen looking back from the circular pond and fountain that is its focal point. Pairs of clipped box bushes give dignity and provide an orderly link from the

Tintinhull House. The pool garden loggia is furnished in summer with flowering plants in a variety of attractive pots many of which were made in Ilminster.

Eagle Court near the house through the azalea garden, where the soil has been specially treated for their culture, to the fountain garden where clipped yew hedges instead of walls form the background to a scheme of silver and white. Although mainly flat, the subtle changes of level into and out from the fountain garden give an added impression of developing enclosure and further reduce the apparent scale.

The neat kitchen garden by contrast allows views out through the surrounding orchards, so important for shelter and the well-being of the garden. Some of the trees are engulfed by climbing roses of the vigorous *synstylae* kind including *R. brunonii* and *R. longicuspis*.

The Pool Garden was converted from a tennis-court after the Second World War and given a new design with a long, formal pool, loggia and flanking borders in memory of the Reiss's nephew, Michael Lucas, who was killed in action. In summer one border has a brilliant association of white and clear, light colours with silver and glaucous foliage, while the other has light blues, pinks and mauves contrasted with dark delphiniums, and coppery foliage. Creamy yellow is in both borders and in the variegated ivy which overflows from big pots around the pool to link the whole scheme together.

The most dramatic colour scheme is on the west side of the cedar lawn where purple and bronzy foliage tints are contrasted with golden variegated dogwood and strong flower colours predominate.

All the borders are mixed and contain shrubs, even small trees, as well as herbaceous plants, ground covers and roses, and clumps of bulbs give an early display. This and the deliberate use of foliage for contrast and texture achieves that elusive year-round interest and beauty that was Mrs Reiss's aim. The walls too are fully exploited with climbing plants and roses to contribute their fragrance and profusion to the enveloping glory.

University of Bristol Botanic Garden

Open for NGS in summer. At Bracken Hill, Leigh Woods, 3.2km (2 miles) W of Bristol. 2ha (5 acre) garden containing 3,000 species. Special collections of Hebe, Cistus, Campanula, Sempervivum, etc., and many British natives. Large area of glass and rock garden.

Wayford Manor

Robin L. Goffe Esq.

At Wayford, 5km (3½ miles) SW of Crewkerne, 1.5km (1 mile) west of Clapton off the B3165. Part terraced and part informal garden of 1.25ha (3 acres) planted by the late Humphrey Baker and partly designed by his uncle, Harold Peto. Fine manor house in Ham stone, mainly Elizabethan, part dating from thirteenth-century. Garden only open for NGS and GS in spring. On lime-free loam up to 152m (500ft) on steep SE slope with fine views to the Dorset hills. Mild climate and only 14.5km (9 miles) from the sea. Rainfall 914mm (36in.). One gardener.

After winding through very English lanes close to the Dorset border there comes a dramatic change on entering the gates of the beautifully mellow Wayford Manor. Here suddenly is a touch of Tuscany. Statuary and pools adorn ordered terraces, where spires of juniper and cypress make foreground to a spectacular view. A stone-pillared balustrade and loggia placed carefully for the enjoyment of the sight and scent of the garden and of distant landscape completes the effect.

The source of this Mediterranean feeling becomes clear from learning that the creator of the garden, Mr Humphrey Baker, was advised and helped by his uncle, Harold Peto of Iford Manor, whose Italianate style is as unmistakable here as it is at Buscot Park.

The original garden, contemporary with the Elizabethan house, existed only in the uppermost terraces and it is here that Harold Peto's architectural influence shows most. The E-shaped front of the house is sideways to the view and separated from it by broad clipped yew hedges which enclose a simple formal paved court, terracotta pots and a central axis to a copy of the Byzantine font at Ravenna in a niche of clipped yew. In this courtyard the decoration is restrained to one large *Magnolia × soulangiana* 'Rustica Rubra', *Cotoneaster horizontalis* on the low walls and Banksian Rose on the house wall but near by is a little intimate enclosure full of figs and Flag Irises.

Running right along the southern garden front of the house and extending further west is a stepped terrace, paved on the upper level and grass on the lower, with a rocky bank between. A magnificent pair of Horse Chestnuts growing together finish the terrace at its western end and balance superbly the bulk of the house at the other.

In the shade of these great trees is a small arbour against the wall and a typical Peto arrangement of formal lily pool set in paving with topiary and an angel and dolphin fountain. At the other end of the terrace the house has been extended to make a conservatory and projecting summerhouse, poised so that one captures the view while sheltered from the east wind. Basking against the house is a gnarled old Wisteria dripping pale blue near to *Magnolia grandiflora*, ceanothus and the strongly-scented *Clerodendrum bungei*. Many dwarf bulbs grow on the terrace, with *Amaryllis belladonna* and *Nerine bowdenii* against the house, and aconites, snowdrops and *Crocus tomasinianus* under the great Horse Chestnuts.

Bordering the grass terrace is a most handsome balustrade divided by a dignified stone staircase leading to the main terrace garden below. A notable feature is another great *Magnolia* × *soulangiana*; the garden is famous for this genus. On a side border is an effective combination of purple berberis and the single *Kerria japonica*. Opening off this large open square through a gate is a walled secret garden. Here is a charming oasis, cool and shady and full of the sound of water from a cherub fountain in a large rectangular water-lily pool. Two splendid Japanese Maples give dappled shade to Plantain Lilies, Solomon's Seal and Irises and a seat niche has been carefully contrived to see all without being seen. This is garden design at its best, a few steps giving a total contrast between openness of the terrace and the intimate enclosure of this sheltered corner.

Continuing down the hill, a path crosses at right angles leading to the kitchen garden but beyond that the garden becomes informal, beginning with a rock garden. The dwarf conifers of the turn of the century are now huge and include notable specimens of the horizontal-growing golden yew, *Taxus baccata* 'Adpressa Aurea', a dwarf Scots Pine, *Pinus sylvestris* 'Beuvronensis', *Juniperus squamata* 'Meyeri' and *Chamaecyparis pisifera* 'Squarrosa'. In the shade beneath, hardy cyclamen, including *C. repandum, C. europaeum* and *C. hederifolium*, have spread along with the purple-blue Gromwell, *Lithospermum purpureo-caeruleum*, Welsh Poppy and *Corydalis lutea*, all blue and yellow in late spring. On the south side the rock garden has a Japanese effect with a stone lantern, bamboos and irises by a pool and a stone Buddha among Japanese Maples.

Beyond the rock garden is a venerable orchard of cider apples wild with daffodils and self-seeded *Crocus versicolor* surrounded by old borders of rhododendrons, cherries and maples. We are now in a real plantsman's paradise. For a garden of its size it contains a remarkable collection of trees and shrubs collected by the late Mr Humphrey Baker and his gardener, Mr Garrett. Sir Eric Savill was a frequent visitor and his influence shows.

Right at the bottom the water garden has gone rather wild to great effect with exotic masses of *Peltiphyllum peltatum*, rodgersias, hostas and Bog Arum holding their own in the boggy ground among superb specimens of *Acer palmatum*, hardy palm and water lilies. The most memorable experience in this garden of contrasts was to follow steps of sawn logs through damp ground and come suddenly upon a whole grove of pale green Shuttlecock Ferns, contrasted against the rugose leaves of

Rodgersia aesculifolia with *Magnolia stellata* beyond. Other Magnolias include *M. denudata* and *M. salicifolia*. All around are naturalized fritillaries, camassias, *Lilium pardalinum* and *L. martagon*.

An area of woodland contains more Japanese Maples and dense masses of rhododendrons including 'Loder's White', 'Pink Pearl' and the cream 'Penjerrick' as well as such species as *R. arboreum*, *R. campanulatum* and the early *R. sutchuenense*. *Malus baccata* has grown into a large tree, indeed everything seems a little larger than usual on this moist and fertile soil. Just when it all seems too oppressive there is an open grove of ilexes with glimpses out into the fields.

A little back toward the house a former tennis-court contains a collection of *Sorbus* species with the green snake-barked *Acer hersii* and the large-leaved *Betula maximowiczii*.

Although it must be a great delight to own, such a complex garden is far from easy to maintain in these times of rapidly rising costs, and Mr and Mrs Goffe are grappling with problems of upkeep only too familiar to most garden owners today. Sensibly they keep the upper formal terraces as well as possible while following a more relaxed regime further down in the informal areas.

Weacombe House
Mr and Mrs A.J. Greswell

Open for NGS in spring. At West Quantoxhead. Medium-sized garden with rhododendrons, azaleas, and other shrubs; lake and lawns.

Weatherham
Mr and Mrs T. Sutcliffe

Open for NGS several times a year. At Brompton Regis, 7.2km (4½ miles) N of Dulverton. 1.6ha (4 acres) around seventeenth-century farmhouse under development only since 1976. Hardy and old-fashioned cottage-garden plants; woodland garden with primulas; moorland views. Pond with ducks and geese; also mares and foals in the paddocks. Plants for sale.

Westholme House

Brigadier and Mrs N.S.E. Maude

Open for NGS in summer. At Pilton, SE of Wells. Large garden around fine Georgian house of Bath stone. Unique setting overlooking lake; terraced garden, woodland and park with outstanding views.

Wootton House

The Hon. Mrs John Acland-Hood

Open for NGS in spring and autumn. At Butleigh Wootton, 4.8km (3 miles) S of Glastonbury. Herbaceous borders, roses, shrubs, trees, bulbs; rock garden and woodland garden.

Yarlington House

Countess Charles de Salis

Open for NGS in summer. 5.6km (3½ miles) both from Wincanton and Castle Cary. New garden being developed around eighteenth-century house; woods and park. Pleached limes, statuary, rose garden, walled garden and laburnum walk.

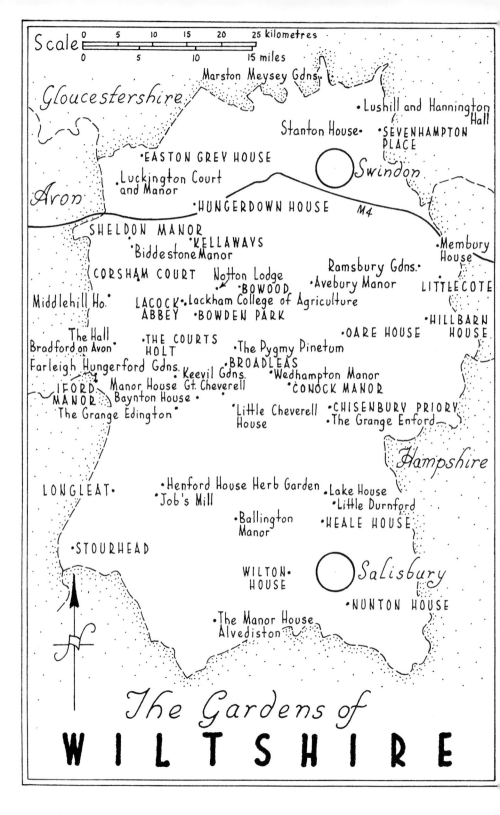

The Gardens of Wiltshire

Avebury Manor

The Marquess of Ailesbury

For opening arrangements see HHCG. In Avebury, 11.2km (7 miles) W of Marlborough.
Extensive garden around romantic Elizabethan Manor house.

Part of an elaborate formal layout of hedges and topiary remains on the west side of the house. The Topiary Garden has a knot garden with an intriguing design of overlapping rectangles, a fountain pool with urns and various shapes cut in yew, including a peacock. Elegant iron railings on a low wall separate it from the park while retaining the view. Beyond the curving tile-capped wall is an impressive arrangement of yew hedges with buttresses forming niches for planting and a splendid lead urn in the centre. The hedges screen a secret walk enclosed on the other side by a vine-covered wall. Here there is a collection of culinary and medicinal herbs, such as might have been used in the Elizabethan house, with an edging of catmint. There is another enclosed walk of yews, a sheep-grazed orchard and a border containing an extraordinary stock of Summer Hyacinth, *Galtonia candicans*.

Ballington Manor

Mr and Mrs D.F.H. McCormick

Open for NGS in early summer. At Wylye, 1.6km (1 mile) E of junction of A36 and A303.
Large garden intersected by two streams and on the bank of the River Wylye. Extensive lawns;
herbaceous and shrub borders. Sixteenth-century house (not open).

Baynton House

Mr and Mrs A.J. Macdonald-Buchanan

Open for NGS and GS in spring. At Coulston, 6.4km (4 miles) E of Westbury. Garden of
6.4ha (16 acres) with spring bulbs; rock garden; wild, woodland and water gardens.

Biddestone Manor

Princess R. Loewenstein

Open for NGS in late spring. 4.8km (3 miles) N of Corsham, 8km (5 miles) W of Chippenham. Large garden around seventeenth-century Manor house with extensive lawns, small lake, topiary and unusual shrubs.

Bowden Park

Sir Arnold Weinstock

At Bowden Hill, 1.6km (1 mile) east of Lacock, 8km (5 miles) from Chippenham via A350 turning east through Lacock village. Mainly informal garden of 4.5ha (11 acres) with productive walled garden, around fine eighteenth-century stone house overlooking the Avon valley and Lacock. Open once a year for GS in late May. Situated at 152m (500ft) on a westerly slope with fine views; light sandy lime-free soil. Rainfall 813mm (32in). Head gardener: Mr. J.A. Brown.

Great garden concepts, however well conceived, can fail for lack of good husbandry, the essential dimension which makes gardening different from the other creative arts. This is not merely 'upkeep' or 'maintenance' but a real concern for plants and an understanding of their needs. Its effect is immediately apparent and gives a pleasure quite separate from any scenic or design merit the garden may have. Such rare horticultural enjoyment is to be had at Bowden Park where the craft of gardening of all kinds is practised at the highest level.

Magnificent beeches shade the drive and opposite is the high western wall of the kitchen garden. In front a raised border contains a well-arranged mixture with purple continus, Weeping Silver Pear and a fine specimen of the choice *Cornus controversa* 'Variegata' among summer-flowering herbaceous plants and low shrubs, giving way at the front to *Cytisus kewensis*, aubrietia, shrubby candytuft and *Stachys lanata*.

Eventually the house is revealed on its balustraded terraces looking out westwards over a park-like view, with cedars and oaks in the foreground. Below is the tranquil valley in which Lacock and Corsham lie and through which Bristol's Avon winds its way.

The older part of the garden lies adjacent to the drive south of the house and consists of a large terraced lawn surrounded by mature trees and shrubs with bulbs and shade-loving plants beneath. Apart from the obviously earlier framework, mainly of beech, there is some good nineteenth-century planting here including Atlas Cedar, Variegated Oak, Copper Beech, Monterey Pine and a Victorian favourite, *Aesculus flava (octandra)*. Behind a pair of enormous London Planes stands the great surprise of the garden: an elaborate rock grotto of brown sandstone, as picturesque and melancholy as any. At the front is a summerhouse glazed with leaded lights and with a fantastic interior of shells and coloured stones, both on the walls and forming a gothic ceiling of terrifying stalactic shapes. All round are mysterious catacombs covered in ferns and draped in creepers.

Further down the slope, in contrast to the cool greenery above, is a rhododendron garden, a stimulating riot of dazzling colours in late May with a large central splash of mixed azaleas surrounded by every shade of hardy hybrid rhododendron the breeders have ever produced, all battling for attention in a Chelsea Flower Show of exciting colours.

Down again is a most beautiful feature, presumably Victorian, where a stream has been harnessed into a series of six stepped pools like watercress beds each overflowing into the next and full of the pure white Water Hawthorn, *Aponogeton distachyon*. All around are Plantain Lilies, Globe Flowers, spireas and clumps of *Primula denticulata*. From here a curving walk, at first set deeply in a cutting, with well-planted sandstone rock banks on either side, returns to the house. There are superb clumps of the sweet-scented *Daphne retusa*, heathers, dwarf conifers, Spanish Broom, dwarf azaleas and the tiny white stars of the moss-like *Arenaria balearica*. Evidently this walk originally formed the garden boundary and it is only in recent years that the lower areas, where there are many more fine young plants, have been taken into cultivation.

Immediately south of the house is a simple formal pool and fountain, and facing steeply west above it are paved terraces containing a series of tiered pools. Around the house large areas have been planted in modern, labour-saving style with weed-smothering ground covers and there is an extensive new heather garden.

But perhaps the greatest pleasure at Bowden is to see a really productive and efficient walled garden where no one needs to make the now familiar excuses for weedy beds and empty greenhouses. This kitchen garden, although adapted to modern needs by the removal of box hedges, really is a going concern with dahlias, chrysanthemums and other cut flowers as well as vegetables and soft fruits, all bursting with health and immaculately maintained. There are greenhouses of pot plants and peaches, early tomatoes 'looping the loop' and cucumbers hanging in bunches from the roof. Obviously this is the powerhouse of the garden, where Mr. Brown demonstrates his skill and from which the air of efficiency and good craftsmanship spreads to the whole garden.

Bowood
The Earl of Shelburne

4km (2½ mile) W of Calne, 8km (5 miles) SE of Chippenham, 1.6km (1 mile) S of A4, separate entrance to rhododendron garden off A342. For opening arrangements see HHCG, closed Mondays. Eighteenth-century house, reduced to its present size in 1955; exhibition rooms open. Park by Lancelot Brown; 32.8ha (82 acres); lake, cascade, terrace garden, pinetum. Separate rhododendron garden. Soil mostly gault clay overlaid on high ground with well-drained fertile Upper Greensand, lime-free, especially in rhododendron garden. Rainfall 813mm (32in.). Altitude 91-152m (300-500ft). Excellent general guidebook in colour and separate·guide to the trees in the pleasure-grounds are on sale. Refreshments available.

Gardens appeal to a variety of interests. Many may come for the appeal of flowers and colour alone, while others may appreciate fine trees and landscape or good buildings, or the historical interest, or rare plants, or the natural flora and fauna. Some may merely want an afternoon out with their families in pleasant surroundings. All will be satisfied here at Bowood.

The park was designed by Lancelot 'Capability' Brown between 1762 and 1768 and remains as one of the most successful and best preserved works of the great man. The total scheme was of vast proportions and, although many of the original tree clumps survive in the outer parts, the woodland belt with its winding ride now encloses mostly arable farmland. The eastern part near the house, with gently undulating lawns sweeping down to the lake, is maintained as mown park. The broad curving sheet of water was formed by blocking two streams with a dam cunningly concealed by trees. Placed here on a promontory to give reflections across a long stretch of water from the house, is a little Doric temple but unbelievably this was not part of Brown's scheme, having been moved there from the pleasure-grounds in 1864. Also amid the trees beyond the dam is a gushing cascade, fascinating and intricate, and a mysterious fossil-lined hermit's cave both designed by Charles Hamilton (of Painshill) in the rococo style and added in 1785, after Brown had finished his work. The rockwork was constructed with great skill by the great eighteenth-century specialist Josiah Lane, who also worked at Painshill and Fonthill.

North-west of the house near the present car park a Pinetum fits unobtrusively into the Brownian landscape. Of quite exceptional quality, it was begun by the third Marquess of Lansdowne in 1848 although there was a nursery there before. It has been added to occasionally by the family ever since and the present Earl of Shelburne is particularly enthusiastic. The collection is remarkably comprehensive and is well described in a guidebook by Mr P.H.B. Gardner. Several trees are either among the 'champions' in height as listed by Alan Mitchell or are notable specimens in their own right, especially several Cedars of Lebanon, *Cedrus libani*; a magnificent *Pinus ponderosa*; a Giant Fir, *Abies grandis*, at 42.1m (138ft) the tallest tree on the estate; a grove of enormous Californian Redwoods, *Sequoia sempervirens*; Monterey Pine, *Pinus radiata*, and many more. All are spaciously arranged and interspersed with a wide range of deciduous forest and flowering trees and shrubs. There are hours of fascination here for the dedicated dendrologist and for the more humble lover of fine trees.

The larger wing of the house was pulled down in 1955 and its site is now represented by a grass terrace. A substantial house still looks over the lake to the east and at right angles facing south is Robert Adam's superb Orangery, now a picture gallery. This is set above formal terraces, of which the top one was designed by Sir Robert Smirke in 1818. The main terrace with its raised walk and pavilion to the west was made in the Victorian Italianate style by George Kennedy in 1851. The layout is now much simplified from the original complexity but still retains its clipped pyramidal Irish Yews, now flat-topped. Between are large colourful beds of bush roses and the urns are also appropriately bright and profuse with geraniums. Against the terrace wall *Magnolia grandiflora* and lavenders revel in the hot sun and climbing roses are trained on the wall below the balustrade.

Quite apart from all this, in a 20ha (50 acre) part of Brown's outer woodland belt, facing north-east towards the house, is Robert Adam's monumental Mausoleum built in honour of the first Lord Shelburne by his widow. In the surrounding mature woodland, principally of oak, beech, Sweet Chestnut and Scots Pine, flourishes a rhododendron garden, which is open via Kennels Lodge on the A342 from mid-May until the end of June, when the rest is closed. The wide range of species and cultivars has been planted in phases and undoubtedly the best way to see them is to follow the planting roughly in chronological order, beginning north at the Mausoleum which commands a breathtaking view from its hill across a corner of the park to the Wiltshire Downs.

The woods on either side of Lady Shelburne's Walk from the entrance to the Mausoleum evoke the proper mood being funereally dense; mostly with *Rhododendron ponticum*, but there is relief at the Quarry where Scots Pines tower above a mixture of the older hardy hybrids such as 'Glory of Littleworth' with 'Lady Chamberlain' and some of the species. Lord Shelburne's Walk below the Mausoleum and Lord Lansdowne's Rides are furnished mostly with gigantic bushes of the hardy hybrids of pre-First World War vintage. The latter is a spacious loop overlooking a spectacular

Left: Bowood. Hamilton's magnificent cascade.

Below: Bowood. An aerial view showing the terraces and parts of the pinetum within Brown's masterly landscape, with its lake.
      Aerofilms

mass of the same types closely planted on either side of a steep valley. Here and along Lord Kerry's and Fitzmaurice Walks are immense bushes of reliable old varieties like 'Cynthia', Loderi, 'Cunningham's White' and 'Duchess of Connaught', together with the *cinnabarinum* hybrid 'Lady Rosebery'. Most of these and the group of large-leaved species in Petty's Walk were planted by the fifth Marquess of Lansdowne in the first two decades of this century.

Further south the woodland opens out into more recent plantings of rhododendrons and azaleas by the present Lord Lansdowne, spaciously arranged with a variety of choice trees and shrubs, dogwoods, magnolias and *Enkianthus* spp. amid carpets of bluebells. Here, near the junction of Pauline's and David's Walks are thriving groups of the less common species such as *RR. augustinii, campylocarpum, callimorphum, orbiculare, haematodes,* the compact *williamsianum* and the handsome-stemmed 'Shilsonae'. Further up towards Abbot's Ride are some of the more subtle coloured recent hybrids such as 'Vanessa Pastel' and forms of Loderi associating beautifully with yellow azalea *R. luteum* and *R. mucronatum,* bluebells, *Cornus nuttallii, Cornus florida* and the incomparable purity of *Magnolia sinensis.* Only the scarlet of *R.* 'Armistice Day' jars.

Broadleas
Lady Anne Cowdray

Near Potterne, 2.4km (1½ miles) SW of Devizes on NW side of A360. For opening arrangements see HHCG ; also open for NGS. Garden of 1.4ha (3½ acres) mainly south and east of late Georgian stone house (not open). Situated at 122m (400ft), open to SW winds but with a sheltered valley and walled area. On lime-free upper Greensand ridge. Rainfall 838mm (33in.). Plants for sale. Staff of head gardener and some casual help but the owner also works full-time in the garden.

A house enjoying a view, especially when it is to the south-west, usually creates problems for the gardener. With the view comes the wind and the limitations it imposes on growth and choice of plants. A visit to Broadleas on a gusty Easter day emphasizes the obvious exposure of the garden near the house, with its open views towards Westbury, and sends the visitor scurrying for shelter. But rarely does a garden offer such a variety of conditions and microclimates in so small a space and even less commonly are these opportunities grasped so eagerly for the cultivation of plants.

Close to the house is a south-facing border of silver plants revelling in the sunshine, whose foliage is well adapted to breezy conditions and dryness. Curry Plants, several *Artemisia* spp., soft-leaved *Ballota pseudodictamnus*, blue-flowered *Teucrium fruticans* and other silvers spill out on to the gravel terrace with Rosemary, Sea Purslane, *Piptanthus laburnifolius (nepalensis)* and *Olearia scilloniensis*.

A moongate pierces the wall behind to give glimpses into the sunken rose garden, a haven of shelter east of the house. Here the paved surface and retaining walls are full of wild strawberries, aubrietia and Snow-in-Summer. Bush roses are arranged in tiered borders around a central sundial with a mass of *Nerine bowdenii* ready to give a late show on the south-facing side. Using the shelter of the house is the beautiful *Abutilon vitifolium* 'Album', while the Banksian Rose hangs from the wall behind.

Beyond the south-facing loggia, where excellent plants can be bought, is a raised rock bank and herbaceous border, punctuated by coade-stone vases and surrounded by shrub roses and Japanese Maples. There is a magnificent specimen of *Clerodendrum trichotomum* at each end. Here, as well many choice dwarf bulbs, are the dwarf lilac *Syringa palibiniana,* and the little mountain ash *Sorbus reducta*.

The long terrace which forms the spine of the garden is closed at either end by free-grown but shapely Irish Yews and supported by a dry stone wall full of aubrietia. It leads to a series of small enclosures hedged for shelter, where all sorts of treasures grow. Near a thatched shelter there is a spectacular group of *Cyclamen* spp. thriving under a beech tree, with the spring-flowering *C. coum* and *C. ibericum* as well as the more common but equally beautiful autumn-flowering *C. hederifolium* (*C. neapolitanum*). Winter and early-spring-flowering plants are a speciality with *Daphne mezereum* 'Alba', the choice dwarf *D. blagayana*, Lenten Hellebores, and *Ribes laurifolium* catching the eye. The unusual, golden *Pittosporum tenuifolium* 'Warnham Gold' is only one of the many exciting plants to be found.

Below the terrace is a total change of character and climate. Unsuspected from the house, a steep coombe drops away to the south, sheltered on either side by old oaks and Scots Pines, under which masses of old-fashioned daffodils crowd the grass. With this shelter and a stream trickling through, the climate is a complete contrast to the bracing terrace above, only a few yards away. The growing conditions have been further improved by dense planting and the clever use of bamboos and tough old hardy hybrid rhododendrons to raise the humidity and increase the shelter. The cold air drains away into the meadow below to reduce the frost risk and the result, on this acidic soil, is an ideal site for ericaceous plants and tender shrubs. This opportunity has been seized with great enthusiasm by Lady Anne, who is particularly keen on the less common species of *Rhododendron*. In this valley the whole unrivalled diversity of this genus can be appreciated in extraordinary juxtaposition: tiny-leaved *R. impeditum* and giant *R. auriculatum*; large-flowered 'Fabia' and choice little *R.*

lepidostylum with its glaucous foliage — all sited with care and obviously loved as individuals.

And not only rhododendrons do well here; the head gardener's favourite camellias flourish too and there are many other choice lime-haters such as the white *Eucryphia* 'Nymansay'; the red lanterns of *Crinodendron hookeranum*; hydrangeas of many kinds; even the tender *Drimys aromatica*. Relieving the evergreens are the unusual cut-leaved Elder, Golden Mock Orange, *Pittosporum tobira*, *Abutilon vitifolium* and *Viburnum plicatum*. The layout is in the classic English wild-garden style with naturalized *Gunnera manicata*, herbaceous ground covers with *Pulmonaria azurea* to the fore and many bulbs including *Erythronium*. But the real high point at Broadleas is the magnolias and especially the water-lily-flowered *M. sargentiana robusta* and the slightly later and equally large-flowered *M. campbellii mollicomata*, two fine and unusually compact trees crowded with flowers at the head of the valley.

You will have gathered that the garden is a joy to visit in spring but summer has not been neglected in Lady Anne's planting. The collection of shrub roses is a delight both in the sunken garden and elsewhere.

Chisenbury Priory

Frances Estelle, Lady Harvey

At East Chisenbury, 1.6km (1 mile) N of Enford, 9.6km (6 miles) SW of Pewsey; across river Avon from A345 by turning E into Enford, then N towards E. Chisenbury. Mainly walled garden around seventeenth-century house with 1767 front of pinkish-red brick. Open for NGS and GS in summer. In valley near Avon, at 91m (300ft) light alkaline, alluvial soil with a high water-table. Rainfall 762mm (30in.). Owner plus one gardener full-time and another part-time. Plants for sale.

There is a string of beautiful gardens along the narrow valley that the Wiltshire Avon has gouged through Salisbury Plain and in which Amesbury lies. Whatever the planting, they all have a timeless quality and a tranquillity that comes from their ancient origins. The valley as a whole has a special atmosphere of remoteness, enclosed as it is by the gently rounded outlines of the chalk Downs.

Chisenbury Priory retains the formal outline of the Tudor garden. Both at the south front of the house and at the back there are garden courts enclosed in the attractive local tradition with walls of clunch and flints, capped with pantiles.

The drive is a tunnel of deep shade beneath sycamores and chestnuts opening out suddenly in front of the house. The attractive gates on either side of the forecourt lead to a symmetrical arrangement of drives, to and from the house, enclosing a trim lawn. On either side are ample borders of herbaceous plants interplanted with vigorous shrub roses such as 'Frühlingsgold' and 'Blanc Double de Coubert' with more roses, 'Albertine' and 'New Dawn', mixed with clematises on the walls. The colour scheme is a fitting one of blues, pinks and light yellow with delphiniums and paeonies outstanding among a profuse mixture of herbaceous perennials.

West of the house, the garden is more intimate with two small enclosed gardens. One near the garden room, where tea is served, is mainly paved and dominated by a large circular bed of old-fashioned border flowers. A crab apple, a purple *Cotinus coggygria* and a Mexican Orange complement a rose-covered wall to shelter this corner. In contrast to this floweriness, the other little garden is a formal arrangement of cool and restful greens which relies on the contrasting foliage shapes of Plantain Lilies, *Veratrum nigrum*, Solomon's Seal, Rue and various grasses.

Further west the arboretum has tempting mown walks through lush long grass past big flowering shrubs to a lily pond, and on to the neat kitchen garden. But the main path leads on to the large walled area north of the house. Here the garden is terraced down to the north-west from the house lawn, where the planting is simple with groups of cherries and a large juniper, to a stream where most of the horticultural excitement is concentrated. The stream, which emerges mysteriously from among enormous old clipped yews, has been skilfully manipulated by Lady Harvey and her gardener to form a pool where a weeping willow makes a feature. The stream has two pretty stone bridges and sides planted with a rich variety of vigorous watersiders, Bugbanes, Day Lilies, the creamy plumes of *Aruncus dioicus* and the fiery giant 'montbretia', *Curtonus paniculatus,* interspersed with Weeping Cherry, quince and *Buddleia alternifolia*. But the main feature of this garden, and the reason for coming in early July, is the glorious array of roses. There are shrub roses like 'Complicata', looking well with violas and 'Nevada' with *Hosta seiboldiana* near the stream. 'Mrs Honey Dyson', 'Filipes' and 'Wedding Day' climb over the walls and into old apple trees, and masses of old shrub roses are mixed among espalier apples and pears with clematises, in delicious confusion. Modern shrub roses like 'Constance Spry', 'Dream Girl', 'Inspiration' and 'Fritz Nobis' have been thoughtfully arranged among weed-smothering campanulas, geraniums and *Alchemilla mollis*. The whole garden is a great spectacle in July.

Conock Manor
Mr and Mrs Bonar Sykes

At Conock, 8km (5 miles) SE of Devizes on north side of A342. Walled garden of 1.2ha (3 acres) mainly east of Bath stone house of 1765, gothic windows and summerhouse on east side added 1820. Open for NGS and GS in spring. Heavy alkaline soil. Level country at 106m (350ft). Rainfall 838mm (33in.). Owners and one gardener.

The handsome Georgian house faces west with a simple arrangement of topiary in front and elegant iron railings at the side to separate the garden from the drive. The garden lies mostly east of the house and beyond an imposing Georgian stable block with a splendid clock and dazzling copper ball on top. It is enclosed on the north side by a high wall backed by sheltering beeches but to the south only the invisible barrier of a ha-ha separates the lawn from the park and a fine view of the Downs.

In contrast to the west front, the garden side of the house is gothic in character with a romantic 1820 thatched summerhouse with tree-trunk pillars, and is very reminescent of Repton. The south-facing wall provides support for a fig, wisterias, magnolias, climbing roses and *Ceanothus* spp., and shelter for a long mixed border of shrub roses and sun-loving *Abutilon, Hebe* and *Hibiscus* cultivars. A wide variety of herbaceous plants includes hellebores, Japanese Anemones, Oriental Poppies and Day Lilies as well as ground covers, making this a border of continuing beauty.

Beyond the stable block is a formal area devoted to magnolias and shrub roses, including the silvery hue of the vigorous *R. souleiana*, around a hexagonal pool. Further on is a smart kitchen garden but the best feature of the whole garden lies south of this where an ingenious formal arrangement of beech hedges and clipped box encloses a grass walk. The long *allée* leads to a fine specimen Japanese Maple through an intriguing variety of spaces alternately broad and narrow and given continuity and perspective by pairs of box balls. A continuous border of shrubs which screens the kitchen garden contains much of interest and fine mature specimens of such subjects as *Viburnum carlesii, Magnolia stellata, Garrya elliptica* with crabs, lilacs, Mock Orange, barberries, cotoneasters and effective ground cover planting of *Galeobdolon luteum, Tellima grandiflora, Geranium macrorrhizum* and the Forget-me-Not-flowered *Brunnera macrophylla*.

Corsham Court
The Lord Methuen

In Corsham village, S of the A4 Chippenham to Bath road, 6.4km (4 miles) W of Chippenham. For opening arrangements see HHCG 3.2ha (8 acre) flower garden (plus 2.8ha (7 acres) walled kitchen garden not open), park of 121ha (300 acres) by L. Brown and H. Repton with later additions; Elizabethan house altered by L. Brown, J. Nash and T. Bellamy. Situated at 106m (350ft) in gently rolling country on open alkaline soil with high water-table. Rainfall 813mm (32in.). Four gardeners, including kitchen gardens.

When Mr Paul Methuen invited Lancelot 'Capability' Brown to assist with the enlargement of Corsham House and its park in 1760 it was then a typical Elizabethan house with a formal garden. Although Brown extended the house to make a symmetrical south front he retained its Elizabethan character. Likewise he retained the forecourt and the Jacobean stables and riding-school at the gates. It remains now much as he might have wished with a vast Lebanon Cedar on one side and on the other a Maidenhair Tree to balance it. The attractive borders are modern with their magnolias, hibiscuses, paeonies and hollyhocks combined with climbing roses like 'Félicité et Perpétue' and 'New Dawn' on the walls. Sadly the elms in the south avenue, replanted by Brown, have recently succumbed to disease but they have been replaced in turn by limes. Another feature of the curtilage of the house is the array of yews along the back drive from the village, making vast sculptural shapes evolved by generations of trimming. The house walls carry climbing plants grateful for the warmth, like the scarlet-trumpeted *Campsis radicans*, lemon-scented *Magnolia grandiflora*, a wisteria and a Banksian Rose. White doves and strutting peacocks enliven the gravel front.

Currently used for croquet, the east lawn was laid out by Brown as a simple foreground to his park, with the low magnificent old Lebanon Cedar perfectly framing the view with its tabulate branches. Both here and on the north side Brown swept away the walled gardens and brought his idyllic countryside right up to the house. He provided for a 5.2ha (13 acre) lake but this was not completed until Humphry Repton came to work at Corsham some forty years later. Now, though partly silted, it still catches the sun, giving life to the middle distance as both great men would have wished. Brown removed an avenue on this side and planted instead the characteristic perimeter belt to obscure the boundary, and clumps to enhance the views. The sunk fence he made on the east side is set well out into the park to include the churchyard, well beyond the existing bounds of the garden, presumably so that it would not be looked into from the upper rooms of the house.

As well as the making of the lake, Repton supervised the planting of several thousand trees — oaks, Spanish Chestnuts, elms, beeches and sycamores mostly from Miller and Sweet's nursery at Bristol. In 1798 Mr Methuen wrote to him: 'Corsham is no doubt much improved in your hands . . . we are much pleased with what you have done there'.

On the north side the ha-ha is sited cunningly where the land falls away and here it does form the boundary of the garden. Brown retained the ancient lime avenue to the Bath road but removed some trees to allow cross views. In place of Thomas Greening's small *ferme ornée* garden with its rectangular pool, he made sweeping lawns and extended the avenue towards the house. The gigantic layered specimen of Oriental Plane, *Platanus orientalis insularis (cretica),* can have few equals in the country and several of the other trees are only marginally less notable. There is a magnificent Black Walnut, a tall Californian Redwood and a group of Horse Chestnuts on the west side sadly now breaking up. The east side has Copper Beeches, a shapely Turkey Oak and, further on, one of the Wing Nuts, *Pterocarya fraxinifolia*, which produces its long green catkins in midsummer. Among these larger trees east of the vista is the so-called Chrysanthemum Walk now planted with a variety of decorative trees, several magnolias including the early-flowering *M. sprengeri*, an Indian Bean, cherries and crabs, and shrubs with Mock Oranges, deutzias and the large-fruited Spindle Tree, *Euonymus latifolius*, prominent. At the end is a grove of tall Gean Cherries.

Beyond the big trees on the west side the path winds round to the exquisite Gothic Bath House with its ogee roof, which Brown designed to overlook Thomas Greening's pool after its conversion to an irregular outline. The pool was filled up in the early Victorian period, at the time the flower gardens were being developed. The Bath House was later altered by John Nash and is ingeniously connected with the flower garden by an inclined passage that opens into the newly re-erected Bradford-on-Avon, fifteenth-century Porch — a dramatic transition. Beyond the Bath House a gravel walk follows the line of the ha-ha with groups of shrubs on either side and leads to another of 'Capability' Brown's features, the North Walk, a 3km (2 miles) long path leading to a handsome classical gateway. It provides fine views over the ha-ha into the park and the opportunity to see at close quarters a number of remarkably fine trees including Turkey Oaks, Oriental Planes, Wellingtonias and Lucombe Oaks. Near the beginning of the walk, in a grove of tall yews, is a little water garden with big hydrangeas around, both *H. villosa (H. aspera villosa)* and *H. aspera* 'Macrophylla'.

The flower garden was brought into the pleasure-grounds by Jane Dorothea who developed the garden from the time she married Paul

Methuen, the first Peer, in 1810 until he died in 1849. Mary Ethel (1860-1941), second wife of Paul Sanford Methuen, the third Peer, was responsible for the present layout of the flower garden. The structure is a good one. Contained firmly between walls and trees, the scale is intimate enough for the appreciation of flowers and plants. In the best traditions of Victorian flower gardens of a modest scale, the layout is formal and dignified with box-edged borders containing a good variety of plants.

The fountain garden has a circle of lovely pale-green, summer-flowering Indian Bean Trees around the caged lily pond. In the borders are great banks of the unusual *Clerodendrum trichotomum* with its fragrant summer flowers and blue berries and the dwarfer and rather more pungent *C. bungei*. Among these are hydrangeas, great clumps of pink *Crinum powellii* and the well-armed Japanese Bitter Orange, *Poncirus trifoliata*, fruiting freely, while 'New Dawn' roses and *Clematis* × *jackmanii* grow on iron supports and on the wall behind.

A straight axial walk from the pond leads past lilacs and between flanking vases to a fine stone urn beyond the deep shade of some yew trees. Off to the west is the charming box-edged rose garden with mixed Hybrid Tea roses in the centre bed and old shrub roses and the plumbago-

blue *Ceratostigma willmottianum* at the sides. A little arbour of Mountain Ash sheltering a pretty Victorian cast-iron seat makes an unusual focal point. There are several ornaments in this area including a stone pedestal-mounted lead bird bath, a Swan at the end of the hornbeam walk and a pair of stone Owls guarding a little rustic shelter containing several pieces of sculpture among wheelbarrows and the other paraphernalia of gardening.

The route returns to the house through box-edged borders containing a mixture of choice shrubs and plants, particularly some of the large *Hydrangea* species, with magnolias, Mock Orange, *Osmanthus delavayi*, Willow Gentians and hellebores.

The Courts, Holt
The National Trust

At Holt, 4km (2½ miles) E of Bradford-on-Avon, S of A3053 Melksham road, 4.8km (3 miles) N of Trowbridge. For opening arrangements see HHCG and NT; usually Monday and Friday afternoons April-October. Twentieth-century garden of 2.8ha (7 acres) around historic seventeenth-century stone house. Sited in the vallage on moist and rich alkaline soil at 61m (200ft). Rainfall 787mm (31in.). One gardener.

The mellow stone house is so named because it is said to have been, until the eighteenth-century, the place where weavers brought their disputes for arbitration. It was only converted into a private house in early Victorian times. But there is no disputing the beauty of the garden which was made by the late Lady Cecilie Goff when she and Major Goff took over the house in 1920.

The 'bones' of the garden — the yew and box hedge, the topiary, the major paths and the garden buildings — are Edwardian, having been made by Sir George Hastings between 1900 and 1911 when he occupied the house. The fine old Deodar Cedar, which dominates the garden, and the stone statuary are also his contributions. On this canvas Lady Cecilie embroidered a garden of considerable beauty and interest, a garden in the Hidcote style and very much of the first half of this century. She combined an admiration of Gertrude Jekyll with a belief that a garden should be full of variety and surprise. This philosophy fitted well Sir George's legacy of hedged enclosures, a firm framework in which she could create an imaginative series of secret gardens and shaded walks.

The garden is entered where the east and most impressive facade of the house overlooks a plain rectangular lawn bordered by pleached limes on

Left: The Courts, Holt. One of the ornaments in the garden. *Iris Hardwick*

Below: The Courts, Holt. The house with its Edwardian loggia and the mighty Deodar that dominates the garden. *Iris Hardwick*

one side and topiary yews on the other, with high beeches and limes as background. The next in a series of garden 'rooms' is entered through an inviting 'doorway' formed under a picturesque multi-stemmed False Acacia by box and yew topiary, the paving here furnished with the contrasting textures of bergenias and *Cotoneaster horizontalis*.

The way leads through a little garden of roses on stone pillars, once perhaps linked by ropes, round a sculptured stone column. Next is the lily-crammed formal pool screened by masses of the purple Smoke Bush whose dusky foliage is echoed all around by *Rosa rubrifolia*, *Berberis* × *ottawensis* 'Purpurea' and the Purple Plum. By the pool are Day Lilies, lavender and pink phlox. Tall lime trees give shelter on the east side and the evergreens beneath provide background to bays of pink and red Floribunda roses separated by broad obelisks of clipped yew; their repetition gives rhythm and unity to the whole area. Towering over the roses, the Golden Rain Tree provides masses of its small yellow flowers and bladder-like fruits in summer and *Xanthoceras sorbifolium*, a rare Chinese tree, gives white flowers in spring.

Beyond the lily pool and past the flaking mahogany stem of *Acer griseum*, a clump of the massive-leaved *Gunnera manicata* confronts the visitor and the way becomes narrower and mysteriously overhung with shrubs. Here, suddenly revealed, is another pond, informal in shape and different in character. Its edges are so densely planted that the path has become an intriguing tunnel relieved only by glimpses of the water. On a little peninsula under a tall Swamp Cypress one can sit and admire a vast spreading Westfelton Yew nearby and a fine specimen of the unusual summer-flowering *Cornus macrophylla*, now a small tree, on the opposite bank.

Passing over a little bridge, the path suddenly emerges in front of a little stone summerhouse of classical design, its front focused on a straight grass walk towards the house. On either side are high mixed borders enclosed by Guelder Rose, Tamarisk and shrub roses with the Golden Variegated Dogwood and *Physocarpus opulifolius* 'Luteus' to give foliage colour throughout the season. The spiky crowns of *Yucca gloriosa* seen against a juniper provide a focal point in the distance.

At the end of the walk an inviting iron gate leads out into the arboretum which surrounds the hedged flower garden on its south and west sides. Formerly a meadow, this was planted by Miss Moyra Goff more than 25 years ago with a variety of trees — limes, Horse Chestnut, walnuts, Copper and Cut-leaved Beech, Turkey Oak and False Acacia — most of which have grown well in the rich, moist soil. An Indian Bean Tree and a Manna Ash are both flowering well.

The lawn near the house is dominated by a grand old Deodar Cedar with yew topiary in green and gold and a little box parterre round a stone urn to balance it. There are narrow paths along perimeter borders of fuchsias and hypericums and one bed has a pink and white mixture of 'Queen Elizabeth' roses and Japanese Anemones. The main vista from the house has as its focal point a finely-worked wrought-iron gate in a floral design set in the yew hedges that divide the garden proper from the arboretum. There is more to see west of the house beyond a raised terrace walk where the purple Teinturier Grape and Coignet's Vine have been trained to make a screen.

In contrast to the house lawn, that on the west side is entirely open and uncluttered, the towering form of a majestic Tulip Tree in the far corner balancing the bulk of the house convincingly. Sentinel Irish Yews with silver Cotton Lavenders at their feet guard the border nearest the house. On two sides there are deep concave niches; the one facing north is paved and the other here comes from bold splashes of the Golden Dogwood, *Cornus alba* 'Spaethii' and Weeping Silver Pears. Yellow is repeated in the borders with, among others, potentillas, Golden Rod and *Helianthus* 'Loddon Gold' to contrast with the prevailing blues and violets of *Aconitum, Echinops, Erigeron* and the herbaceous *Clematis integrifolia*.

Crinums grow well at The Courts, appearing time and again in the borders, but undoubtedly their best use is near Sir George Hastings' charming little classical conservatory. Here a box-edged border is given over to a mass of the deep pink *Crinum powellii* with clumps of the elegant *Nandina domestica*, the coppery red of its translucent young shoots shining against the dark background.

Here is a garden which for more than a lifetime has been formed and developed and then elaborated. It has all the tranquillity of old age, a softness and charm that comes from settled maturity. Today, while the vital structure of trees and hedges remains, we can enjoy its beauty, all the more precious because we know that all gardens are transient, continually being altered and born again.

Easton Grey House

Mr and Mrs Peter Saunders

At the village of Easton Grey, 5.6km (3½m) W of Malmesbury on B4040, 2.4hrs (1½ miles) from Westonbirt. Garden open in spring for NGS but in conjunction with Peter Saunders' Boutique the garden is also open daily, except Sundays in aid of the Church. 3.6ha (9 acre) informal garden surrounding Cotswold stone Queen Anne manor house sited above the south slope to the river valley of the Avon, at 91m (300ft) on well-drained heavy alkaline soil. Rainfall 864mm (34in.). Excellent illustrated booklet on sale, giving history of the house and garden. Garden staff of two full-time, and one part-time.

The best way to approach the house is from the village, through the wrought-iron gates of the drive and past the little Cotswold stone village Church with its Norman tower. The curving drive follows the contour through paddocks, with masses of daffodils on either side, giving a taste of views into the valley that can be enjoyed to the full from the house. Groups of shrubs including Guelder Rose, dogwoods and musk roses decorate the approach and in the paddocks are old limes and oaks and a Wellingtonia dating from late Victorian times, together with some young trees for the future.

Easton Grey is a deliciously mellow Queen Anne manor ingeniously sited so as to command superb views across and along an unspoilt valley of the Avon. Climbers on the walls soften the outline and a good legacy of Victorian trees gives shelter and relates the house to its surroundings; this is a perfect house in a perfect setting.

The drive sweeps to the east front around a circle of lawn and sundial past a venerable old False Acacia to the portico decorated with two splendid stone vases.

The main south front is set above dignified nineteenth-century terraces with Cotswold stone dry walls and stone-edged beds all of which have been recently replanted with roses and dwarf *Artemisia* by Mr Saunders. The central stone steps lead to a sundial set in a star-like pattern of paving and on to the park and river below.

A paved area on the west of the house is sheltered by a projecting loggia on the north side which houses outdoor sitting and dining rooms. On the house are vines, enormous wisterias stretching right round to the south side and a fine *Akebia quinata* filling the air in spring with a subtle fragrance from its pendant purple flowers. By the paving, beds are filled with an effective mixture of purple and silver foliage: rue, Cotton Lavender, *Senecio* 'Sunshine' and the white flowers of 'Iceberg' roses.

The informal west garden flows apparently endlessly on into the pasture beyond, separated only by a ha-ha from the valley. The prospect in any direction, either back towards the village or west along the Avon valley, is all beauty and tranquillity. In spring there are masses of daffodils in named varieties naturalized in the grass among the informal groups of shrubs, conifers, maples of many kinds and a well-planted pool. A feature of the garden is the juxtaposition of old and new, arranged to be in scale and in sympathy with each other. Here is a striking modern sculpture set against the sky and equally well sited old stone vases.

The kitchen garden now houses a tennis-court and a swimming-pool as well as vegatables, all set within the firm framework of the old walls, and a striking central vista of twin herbaceous borders from the Queen Anne gates to a classic portico containing a fine eighteenth-century statue. Outside the walled garden is the Long Walk once trodden by Lord Asquith and his cabinet colleagues. Here the surrounding trees — *Parrotia persica*, cedar, walnuts, False Acacia, limes and Horse Chestnuts — are appropriately mature and a little stone bridge surrounded by a rock garden with ferns and periwinkle leads back to the house.

Farleigh Hungerford Gardens

Two gardens open for NGS in late spring. 5.6km (3½ miles) W of Trowbridge. CASTLE HOUSE *is a cottage garden made since 1966 beside a mill-stream.* ROWLEY GRANGE *has 2ha (5 acres) of terraces with herbaceous borders along the River Frome.*

The Grange

Colonel and Mrs J.S. Douglas

Open for NGS in early summer. At Edington, 6.4km (4 miles) E of Westbury. 0.3ha (¾ acre) garden with varied shrubs mostly planted since 1972 around an eighteenth-century house.

The Grange

Major and Mrs A.M. Everett

Open for NGS in early summer. At Enford, 9.6km (6 miles) S of Pewsey. Garden on River Avon surrounding Queen Anne farmhouse; ornamental pool; trout stream; walled gardens; shrubs and water-loving plants; large conservatory, climbing plants and shrubs.

The Hall

A.E. Moulton Esq.

Open for NGS in summer. In Bradford-on-Avon. Large garden by River Avon with lawns and fine trees, herbaceous and rose borders; acoustic baffle fence. Fine Jacobean house, part open.

Hannington Hall

Mr and Mrs A.F. Hussey-Freke

Open for NGS in summer. At Hannington, 8km (5 miles) N of Swindon. 1.2ha (3 acre) garden, largely lawns and trees. Very interesting 1653 house, part open.

Heale House

Major and Mrs David Rasch

On NE side of Woodford village, 5.6km (3½ miles) NW of Salisbury; on A345 Amesbury road turn at High Post Filling Station. Garden of 3.2ha (8 acres) around sixteenth-century brick house with stone quoins, with late nineteenth-century wing by Detmar Blow. For opening arrangements see HHCG; also open for NGS and GS. Deep alluvial soil, containing chalk, with a high water-table, in the Avon valley, at 61m (200ft). Rainfall 762mm (30in.). Maintained by the owners who are keen gardeners, plus one gardener full-time and extra help for mowing.

At Heale House there is an atmosphere of tranquillity that comes partly perhaps from the mellowed brick and weathered stone but mainly from the sheltered seclusion and maturity of the garden. This unmatched aura of relaxed calm would not be the same but for the river winding its way lazily through a flood plain on the eastern boundary, its shallow valley seemingly missed by the modern world.

The garden is Edwardian, made by the great-uncle of the present owners after he bought the house in 1890, and like most of its kind it has had to be adapted to the entirely different circumstances of the present day. Although its area has been reduced by about one third, the transition has been a success, the garden being well maintained with a quarter of the labour needed in 1910.

All around, elm disease has taken its toll but an avenue of poplars makes an impressive approach and a pattern of yew topiary flanking the gates forms a boundary to the garden on the west front. Here the ground rises away from the house. The lower terrace level near the house includes two stone lily ponds and is enclosed by a balustraded retaining wall. In front of this is an attractive border with roses 'Spek's Yellow' and 'Rambling Rector', clematis and honeysuckle on tripods 2.7m (9ft) high, delphiniums, irises, paeonies and purple cotinus. Shallow steps lead up to a very wide path now a laburnum avenue the paving full of yellow stonecrop. This passes through a lawn bordered by yews to a terrace walk at the far western end. Here are stone seats in sheltered corners at either end and mature shrub borders containing some effective associations of shrub roses, especially the Rugosas, 'Nevada' and 'Fantin-Latour', with *Viburnum plicatum* 'Mariesii', Weeping Silver Pear and Golden Mock Orange. The giant seakale, *Crambe cordifolia* is well placed near the purple forms of *Cotinus coggygria* and Myrobalan Plum.

South of the house the garden is on two levels, the higher part consisting of a square lawn before the house setting off a fine tree group composed of a Copper Beech and some old Horse Chestnuts. The angle of the house encloses a wide terrace of paving in which grow spurges, rues, and foaming masses of greeny-gold *Alchemilla mollis*, overlooked by a large *Magnolia grandiflora* beside the high pedimented door and some superb climbing roses on the house including 'Paul Lêde' and 'Kathleen Harrop'. Balustraded steps lead down to the river on the east side and a formal walk continues beside the river below a lavender hedge bordering the lawn. South of this great lawn steps descend to the second level through a border of primarily Hybrid Musk roses with more purple cotinus, another Weeping Silver Pear, variegated weigela, standard wisteria and *Rosa rubrifolia*. The lawn shelves down gently to the river, a tributary of the Avon, which winds around to enclose the garden on this side too.

Following the direction of the river the way leads through a gateway in a tile-topped wall covered with 'Mermaid' and 'Mme Grégoire Staechelin' roses and honeysuckle into an orchard garden with a sundial and dominated by a splendid old mulberry. In a suitably sunny place near the stables a comparatively recent group of mainly white-flowering shrubs and silver foliage has been assembled.

Japanese gardens were a short-lived Edwardian fashion and at the time every ambitious country house garden owner had to have one. This one, sited in a bend in the river, must have been one of the most successful with its pretty thatched teahouse set over the river and its red lacquered bridge, all made with the help of four Japanese gardeners in 1901. Although much of the original planting and many of the stones have been removed in the interest of economy, the character remains. In the damp ground thrive superb groups of Shuttlecock Ferns with the bold leaves of Bog Arums and *Rodgersia aesculifolia*. Even they are hardly a match for the enormous *Gunnera manicata* on the island and the giant Cartwheel Plant, *Heracleum mantegazzianum*. Candelabra primulas and bog irises provide colour, together with a large *Magnolia × soulangiana*. Several other choice trees are here including a fine *Cercidiphyllum japonicum* and a young Tulip Tree.

So many traditional, walled kitchen gardens have gone that it is a great pleasure to find one which has been retained and adapted so well for pleasure and beauty. On a south slope it is open on the sunny side except

for a pergola and enclosed on the other three sides by more tile-topped walls covered with climbing roses and clematis. Facing south is *Abutilon vitifolium* and a fine old fig. The plots of vegetables and nursery plants are divided by paths, wide tunnels formed by espalier apples and pears, and pergolas richly hung with vines and roses. In the centre is a little lily pond. It is all very relaxed and the epitome of the English country house garden.

Henford House Herb Garden
Commander and Mrs V.J. Robinson

Open for GS in early summer. At Henford's Marsh, 1.6km (1 mile) S of Warminster. Large herb garden set in lawns; rhododendrons, roses, etc. Plants for sale.

Hillbarn House
Mr and Mrs A.J. Buchanan

At Great Bedwyn, on N side of main village street. S of A4 Hungerford to Marlborough road. Mainly formal terraced garden of 0.8ha (2 acres) behind converted village house and cottage. Garden only open for NGS and GS in early summer. Light gravelly soil over chalk facing south-west at 122m (400ft). Rainfall 762mm (30in.). Owners plus one full-time gardener and a part-time pensioner.

It is unusual to come across a garden where successive owners, while making their own contribution, have so faithfully respected the tradition of their predecessors. The result is a tribute to their understanding, and here provides the abiding satisfaction of unified design as well as the interest and beauty of flowers and plants. It is immaculately maintained and despite its modest size there is a good deal to see. Indeed this garden is an object lesson as to what can be successfully fitted in, given a firm framework of unavoidably labour-intensive clipped trees.

When the Earl of Wilton converted the dilapidated house and adjacent cottage in the village street in the 1950s, the garden was in two parts, the larger area shelving up steeply behind the house and the other part, connected by steps, running parallel with the road. The garden entrance is through Virginia Creeper to this second area where a sunny terrace of cobbles and paving faces south-east. The terrace is decorated with clipped bays and tubs of Agapanthus looking well against mounds of *Senecio* 'Sunshine'. It overlooks a simple formal lawn with limes pleached above the roadside wall under which pink and white roses and foxgloves and, later on, Japanese Anemones show up well. On the other side, taking up the sharp change of level, is a raised border furnished with hebes, senecios, hollies, *Viburnum davidii* and other evergreens, but the main feature is an enormous white rose, possibly 'Kiftsgate', growing through an old pear tree.

The steps lead up almost to roof level behind the house past fragrant 'Blanc Double de Coubert' roses and 'Alberic Barbier', growing well in the shade. A fine Weeping Silver Pear leads to a large croquet lawn fringed with old fruit trees. At the far end two old yews give an atmosphere of permanence and of mystery by disguising the boundary. In the borders bold foliage shapes of *Bergenia, Euonymus* 'Silver Queen' and *Mahonia* have been used to complement summer-flowering shrub roses and *Kolkwitzia amabilis*.

Against the boundary the Earl of Wilton made a trim parterre garden of gravel and clipped box centred on an attractive little pavilion of white weather-boarding with a steep shingled roof. In the parterre the present owners, who came in 1971, have planted hybrid musk roses on one side and paeonies edged with silver Cotton Lavender on the other.

The former L-shaped garden was extended into a rectangle when Lord and Lady Bruntisfield bought the house and an adjoining cottage and plot in 1962. This allowed the construction of tennis-courts and a potager at the top and a swimming-pool below a steep terrace wall. Forming a spine between the two is a hornbeam tunnel, a highly successful device with 'windows' to give views down to the pool, where visitors can take a dip for a few pence extra.

On the other side of the tunnel is a meticulously designed and main- tained formal fruit and vegetable garden arranged around a central lawn. Clipped hedges provide background and shelter and neat espalier pears have been trained as arches over the smart board-edged path on one side, where there is also a seat arbour and a border of roses and ground covers spilling onto the path. Even better manicured is the ingenious chequer- board pattern of herbs with standard roses standing like chessmen, made by the Buchanans. The border this side makes a welcome contrast, being informally planted with a beautiful mixture of shrub and bush roses, geraniums, stonecrops, catmint, delphiniums and wormwood. These distinctive colours of silver, pink, light blue and mauve with shrub roses betray the skills of Mr Lanning Roper, whose influence is clear in the garden.

The path leads to a nut walk underplanted with hellebores near the tennis-courts. Beside the tennis-courts is a flower border and a walk screened from the potager by a yew hedge, while a brilliantly original hornbeam hedge on stilts, cut in a series of arches, hides the netting and gives a pattern to the border.

Hungerdown House

Mr and Mrs Egbert Barnes

---

*At Seagry, north of the A420 Chippenham to Swindon road, turning at Sutton Benger church.
Part formal terraced garden by Percy Cane and part informal plantsman's garden of 1.6ha (4
acres) around brick Georgian-style house of 1914. Garden open for NGS, usually in April and
October. Light alkaline alluvial soil on gentle south slope above the upper Avon valley, at 91m
(300ft). Rainfall 813mm (32in.). Mr Egbert Barnes and one gardener.*

Although the great eighteenth-century landscapes were designed by now
famous landscape gardeners they could not have been realized but for enlightened landowners who pursued the same ideal consistently and with
understanding. So it is in this century. Often the best gardens are made by
the combined talents of inspired designer and expert client. It is no
accident that the garden at Hungerdown is one of Percy Cane's finest, for
he and Mr and Mrs Egbert Barnes were in complete sympathy and
became firm friends. The house too fits the scene perfectly, a unity rarely
seen in gardens of the period. Only the M4 motorway in the valley mars
the scene with its dominant scale and noise.

From the road to the north the house is approached through scattered
orchard trees covered with vigorous climbing roses. In the grass drifts of
the choicer *Crocus* and *Narcissus* cultivars appear in spring. Several good
hollies and various conifers furnish a winter background and groups of
strong-growing shrub roses like 'Cerise Bouquet' give summer colour.
The way leads east around the house past birches contrasted against a
splendid group of Scots Pines and past the scented *Ptelea trifoliata* to the
young arboretum begun in 1962. Here a great variety of trees are already
beginning to mature around undulating glades of rough-cut grass.
Autumn colour is the main theme with *Cercidiphyllum japonicum*,
Liquadambar styraciflua, *Parrotia persica*, *Crataegus prunifolia* and many
species of *Sorbus* and *Acer*. But there is colour and interest at other times
from Incense Cedars, Western Arbor-Vitae, willows, alders and cherries,
with Pampas Grass, New Zealand Flax and *Gunnera manicata* to give
variety of form in the foreground.

The flower garden lies south and west of the house and incorporates all
the principles that Percy Cane held dear: a firm podium for the house;
formal terraces both linked with and contrasted with informal areas;
simple areas of mown lawn and paving set against dense and complex
planting; changes of level by characteristically generous steps, and a pool

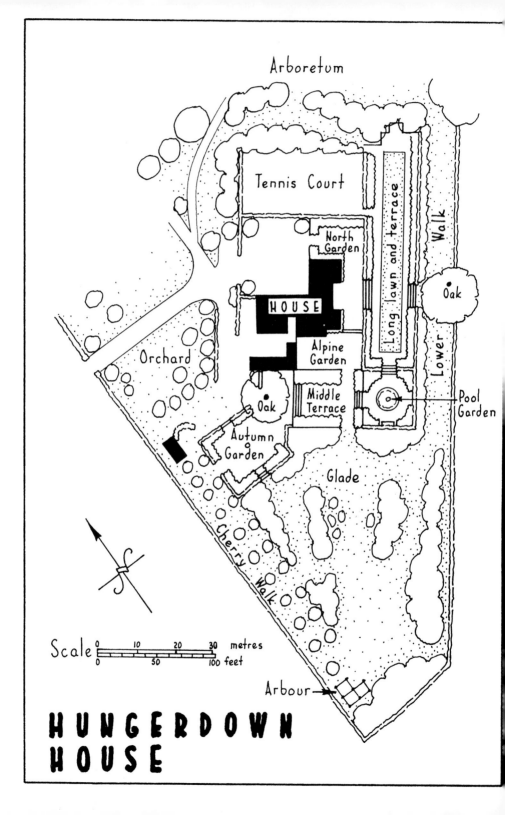

Arboretum

Tennis Court

North
Garden

HOUSE

Long lawn and terrace

Oak

Walk

Lower

Orchard

Alpine
Garden

Oak

Middle
Terrace

Pool
Garden

Autumn
Garden

Glade

Cherry Walk

Scale

| 0 | 10 | 20 | 30 | metres |
| 0 | 50 | | 100 | feet |

Arbour →

HUNGERDOWN
HOUSE

and fountain set in finely detailed paving to give light and movement. Above all, a strong respect for the site is evident and the need to relate the enormous variety of plants used to the overall design has been achieved.

The house terrace is simple with *Dorycnium hirsutum* seeding itself in the paving, sun-loving *Cistus* spp. by the house and two giant vines on the walls, *Vitis vinifera* 'Purpurea' and 'Brant', superb in their autumn finery. At the east end is a yew-hedge sheltered garden of fragrance and good foliage including *Sarcococca* spp., *Viburnum* × *bodnantense* and *Choisya ternata* with thymes in the paving, white at the sunnier western end a fascinating series of raised beds, tended by Mrs Egbert Barnes from her wheelchair, contains a variety of dwarf sun-loving plants with *Daphne cneorum, Convolvulus mauritanicus* and silver plants prominent.

The Long Terrace is reached by broad steps through which, uniquely, *Verbena bonariensis* is allowed to spring. The unbroken ribbon of grass is edged with paving so that the generous mixed borders can spill over the edge. Here is a vast array of plants carefully schemed for colour and given unity by the repeated use of the Mount Etna Broom, *Genista aetnensis*, and given character by a preponderance of grassy-leaved subjects including *Miscanthus saccharifolius*. Two biennials, the Scotch Thistle, *Onopordon acanthium,* and the mullein, *Verbascum bombyciferum,* provide accents of silver. Further steps extend the main axis down to a grass walk overlooking the meadows beyond but the eye is drawn westwards to a glimpse of water.

The sunken Pool Garden acts as cornerstone to the whole design by finishing the main east/west terrace and beginning a new north/south vista up successive flights of steps to incorporate a magnificent oak tree with complete success. The circular lily pool has a plain, paved surround to reflect its shape and the bold leaves of *Vitis coignetiae* make a splendid contrast, sprawling against the steps and paving, — here is a touch of genius. Again, two large *Genista aetnensis* dominate and the foliage of tree paeonies, ceanothuses, the graceful *Dierama pulcherrima* and *Aralia elata* contrast well against the clipped yew 'beehives' and the background hedges.

The way leads up through the Middle Terrace, a broad square of lawn edged with roses where a collection of quinces also grow. Then up again to the great oak which forms a huge canopy over a glade of plain lawn. At each point in the garden a new goal beckons and here it is an octagonal well-head a little way off with herbaceous borders forming a square around it. The next vista leads down a walk of flowering cherries, screened from the road by a hedge of Laurustinus, to the far western corner of the garden. Here a pergola-style arbour of highly original design has been built to incorporate a tree as well as the yew hedges behind.

A charming glade leads back to the house between carefully balanced

groups of birches and a fine Weeping Silver Pear is a telling feature near
the house. Either side of the glade are broad groups of shrubs traversed by
winding paths where one can wander for a long time admiring the rich
variety, of particularly *Mahonia, Elaeagnus, Choisya, Viburnum, Cornus,
Cistus, Cytisus, Juniperus, Abutilon, Abelia, Berberis* and *Magnolia*, and an
almost equally wide range of underplanting including *Hemerocallis,
Geranium, Brunnera,* and *Tiarella* with bulbs between.

Here is an ideal garden to visit. The design is disciplined yet full of
personal touches; it is crammed with good plants but arranged with
discrimination.

Iford Manor

Mrs J. Cartwright Hignett

*4km (2½ miles) SW of Bradford-on-Avon, through Westwood village, entrance only through
gates near Iford Bridge. Terraced and woodland garden of 1ha (2½ acres) made by Harold Peto,
above a beautiful old house with an early eighteenth-century front behind which the county
boundary of Somerset and Wiltshire passes. Garden only open for NGS, GS and occasionally
for local charities in spring. Well-drained alkaline soil over limestone on a steep SSW slope at
30-46m (100-150 ft), overlooking the Avon valley and the ancient bridge crossing the river.
Rainfall 787mm (31in.). Owner and two gardeners. Booklet-guide available gives an excellent
account of architectural features and statuary.*

An architect by profession, Harold A. Peto believed that for the highest
development of beauty a garden must be a combination of artifacts and
plants, the hard and the soft in juxtaposition. He was particularly
influenced by Italian gardens and his finest work was on steep slopes
where he could exploit the dramatic changes of level with steps, terraces
and planting in the Italianate manner. Although his aim was for a combination of stone and plants in just proportion, he filled his gardens with
old buildings and fragments of masonry almost to the point of excess. But
Harold Peto was undoubtedly one of the great garden designers of
Edwardian times and his own garden at Iford Manor is probably his
masterpiece. He had a distinctive style which has stood the test of time and
a remarkable capacity for creating a developing series of spaces and views
linked by a strong architectural framework. He was the master of mood
and his gardens always provide a satisfactory progression of experiences:
contrasts of scale, texture and perspective; shady corner to open terrace;
tall cypresses to accentuate the view, and smooth unyielding stonework
set against soft foliage.

Left: Hillbarn House. The problem of fitting the tennis courts into the garden scene has been ingeniously solved by the pattern of the raised hornbeam hedge and the generous mixed border in front.
Country Life

Below: Iford Manor. The round pool below the terrace walk.
Jonathan M. Gibson

The house stands only just above the river looking out across it and the medieval bridge on which stands Mr Peto's statue of Britannia. A narrow forecourt with a gnarled old wisteria, climbing roses, ceanothus and a myrtle leads east through a wrought-iron gate to a small terrace and D-shaped goldfish pool with a lion-mask fountain and statue of a river god, overlooked by the loggia. The way leads up via an impressively steep staircase with lead urns, statues on pillars, columnar cypresses and the black shade of a large yew all contributing to the Italianate impression. Between each flight of steps is a small terrace of different design, the first with 'Iceberg' roses, *Acanthus mollis* and a large Pfitzer Juniper. The second terrace relates to an orangery in the house and has a cool arrangement of silver foliage with rue and lavender, and the white and green flowers of rose 'Blanc Double de Coubert' and *Itea illicifolia*; alongside is the rock garden where one of the many springs has been tamed into rills and pools surrounded by Mountain Pines and Junipers.

A long flight of steps leads up between marble lions to an open grass terrace and the big oval lily pool and fountain furnished by wisteria and the distinguished dark shape of *Phillyrea latifolia*. The steps divide around the pond up to the main terrace but the axial staircase continues right into the woods above to a column dedicated to King Edward VII.

The main terrace is an architectural and scenic triumph with horticulture playing an important but inevitably subordinate role. Enclosed by columns, it consists of a gravel promenade edged with paving which once covered the whole path. The walk leads from a charming octagonal eighteenth-century garden house at the east end to an open view of the sky framed by columns above a semicircular seat and a well-head at the other. The favourite Italian Cypresses, phillyreas, junipers, box and yew are repeated to add dramatic deep shadows and contrasts of form to the distant views. Each step of the way is a new architectural revelation. At the west end are the Blue Pond and a Spanish kind of loggia overlooking more wisteria and big beds of *Acanthus*, the giant *Euphorbia veneta*, brooms, lavenders and roses. Borders with purple berberis, purple cotinus, potentillas, Jerusalem Sage and shrub roses are underplanted with geraniums, *Alchemilla mollis, Iberis sempervirens* and irises, and bulbs create interludes between stone sarcophagi, terracotta oil jars, statuary and marble seats.

From the eastern end of the terrace a path leads past giant chestnuts and underneath a delightful flowery mead of naturalized bulbs including Martagon Lilies, Bluebells, *Anemone appennina* and *Narcissus* 'Actaea'. This path leads to The Cloisters, an Italian Romanesque building designed by Mr Peto to make use of the remainder of the ancient fragments he had collected in Italy. Apart from its architectural and antiquarian interest the atrium makes an admirable interlude in a tour of the garden and provides superb views both out over the valley from the little balcony and back toward the house.

The walk beyond winds through green, ivy-carpeted woods where masses of snowdrops, garlic-scented Ransomes and Martagon Lilies are naturalized with groups of Stinking Gladwyn, Butcher's Broom and Lesser Periwinkle.

For the energetic who climb to the top the reward is a breezy walk with fine diagonal views down to the house amid giant beeches (full of rooks), yews and box. The walk eventually returns to the terraces by way of the remains of a little Japanese garden containing bamboos, tree paeonies, cherries and the hardy palm *Trachycarpus excelsus.*

Job's Mill

The Marquess and Marchioness of Bath

Open for NG   in late spring. At Crockerton, 2.4km (1½ miles) S of Warminster. Medium sized with small terraced garden through which the River Wylye flows; swimming-pool and kitchen garden.

Keevil Gardens

Three gardens for NGS late in spring. 6.4km (4 miles) E of Trowbridge. Fine trees, some unusual plants and a kitchen garden are the attractions.

Kellaways

Mrs D. Hoskins

4.8km (3 miles) NE of Chippenham, E of A420 between M4 exit 17 and Chippenham, on road to East Tytherton. Open for NGS and GS during summer and by appointment. Cottage garden of about 0.4ha (1 acre), partly walled, around beautiful early-seventeenth-century Cotswold stone farmhouse. In open flat country near River Avon, at 46m (150ft). Well-worked alkaline alluvial soil. Rainfall 813mm (32in.). Maintained by the owner with a little part-time help.

Planting in the English cottage garden style makes it possible to accom-

modate infinite variety and year-round beauty in the smallest space.
Unless great care is taken it can also create infinite work of the most
meticulous kind. To minimize work, forethought and constant adjustment
are necessary but the trick is to make it all appear artless and unforced. At
Kellaways, Mrs Hoskins can demonstrate her success not only in the
charm of her garden but also in the fact that she maintains it almost
entirely alone. The influence of Graham Thomas's writings is evident in
the intelligent and imaginative use that has been made of ground cover
plants among the old shrub roses that clearly are Mrs Hoskins's great love.

Although there are many lessons to be learned at other times of the
year, the best time to visit is in June when the roses are beginning. The
approach along the drive is past clumps of Martagon Lilies and the farm
buildings are screened by a mass of flowering shrubs and trees, magnolias,
lilacs, *Kolkwitzia amabilis* and Judas Tree. White doves and wandering
whippets give a homely touch near the house where honeysuckles and
clematises grow on the warm stone walls.

The main flower garden is west of the house where a walled garden and
an adjacent former vegetable plot have been intensively planted to great
effect. The walled garden is the largest and apart from a central area of
lawn with a statue of Mercury no opportunity for planting has been lost.
Near the house a stone-paved terrace is too richly strewn with thymes,
aubrietias, periwinkles, wild strawberries and even Japanese Anemones for
walking. Perimeter-wall borders are crammed with good things, the
south-facing side having summer-flowering sun-lovers like *Carpentaria
californica*, the unusual *Indigofera pseudotinctoria* and Sun Roses as well as
roses and clematises festooning the wall.

At the far end is a big *Hoheria* and a border of old roses including 'Rose
de Meaux' and 'Belle de Crécy' with Flag Irises and species and varieties of
Ceanothus, Clematis, Syringa and *Akebia quinata* against the east-facing wall.
The remaining border is given over to an enthralling collection of
herbaceous plants. As well as old-fashioned favourites like Oriental
Poppies, Lamb's Ears and *Lychnis chalcedonica*, Mrs Hoskins has wisely
chosen plants that both look well in foliage and in flower, like *Ligularia*
'Desdemona', Giant Oat Grass, Plume Poppy and that treasure from
Japan, *Kirengeshoma palmata*.

Only a low wall, smothered in Variegated Honeysuckle and the dark
blue *Clematis* × *durandii*, separates a large area given over principally to old
shrub roses. Here is the collection of an enthusiast, growing with the
vigour and profusion that is essential if they are to look their best. One
area has the pick of the rugosas with R. *alba* 'Maxima', 'Schneezwerg' and
'Fantin-Latour' looking lovely with herbs like angelica and rosemary. A
long walk leads through moss roses where the unusual *Mitella breweri* is
ground cover and past 'Koenigen von Danemarck' to a sunny corner near

a little greenhouse and a mulberry where there is a refreshing view into the meadow beyond a gate. Here there are some more modern shrub roses like 'Gold Wings' and 'Aloha' as well as 'Penelope' and *R. alba* 'Celeste' with potentillas and epimediums. Near the vegetable garden is a particularly successful association of the purple-leaved crab, *Malus* 'Lemoinei' with the silvers of *Senecio* 'Sunshine' and *Stachys lanata* and roses 'Alan Blanchard' and 'William Lobb'.

Throughout the whole area weed-smothering ground cover plants are employed with understanding and discretion and further south the garden develops into a comprehensive demonstration of how effective they can be. An unpromising area under boundary sycamores has been made a positive asset to the garden using the full range of foliage texture and colour in broad masses under the trees. Here are Plantain and Day Lilies; all kinds of *Geranium* including the rampant *G. collina* and the paragon of all ground covers, *G. macrorrhizum*; the evergreen *Euphorbia robbiae* near *Stephanandra incisa* 'Crispa', and the glaucous *Helictotrichon candidum* and Bowles' Golden Grass. Indeed this garden is almost the A-Z of ground cover plants and a compelling demonstration of their value.

However much you enjoy the garden, do leave time to go into the house for tea with delicious home-made cakes and scones containing butter from the milk of Mrs Hoskins' Jersey cow. Like the garden, the tea would be a bargain at twice the price.

Kewleys

See Ramsbury Gardens

Lackham College of Agriculture
Wiltshire County Council

Open for NGS in summer and GS in spring and autumn. At Lacock, 6.4km (4 miles) S of Chippenham.

The long drive from the A350 road has been planted with a variety of unusual trees to make a linear arboretum in an area denuded of the once dominant elms by Dutch Elm Disease. The Georgian house is used as the administrative offices without being spoilt. Set above terraces it faces south with fields towards Lacock village and the Wiltshire Downs. Around the house are fine trees: beeches, limes, Atlas Cedars, oaks, limes and Corsican Pines for shelter. The well-proportioned terraces with pool, steps and balustrade are appropriately and tastefully planted with a wide range of interesting shrubs and climbers, all labelled. An attractive little garden at the east end has paving and lavender around a fine stone sundial. The student accommodation has been fitted in decently to one side of the old house with lawns and shrubs around. Further east is the large, walled garden with greenhouses of tomatoes, carnations, pot plants, warm-greenhouse plants, propagation, fuchsias and begonias. Neat grass paths separate plots containing a variety of interesting shrubs, vegetables of all kinds, herbaceous plants and fruit, all accurately labelled. The pleasure-gardens have the whole range of mixed borders, herbs, shrubs and lawns and in the woods there is an ancient hornbeam walk which may be unique in the Kingdom. The famous Lackham museum of old agricultural machinery is another attraction. A visit to Lackham makes a fascinating outing for the keen gardener.

Lacock Abbey
The National Trust

In Lacock village, 4.8km (3 miles) N of Melksham and 4.8km (3 miles) S of Chippenham, E of A350 road. Garden and grounds of 3.2ha (8 acres) around thirteenth-century abbey converted into a house also open in 1540 with eighteenth-century façade. For opening arrangements see HHCG and NT. Light, alkaline alluvial soil with high water-table; views to River Avon in the park; situated at 30m (100ft). Rainfall 813mm (32in.). One gardener.

Apart from his inventiveness in the realm of photography William Henry Fox Talbot was also a keen gardener. His photographic work is now amply commemorated in the Museum that bears his name, housed in a splendid old barn just outside the gates of his home, Lacock Abbey. If you go inside the gates you will see a glorious view of the house and some of the trees that he knew and planted.

William Fox Talbot kept a garden diary concerned mostly with ephemeral plants long since gone. It seems highly likely, however, that some of the fine trees in the grounds were planted by him, especially a Tulip Tree and a superb Black Walnut, *Juglans nigra*, which grow just behind the Museum and can be seen over the wall on the left of the drive. A number of trees do exceptionally well at Lacock, presumably because of the fertile open soil and the endless supplies of water available not far below the surface. The moisture-loving Black Walnut, Swamp Cypress, London Plane, Horse Chestnut and the Wing Nut, *Pterocarya fraxinifolia*, enjoy these conditions and the last-mentioned has made a vast suckering clump. There are several smaller trees including the Nettle Tree, *Celtis australis*, in the orchard and an old Judas Tree on the south wall of the house.

The drive provides a pleasant walk to the house past groups of shrubs with the park to the right seeming to ebb and flow into the garden across the recently restored ha-ha. Around the house and the courtyard are many an attractive shrub and several climbers including a tall Banksian Rose near the first-ever photographed oriel window.

The main floral pleasure at Lacock comes in very early spring when masses of snowdrops and Winter Aconites are followed by many thousands of the wild type of *Crocus vernus*, in every shade of purple through to white, naturalized in all the wilder grassy areas along the drive and in the woodland walk to the river and cascade.

Lake House
Captain O.N. Bailey, RN

Open for G S in spring and NGS in summer. At Lake, 11.2km (7 miles) N of Salisbury. Large, mainly informal grounds; rose, herbaceous and woodland gardens; water; old yew hedges, pleached lime alley; peacocks. Jacobean house (not shown).

Little Cheverall House
Joyce, Lady Crossley

Open for NGS in summer. S of Devizes, 0.8km (½ mile) W of West Lavington. Medium-sized old garden with mixed borders, unusual shrubs and plants and a rock garden.

Littlecote
D.S. Wills Esq.

Near Chilton Foliat, 4.8km (3 miles) W of Hungerford, S of A419 and N of A4, turning off at Froxfield. For opening arrangements see HHCG Formal garden of 2.4ha (6 acres) within the original walled enclosures around historic Tudor mansion (also open). Situated overlooking the shallow river valley of the Kennet at 122m (400ft) an open chalky soil with flints. Rainfall 838mm (33in.). Two gardeners.

The great Wiltshire manor houses seem often to be associated with rivers and Littlecote, one of the oldest, is no exception, being situated so close as to enable a trout stream from the Kennet to be diverted through the walled garden. Between the Lambourn Downs and Savernake Forest, the estate is situated in gently rolling, wooded countryside with fine old oaks in the valleys and beech clumps on the hills. A first view of the house across the water meadows from the Swindon road is tempting but the river has to be crossed by the picturesque bridge at Chilton Foliat downstream, an attractive diversion through entirely unspoilt country.

The approach down the well-mown verges of an avenue of healthy young limes, *Tilia* × *euchlora*, gives a good impression and indeed the upkeep of the whole place is creditable by any standard.

The garden lies mainly north of the house in walled enclosures typical of the sixteenth-century, extending the lines of the house. Some parts have been converted for other uses but the largest, an L-shaped piece adjoining the north front, is still gardened. The grass terrace gives a long axial view over lawns and a pond, through a gate in the bottom wall and across the river valley. In the lawns on one side is a Handkerchief Tree and on the other three magnolias. The walls, splendidly built in flint and capped with tiles, support masses of old rambler roses with a cheerful kaleidoscope of bedding plants at their feet.

Most of the flower-growing is at the bottom of the slope where large beds in the grass flank a central pool and contain a brilliant display of bedding plants: dahlias, alyssum, lobelia and silver *Cineraria maritima*. In the corner is a charming gazebo placed so that it could overlook the countryside, the kitchen garden and the flower garden, with its remarkable trout stream. This swiftly-flowing formal canal cannot be seen from the house terrace and comes as a delightful surprise with the sound of water from a series of shallow cascades. It forms a unique foreground to a long herbaceous border, an unsophisticated mixture of colour, facing south and interrupted only by splendid gates surmounted by finials of lion and unicorn.

There is more colour and another pond around the corner but unfortunately one cannot complete the logical circuit to the house this way because an exhibition area intervenes.

Little Durnford Manor
The Earl and Countess of Chichester

Open for GS in late spring. 4.8km (3 miles) N of Salisbury. Lawns with Lebanon Cedars, lake with water lilies; walled garden with flowering trees, small rockery and waterfall. Stone and flint house of 1725 (not open).

Longleat
The Marquess of Bath

6.4km (4 miles) SW of Warminster, 7.2km (4½ miles) SE of Frome, on A362 Bath-Salisbury road. For opening arrangements see HHCG ; normally daily, except Christmas Day. Park of 280ha (700 acres) by L. Brown and H. Repton and formal garden of 2.4ha (6 acres) around great Elizabethan house of 1568-80. Situated at 91-122m (300-400ft) on well-drained, lime-free greensand soil. Rainfall 964mm (38in.). Six men employed: three in the formal garden and three in the park. Guidebooks available.

Although the popular image of Longleat is an exotic one of lions and big game it is in fact one of the most English of our great parks. So thoroughly did Lancelot 'Capability' Brown do his job that nothing remains of the elaborate French and Dutch-inspired formal layout of the early eighteenth century.

When Sir John Thynne built the magnificent Renaissance style house between 1566 and 1580 on the site of a priory he provided it with a garden as comprehensive as could be wished for at that time and took care to supervise the work himself. There are letters in the Red Library from Sir John, written while he was campaigning in France, to his Land Steward, John Dodd, demanding that the garden should not be level but 'sumwhat falling towardes the waterside wherby it wol always be the drier' and telling Dodd to water his cherry and peach stones well and to 'suffer no grasse to grow about theym'. In this and other matters he showed a sound grasp of the principles of horticulture and, although impatient for results, he was diligent in cultivation. The design of this first garden was in the pattern of Montacute and other great Elizabethan houses, typically enclosed and related to the main lines of the house, with a forecourt, walled garden to the east and stable block to the west. The layout, shown in a painting of 1675 by Jan Siberechts in the house, indicates in its simplicity that the gardening interest of Sir John was not shared by his immediate successors.

The next phase of gardening at Longleat began in 1682 with the succession of Thomas Thynne, who was soon created Viscount Weymouth. He was a passionate and committed gardener and under his direction was created one of the most impressive and elaborate formal gardens ever made in these islands. It cost more than £30,000 — a vast sum in those days. He employed George London and Henry Wise of the famous Brompton Nurseries (on the site where the Victoria and Albert Museum now stands) to design and plant a rigorously symmetrical scheme of no less than 28ha (70 acres) mostly east of the house, straddling the valley and extending up to the hillside beyond.

The garden was French in its grandeur but more Dutch in its emphasis on the horticultural detail of fruit trees and bushes, flowers and clipped evergreens. It had straight axial vistas but not on the scale of André Le Nôtre. One was from the house to a *patte d'oie* and formal 'wilderness' among trees on the hillside across the valley. The other, at right angles, was formed from the stream at the bottom of the valley now converted into a regular canal with a central fountain. The huge, walled rectangle was also divided, in a way reminiscent of Villandry, into smaller enclosures and plots each intensively planted. The 'bird's eye' view by Leonard Knyff of circa 1700 shows an enormous complex layout but it was largely self-contained and not, like Versailles, the prelude to limitless vistas stretching to the horizon and beyond.

After Lord Weymouth's death these great formal gardens declined through neglect until the third Lord Weymouth succeeded in 1751 when he found not only a decayed garden but also an unfashionable one. By then the English Landscape Movement was in full swing and Henry Hoare was deeply involved with creating his great Elysium at nearby Stourton. In 1757 Lancelot Brown was summoned and he found 'capabilities': the juxtaposition of hills, house and water ideally suited his style. Lord Weymouth was evidently enthusiastic for the new fashion, for under Brown's direction (the contract is in the house) £8,000 was spent, mainly in the three years to 1760. Brown completely swept away the derelict formality and converted the canal into a chain of lakes along the valley. He planted many thousands of beeches, oaks and Spanish Chestnuts and fashioned the formal woodland into his characteristic clumps and hanging woods. He made sunken fences and new drives but his greatest triumph is the panorama from Heaven's Gate where, through dramatic curtains of beech woods, the whole valley and the wooded hills beyond are revealed. The romantic splendour of the house is set hazily amid the gently flowing contours of the park and the glint of the serpentine water enlivens the view. This is the very quintessence of the English landscape and one of the great glories of the age. Although it can be reached by turning south off the entrance drive, the best approach is on foot from a little car park by

Above: Longleat. Humphry Repton's proposed view from Heaven's Gate from his Red Book which is in the house.   *Marquess of Bath*

Below: Longleat. The view from Heaven's Gate today.

the road near Newbury. From here the way is along Green Drive, a broad grassy walk reminiscent of Westonbirt, through magnificent old beeches and pines with groups of conifers, cherries, azaleas, rhododendrons, dogwoods and *Parrotia persica*. Then the walk leads through a group of towering Douglas Firs, for which the estate is justly famous, to emerge suddenly into a meadow and the prospect from Heaven's Gate.

In 1760 a Mrs Delany, returning after several years' absence recorded that '. . . The Gardens are no more! They are succeeded by a fine lawn, a serpentine river, wooded hills, gravel paths meandering round a shrubbery, all modernized by the ingenious and much sought-after Mr Brown!' Here was Brown responding not only to the changing taste of the day but also to the contemporary requirements of economy and good husbandry. He was selling not just a new art-form but also a cheap and practical system of upkeep which has ensured the survival of the basic character of his scheme for more than two centuries.

Humphry Repton was consulted in 1804 and produced an exquisite Red Book, which also resides in the Old Library. Walpole had complained with some justification about Brown's landscape that the '. . . water is not well contrived and the ponds do not unite well'. Repton's proposals for deepening and broadening the lake near the house, joining two lakes together and making a tree-covered island were completed by 1814. But little of the remainder of the far-reaching proposals in his Red Book was accepted. His work was complementary to alterations to the house by Sir Jeffrey Wyattville, who possibly designed the Boathouse. The architect responsible for the superb Orangery also in the style of the house is not known. By Repton's time 50,000 trees had been planted and by his influence many that had begun to choke the valley were removed. The park, however, remains essentially Brown's creation; the smooth uncluttered turf and the gently swelling gradients, at one time perhaps uncomfortably bald, now balanced and contrasted superbly against the mature tree clumps and hanging beech woods.

In the 1870s the fourth Marquess began the extensive forestry for which the estate is famous and the long drives were planted with exotic trees like Wellingtonias and Monkey Puzzles and with rhododendrons and azaleas, mostly the yellow azalea *R. luteum*, the tree-like, red *R. arboreum* and the ubiquitous *R. ponticum*, which spread quickly through the woods. Less desirable were the mixed clumps of conifers and deciduous trees in the park, as they grew larger their hard striking shapes and spiky tops disturbing the rhythm and unity of the English scene. Helped by Russell Page the present Marquess had the courage and foresight to set about removing most of them during the 1930s and reinforcing and replanting clumps at the same time. Rightly they replanted deciduous trees, including many London Planes and Scarlet Oaks, with *Populus szechuanica* on the island. South of the house they replaced Brown's ageing elms with a clumped avenue of Tulip Trees now already promising well for the future.

Mr Russell Page has advised the sixth Marquess for many years. As well as remodelling the park in the pre-war years, together they replanted the Longcombe Drive. Its present beauty, the first taste of Longleat for visitors to the house, is testimony to their foresight. They cleared out much of the rampantly spreading Pontic Rhododendron and left some of the best specimens of the old red *Rhododendron arboreum* and drifts of the scented, yellow azalea. They also kept well-placed mature beeches, and a few Monkey Puzzles and Western Red Cedars and then enriched the planting, using Incense Cedars and Wellingtonias as vertical accents among Tulip Trees, Snowy Mespilus, *Liquidambar styraciflua* and other trees and shrubs for spring and autumn colour. Big drifts of Knap Hill and Exbury Azaleas make a colourful display in spring with *Pieris forrestii*, *Mahonia japonica* and *Hydrangea aspera* 'Macrophylla' for variety of leaf shape. More recently many more spring-flowering trees have been planted and *Sorbus* added to give early autumn colour and interest.

As well as the planting of exotics in the park, the middle of the nineteenth-century saw a return to formal gardening around the house. By 1856 there were beds of dwarf flowering shrubs and herbaceous plants both on the east side and between the house and the Orangery. In 1860 the fourth Marquess called on Markham Nesfield to advise on the layout but it seems that his ideas were not accepted. Nevertheless, soon after, an elaborate and complex flower garden, the 'bones' of which still survive, was laid out. The origin of this highly architectural scheme of parterres, gravel walks, fountains and stonework is not clear but it was certainly planted by the head gardener, William Taylor. In the fashion of the time he put the emphasis on bedding plants, at the rate of 40,000 a year, as well as cultivating a 4.4ha (11 acre) kitchen garden. A *Country Life* article of the time refers to 'excellent pattern gardening in quaint beds edged with box, full of summer flowers'. The pictures show box parterres full of bedding plants and gladioli and roses trained on ropes and over arches, some of which survive today in the Pheasant Garden behind the Boathouse.

Today the flower gardens are full of colour and interest. While the Victorian layout has been considerably simplified in accordance with the modern need for labour economy, the firm and dignified structure remains and under the guidance of Mr Russell Page many fine features and plantings have been introduced. He has increased the widths of paths and given beds and borders a larger scale to match the larger number of visitors. Overlooking the lake on the east side there are stone urns and box-edged beds filled entirely with the spectacular rose 'Elizabeth of Glamis'. Bordering the paths is a complex ribbon parterre of dwarf box with alternate pyramids and mushroom shapes of clipped yews and Portugal Laurels respectively, surviving intact from the one-hundred-year-old scheme. Near where pleasure-boats ply on the lake there towers a

magnificent Tulip Tree, the largest tree in the garden other than a
venerable old divided False Acacia at the back of the house which was
fully mature a century ago. The rose garden where this old tree grows lies
beyond the cool green interlude of an *allée* of neat yew hedges backed by
pleached limes leading to a large stone urn. The rose garden paths are
shaded by a canopy of the spring-flowering crab *Malus floribunda* and
through their stems pale pink 'Summer Queen' roses are seen with clipped
topiary among them.

The superb Orangery overlooks a terrace with tubs of agapanthus and a
trim formal garden with a central fountain. Here the urns, full of colourful
summer flowers, look well against the plain clipped yew background. The
atmosphere inside the Orangery is an entirely successful contrast, being
full of the luxuriant foliage of palms, oranges and magnificent giant
standards of Lemon-scented Verbena, *Lippia citriodora,* with camellias and
Impatiens in the borders. Budgerigars chatter from the elegant aviary and
the effect is splendidly exotic and just as it should be.

There is more to be seen beyond the Orangery in the walled Pheasant
Garden where big Handkerchief Trees and Indian Bean Trees reign
supreme among hydrangeas, roses and a variety of other shrubs and
flowers. In the centre of one square is a statue of the famous dwarf, Sir
Jeffrey Hudson (1619-82), who was first presented to King Charles the
First and Queen Henrietta Maria at a banquet served in a pie!

Luckington Court

The Hon. Mrs Trevor Horn

---

*For opening arrangements see HHCG ; also open for NGS in spring. At Luckington,
10.4km (6½ mile) SW of Malmesbury. An exquisite group of ancient buildings with Church and
Queen Anne house, which is partly shown.*

Medium-sized garden with flowering cherries along the drive and fine
trees notably a Lebanon Cedar, also a Corsican Pine and a number of False
Acacias in the garden. A sunken terrace, with Coignet's Vine on the
retaining wall and wisteria, clematis and climbing roses on the house,
leads to an attractive garden room, overlooking a lawn enclosed by stone
walls with an imposing classical-style gateway. There is a variety of
shrubs and a small rose garden.

Luckington Manor

W. Greville Collins Esq.

Open for NGS in spring. At Luckington, 12km (7½ miles) SW of Malmesbury.

In 1920 Admiral Neeld, of a local landowning family, bought the old farmhouse, which is mentioned in the Domesday Book, extended it and made the formal garden around the house, including a great deal of effective stonework. On the east front of the house is a formal rose garden enclosed by dry-stone walls; in spring it is colourful with aubrietias, daffodils and tulips. Indeed, spring bulbs are a feature with a gorgeous splash of hyacinths along the drive and big drifts of daffodils in a newly-developed area of mixed borders and in a newly-planted arboretum on the west side. The garden has a good variety of spring-flowering trees and shrubs — cherries, crabs and laburnums — especially on the south side where there are lawns and borders. Every year many thousands of plants are grown from seeds. Near the drive is a unique well garden, consisting of a deep sunken pool, containing water lilies and big golden carp, surrounded by elaborate walling. There is much to see and plenty of colour in this 1.6ha (4 acre) garden, which is maintained by two gardeners.

Lushill

Captain and Mrs F. Barker

Open for NGS in early summer. At Hannington, 9.6km (6 miles) N of Swindon. Garden of 2ha (5 acres); fine trees including a Weeping Silver Lime and a Judas Tree; extensive lawns; old shrub roses; heated plant house.

The Manor House

The Countess of Avon

Open for NGS and GS in late spring. At Alvediston, 19.2km (12 miles) W of Salisbury. Garden of 1.2ha (3 acres) with lawns, yew hedges, herbaceous borders; old-fashioned rose collection; conservatory.

The Manor House
Brigadier and Mrs Oliver Brooke

Open for NGS in early summer. At Great Cheverell, 8km (5 miles) S of Devizes. Medium-sized with herbaceous borders; roses; interesting old yew and box hedges.

Marston Meysey Gardens

Two gardens open for RC in late spring. 6.4km (4 miles) SW of Fairford. THE MANOR HOUSE *dates from 1611 and has a formal garden with clipped hedges.* GRANGE FARM HOUSE *has shrubs and roses and both gardens have herbaceous borders.*

Membury House
Alistair Horne Esq

Open for NGS in early summer. 4.8km (3 miles) NE of Ramsbury and 4.8km (3 miles) SE of Lambourn. 0.8ha (2 acre) garden and park; walled garden, shrubberies and herbaceous border virtually all created since 1970.

Middlehill House
Miss K. Harper

Open for NGS in summer. At Box, 8km (5 miles) W of Bath, north of A4. An intensive and colourful garden with much of interest.

The eighteenth-century house faces south on a slope with a fine Copper Beech and Western Red Cedars as a setting. There is a rose garden and many more climbing and bush roses near the house. Beyond is a rock garden and pools with ornamental fish a special feature. Up the slope a variety of shrubs form a background to free-standing herbaceous borders which curve around an open lawn. There is also a well-worked kitchen garden and greenhouse.

Notton Lodge
Mr and Mrs Gilbert Holliday

Open by appointment; telephone Lacock 282. At Notton, Lacock 4.8km (3 miles) S of Chippenham. Within a framework of established trees, giving ample shelter, Mr and Mrs Gilbert Holliday have created a garden conforming to clear landscape principles.

The house, which is almost on the narrow road, faces west and the 1.6ha (4 acre) garden is almost entirely to the east of the house where there is a large lawn and ha-ha. Two spinneys and some splendid Turkey Oaks have been retained beyond the ha-ha to frame both the views and a central V-shaped plantation of unusual shrubs and trees. Using the main Chippenham - Melksham road as a second giant ha-ha, two vistas have thus been created: to Lackham on one diagonal and to Bowden Hill on the other.

The lawn near the house is bounded on the north side by a large herbaceous border containing shrub roses and generous clumps of herbaceous perennials matching the scale of the lawn. Here are rose 'Nevada', *R. farreri persetosa*, the Threepenny-bit Rose, the dusky-leaved *R. rubrifolia*, with contrasting foliage of *Acanthus mollis, Ligularia, Achillea filipendulina, Sedum spectabile*, artichokes, irises, Plume Poppies and Day Lilies. On the south side is a large shrub border with pink-flowering thorns, Mock Oranges, Firethorns and the graceful pink-flowered *Kolkwitzia amabilis*. A stone wall behind is covered with an interesting collection of ivies.

In shade on the northern fringe are some azaleas and hybrid rhododendrons such as 'Loder's White', tolerating, if not enjoying, the conditions. A catholic collection of shrubs and trees has been established along the southern boundary with masses of the rampant variegated nettle *Lamium galeobdolon* 'Variegatum' used effectively as ground cover. Here are many barberries, both the dwarf purple form of *Berberis thunbergii* and the strong-growing *B. × ottawensis* 'Purpurea' with *Daphne mezereum* and *Elaeagnus × ebbingei*; also many vigorous young trees, birches, larches and *Robinia pseudoacacia* with a fine old walnut on the road boundary. Against the tennis-court hedge are many *Cistus* and *Berberis* raised by the owner who has lived in countries where they grow wild.

Two outstanding features are the glorious sea of daffodils beneath the oaks in spring and the magnificent 80-year-old *Wisteria sinensis* embracing the small, walled garden south of the house.

Nunton House
Mr and Mrs H.E. Colvin

At Nunton, near the Church, 4.8km (3 miles) S of Salisbury; 400m W of A338 Salisbury-Fordingbridge road. Open for NGS. Enclosed garden, with paddock, of 1.4ha (6 acres) beside classic house dated between 1690 and 1710. Low-lying site at 46m (150ft) by the River Ebble, near its confluence with the Avon, on sandy alluvial soil with flints, mostly alkaline but with occasional lime-free patches. Rainfall 762mm (30in.). Owners and one full-time gardener.

For anyone even remotely interested in landscape design the name of the owners of Nunton House has a special significance for Mr Colvin's sister is Brenda Colvin, the distinguished landscape architect and Past-President of the Institute of Landscape Architects. Her charming garden at Filkins is also open regularly for the NGS. After the Second World War Mr and Mrs Colvin acquired this beautiful Carolean house of mellow pink brick and asked Brenda Colvin to design the garden.

The house is set sideways to the road with its principal façade facing south over an area that had always been garden. There is a fascinating tradition that the house was built by a rich merchant from Salisbury who fell in love with a beautiful farmer's daughter who lived with her parents in a little farm just north of Nunton House. She would only marry him on condition that he built a house within sight of her mother's. But he took care to face it in the other direction!

As befits a house approaching 300 years old the dominant impression of the garden beyond the gravel forecourt is of maturity. The layout is dignified and relies for its effect upon the magnificent trees that surround it. By the road there are hornbeams including the unusual cut-leaved form and a magnificent multi-stemmed specimen of *Zelkova carpinifolia*, a close relation of the elms. There is a lofty group of limes, an unusual oak and many old yews to give an atmosphere of antiquity. Around a rectangular, mown lawn is taller grass full of spring bulbs. The effect is cool and restful with only climbers and a few shrubs like *Cornus kousa* and *Viburnum rhytidophyllum*, chosen principally for their shape and texture, to complement the simplicity.

The rest of the garden lies to the east beyond the yews under which is a carpet of Irish Ivy strewn with Honesty and Spurge Laurel. The rose garden is enclosed by a wall-backed herbaceous border on one side and separated from the kitchen garden on the other by a beech hedge. The bush roses are set in a formal key pattern of dwarf box designed at once to separate and to link the blocks of different varieties. The south-facing border is backed by *Clematis* × *jackmanii*, the purple Teinturier Grape, nasturtiums and old wisterias on the wall and is colourful with dahlias and perennials. The summer fragrance of *Phlox* is stronger than any of the roses. At the end are Rugosa roses and a striking combination of colour and texture from Weeping Silver Pear, Tamarix, *Cotinus coggygria, Iris pallida* and Hidcote Lavender.

The sound of water draws the eye to where the Colvins broke into the wall to make a straight vista to the delightful little Orangery, contemporary with the house. The so-called Dutch garden in front of the Orangery contains a sunken lily pool and a pattern of stone paving surrounded by four drum-shaped clipped yews and two pairs of Irish Junipers which link the steps through the wall to the Orangery. The Dutch garden is flanked on one side by the Pastel Border with heathers, paeonies and *Campanula lactiflora* and on the other by the Yellow and White Border.

The mown-grass Woodland Walk leads logically on from here under a promising young *Magnolia kobus*, big beeches, yews, Horse Chestnuts and an enormous London Plane. In the cool shade the natural woodland plants have been enriched by Periwinkles, Butcher's Broom, the wild Bellflower and the giant Cartwheel Flower, *Heracleum mantegazzianum*. Shrubs like Variegated Dogwood, *Rosa rubrifolia* and the landscape architect's favourite, *Viburnum rhytidophyllum*, are placed where their foliage is most telling. At the end is a bench seat sheltered by a box hedge and near by is a group of rhododendrons on an isolated patch of lime-free soil.

Glades with shrub roses, *Hydrangea villosa* and *Viburnum tomentosum* 'Mariesii' lead back past a paddock and a tennis-court well screened with glistening foliage of *Crataegus prunifolia*. The extensive kitchen garden with cordon apples in rows and its espalier pears on the walls is productive and well maintained.

Here is a garden of great charm, full of interest and with many plants. It is held together by a firm plan which makes the most of its buildings and features and provides the maximum of variety.

Oare House
Henry Keswick Esq.

At Oare, 3.25km (2 miles) N of Pewsey on the A345 Marlborough road. Formal garden of 3.25 ha (8 acres) created by Sir Geoffrey Fry between 1920 and 1960 to complement a beautiful mellowed red and grey brick house of 1740, extended by Clough Williams Ellis in the 1920s. Garden open for NGS once in spring and again in summer. Situated on almost lime-free, light, alluvial soil at 152m (500ft) on a gentle slope to the west, overlooking a shallow valley. Rainfall 787mm (31in.). 2½ gardeners.

Before the English Landscape style of the late-eighteenth-century a close formal relationship between house and garden was axiomatic. Rarely does one see such unity achieved as here where the garden, an almost perfect blend of discipline and exuberance, perfectly complements one of the most handsome houses in Wiltshire.

The approach is down a soaring lime avenue of majestic proportions, set axially on the east front. In spring the grass beyond the boles of these splendid trees is a mass of daffodils, and is a wonderful sight with the lime shoots bursting pale green above. Against the house the small railed courtyard is paved with setts and has a simple formal arrangement of bays in tubs and *Magnolia grandiflora* on the wall. A door leads south to the Library Garden via a brick-and-timber pergola supporting an enormous wisteria with a little formal lily pond, irises and New Zealand Flax alongside. The south-facing Library Garden is a satisfying architectural composition of clipped yew hedges and a handsome seat. A vista from the house passes through a gap in the hedge and along an avenue of pleached limes to a loggia, the shape of which echoes the house door at the other end. Alongside is a narrow secret garden known as 'The Ship' with clematises and a ceanothus on the wall and a seat at one end.

In contrast the main west front looks over an open rectangle of two acres entirely uncluttered except for a central blackboy sundial, an old apple and a sprawling *Amelanchier laevis*. At the far end a *clairvoyée* separates it from the pool garden but the prospect continues uninterrupted across the valley to a vista cut in the woods beyond, thus completing the axis from the lime avenue and through the house. On the garden front the house is supported by a raised terrace with a grass ramp leading to the lawn. The sheltered west walls of the house carry a variety of clematis, a purple vine and the tender *Raphiolepis japonica*.

The mixed borders either side of the Great Lawn indicate the work of a discerning plantsman with cherries including the lovely *Prunus* 'Shimidsu Sakura'; *Viburnum × burkwoodii, V. carlesii, V. × carlcephalum* and others;

lilacs, including *Syringa komarowii*; the Japanese Bitter Orange, *Poncirus trifoliata*; the unusual *Berberis chillanensis; Lespedeza thunbergii*, and even a few rhododendrons — all newly interplanted with the now popular shrub roses. At the bottom the railed wall carries a pattern of trained pear trees on the buttresses with *Clematis macropetala* and the deliciously scented *Osmanthus delavayi*.

Swimming-pools are never easy to assimilate into the garden scene but here the pool garden is a triumph, the water surface being large enough to give life to the view from the house and to give a reflection of its mellowed west façade when looking back. A dignified setting of sculptured yews completes the effect. Beyond the pool is an herbaceous border where, very sensibly, the plants are arranged in large drifts, which is essential to make an impact on the broad scale of this part of the garden.

Adjacent to the great lawn and similar in area is the kitchen garden, a traditional four-square arrangement with the vegetables grown in one quarter and fruit trees in the other three. Through the centre, east-west, runs a colourful herbaceous border edged with lavender and the central path on the other axis has bush roses backed by old espalier fruit trees on either side. Sentinel Irish Yews in pairs give a firm pattern and each path has a gate as a focal point.

Before leaving this delightful garden, spare a moment to look at the splendid collection of magnolias sheltering behind beech hedges south of the lime avenue. Here, set against the ideal background of Holm Oaks, are several cultivars of *M.* × *soulangiana,* two excellent *M. kobus*, the butterfly-flowered *M. salicifolia*, the early-flowering *M.* × *veitchii*, and others, with a big Tulip Tree, the rare *Styrax hemsleyana* and the late-flowering Buckeye, *Aesculus parviflora*.

The Pygmy Pinetum

Mr and Mrs H. Welch

Open for NGS in spring. In Hillworth Road, Devizes. Small, specialist nursery and pinetum containing the largest commercial collection of dwarf and slow-growing conifers in the British Isles and many other interesting plants. Young trees for sale.

Ramsbury Gardens

A group of village gardens sometimes open for NGS in early summer. 8km (5 miles) NW of Hungerford. There is a variety of features and waterside planting, roses, interesting hedges and herbaceous plants. KEWLEYS is a 0.1ha (¼ acre) cottage garden formerly owned by Miss Grace Hooker, daughter of Sir Joseph Hooker, one of the founders of The Royal Botanic Gardens, Kew. An old Chinese Wisteria grows on the flint walls. There is an old mulberry and a walnut and many shrub roses have been planted recently. The garden is open by appointment.

Sevenhampton Place

Mrs Ian Fleming

At Sevenhampton, 9.6km (6 miles) NE of Swindon, turning E from A361 Swindon to Highworth road at Stanton Fitzwarren. Informal garden and lakeside walk south and west of exceptionally beautiful Georgian house, the remaining part of a larger house, with modern extensions to the east. Open for NGS in spring and summer. In valley of River Cole on heavy alkaline soil at 91m (300ft). Rainfall 787mm (31in.). One gardener.

For several centuries Sevenhampton Place was the home of the Warneford family and it was they who built the house in 1734 and extended it subsequently. In those days the principal approach must have been from the west, where church and village lie. An abandoned drive goes across a field, into the grounds, to an obelisk and alongside the lake to the house in the best traditions of the eighteenth-century. Now one enters from the east through a farmyard and past recently rebuilt stables. The infinitely more beautiful way can still be followed on foot and this walk around the lake is the principal pleasure of a visit. In 1910 there were thirty gardeners but now Mr Beckett manages alone.

The 1734 pavilion and house of mellowed brick, the remains of a larger mansion of many dates, was converted by Mr Ian Fleming of James Bond fame. It faces south in the most tranquil of valleys over an extensive lake made by damming a tributary of the River Cole, which itself joins the Thames at Lechlade. The setting is idyllic, with the house sheltered by beeches, limes and Holm Oaks and the whole valley enclosed by vast trees. Despite the loss of elms there are still fine groups of lime, Horse Chestnut, beech, yew and Corsican Pine, and there are superb individual specimen Copper Beech, London Plane, Atlas Cedar and Wellingtonia, all presumably planted late in the last century. Broad lawns lead to a waterside of relaxed informality fringed with native plants and splendid clumps of *Polygonum cuspidatum*, a rare case where this invasive plant is a total success. Further along among the trees vigorous herbaceous plants like *Crambe cordifolia*, the giant Cartwheel Flower, *Heracleum manteggazzianum*, Plantain and Day Lilies have been naturalized in the tradition of William Robinson, the 'Wild Garden' getting wilder further from the house with Foxgloves all around.

Apart from some well-considered planting of *Hydrangea villosa*, Japanese Anemones, rosemary and climbing wisterias and *Clematis montana* near the house, the purely floral interest is concentrated in the rose garden on the south-facing bank not far away. A path bordered with fragrant 'Blanc Double de Coubert' roses leads up to a little box-edged flower garden sheltered by an old kitchen garden wall. It is a charming cottage-garden jumble of old roses, paeonies, campanulas, Day Lilies and herbaceous geraniums with hostas and Lilies of the Valley in the shade. In one place there is a more organized arrangement of Hidcote Lavender backed by Regal Lilies and musk roses — a fragrant mixture made the more intoxicating by a whiff of Mock Orange from nearby. Here is captured that illusive peacefulness that comes from a garden mature enough to seem on the brink of gentle decay; it is an atmosphere difficult to achieve and even more so to maintain.

Sheldon Manor

Major M.A. Gibbs D.L., J.P.

4.8km (3 miles) W of Chippenham, S of A420 Bristol road at allington crossroads. Formal garden of 1ha (2½ acres) and additional orchard and small arboretum around Plantagenet manor house of exceptional interest (also open) with thirteenth-century porch and fifteenth-century chapel. For opening se HHCG; also open for NGS. Gentle slope to the south-east at 106m (350ft) on heavy, mainly alkaline soil. Rainfall 813mm (32in.). Maintained by one gardener.

For 600 years this fascinating house, one of the oldest in Wiltshire, has survived through the changing fortunes of its owners. For half that time it was owned by the Hungerford family and one of their tenants, William Forster, rebuilt it after the great rebellion of the 1640s. The walled court in front of the house no doubt received attention too but it would almost certainly have been a feature of the garden layout from the earliest days. Within its walls there is a strong sense of antiquity imparted not only by the house and chapel but also by the pair of ancient yew trees (once topiary perhaps?) which straddle the path. The splendid ball-topped gate piers are attributed to William Norris who bought the house in 1710. The layout is on two levels with a dry-stone terrace wall between. There are stone-paved paths embellished with rosemary and some interesting shrubs including yellow-flowered *Piptanthus laburnifolius* and pineapple-scented *Cytisus battandieri*. On the terrace west of the house is a small summerhouse with a fig and the rare *Rosa gigantea* 'Cooperi' nearby. There are many more old climbing roses on the fine old stone barns further west. Well-planted sink gardens placed on the paving give an interesting homely touch.

To the south-east the main axis from the forecourt has been extended across the drive into a large sunken garden and between formal yew hedges to a fine stone seat. The screening of modern farm buildings is never easy and here the Lawson's Cypresses, which were planted *circa* 1911 by the Bailey family, only partly achieve their purpose. In this sheltered area some unusually tender and exotic shrubs grow by the walls. They include the Australian *Grevillea sulphurea*, species of *Callistemon*, *Romneya* and *Hoheria*. Through the hedges beyond, in place of an elaborate formal water garden laid out *circa* 1935, is an oblong swimming-pool complete with gushing lion-masks, fine lead urns and statues including a winged Mercury and a benign lion.

The main feature of the garden is the remarkable collection of shrub roses of every kind. The most vigorous kinds like *R. moyesii*, *R. alba* 'Maxima', *R. rugosa* cultivars and 'Fantin-Latour', take better to growing in grass than the Gallicas but together they make a visit worth while in late June or early July.

Many other interesting and unusual trees and shrubs grow in the garden, including a big white Judas Tree, collections of *Sorbus*, *Crataegus* and *Eucalyptus* species and cultivars, the Fringe Tree, *Chionanthus virginicus*, *Eucryphia* × *nymansensis* 'Nymansay', and a form of the Chilean Fire Bush, *Embothrium coccineum* 'Longifolium', which produces its orange-scarlet flowers in profusion — proof of an unexpectedly mild climate for this part of Wiltshire.

Stanton House
Sir Anthony and Lady Tritton

Open for NGS in summer. At Stanton Fitzwarren, 4.8km (3 miles) N of Swindon. 2ha (5 acre) garden with lake, extensive lawns, herbaceous borders; walled kitchen garden and greenhouses.

Stourhead
The National Trust

---

*At Stourton, 4.8km (3 miles) NW of Mere on the B3092 road to Frome. For opening arrange-
ments see NT and HHCG; daily all year. World-renowned landscape garden of about
16ha (40 acres) within a related park, woodlands and estate of 1010ha (2,500 acres) by Henry
Hoare between 1722 and 1787, Richard Colt Hoare between 1787 and 1838 and their successors
thereafter. Temples by Henry Flitcroft. House by Colen Campbell (modified later). Occupying a
valley below the source of the River Stour on the western scarp of the Wessex Chalk Downs, at
152-183m (500-600ft). Deep lime-free soil of the Lower Greensand. Rainfall 991mm (39in.).
Five gardeners. Excellent guidebooks available.*

The greatest works of art are distinguished by their ability to appeal to the
widest possible range of people, each at his own level. So it is with
Stourhead. In a garden as cohesive in structure and as rich in history every
visitor must find something to enjoy, perhaps to criticize, but few go
away unmoved. If works of art are about arousing the emotions then there
can be no doubt about the status of Stourhead.

Stourhead has features that appeal to all the senses. There is the architectural satisfaction of seeing fine buildings imaginatively sited, the
country joys of bird song and wild flowers, the fragrances of the seasons,
the fascination of water both moving and still, the excitement of botanical
rarity and the sheer sensual pleasure of the colourful masses of flowering
shrubs. But above all Stourhead is one of the most precious works of the
English Landscape Movement of the eighteenth-century, a philosophy of
landscape design that has been this country's major contribution to the art.
The deeper beauty of Stourhead lies in the composition of buildings, water
and plants, always changing with the seasons, always developing and
decaying. But its success is also dependent upon the unique nature of the
site: the genius of the place.

Siting is even more important for gardens and designed landscapes than
for houses. The finest natural landscape often occurs along the lines of
geological change: the shores of lakes; coastal cliffs; the edges of mountain
ranges and hills, and the courses of rivers. Stourhead is situated on the
western scarp of the Wiltshire chalklands, a watershed where the soil
changes suddenly from thin chalk to deep, lime-free loam. Three rivers
rise here, the Dorset Stour giving its name to the estate.

The history of the garden is a fascinating story, well described in all its
detail in *The Stourhead Landscape* by Kenneth Woodbridge. Saddened by
the death of his wife, Henry Hoare II conceived the layout, beginning at
the house, as an allegorical sequence of pictorial views and experiences

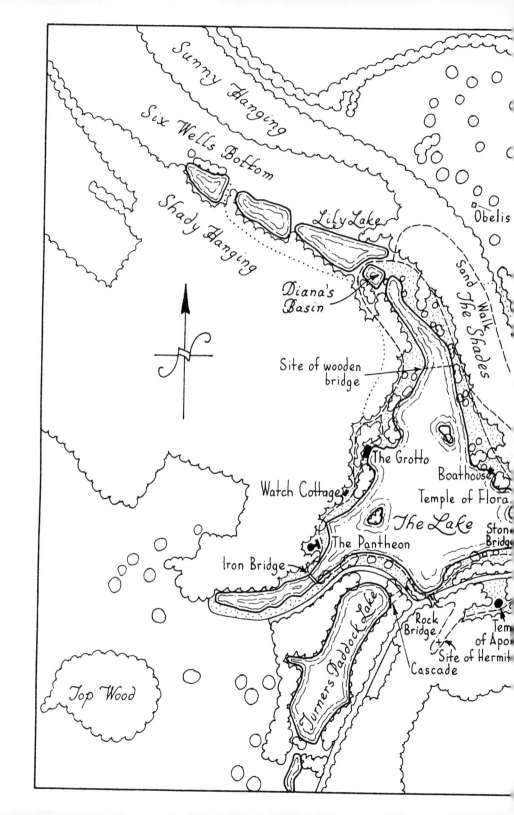

Summy Hanging

Six Wells Bottom

Shady Hanging

Lily Lake

Diana's Basin

Site of wooden bridge

Obelis

Sand Walk

The Shades

The Grotto

Watch Cottage

Boathouse

Temple of Flora

The Lake

Ston Bridge

The Pantheon

Iron Bridge

Turners Paddock Lake

Rock Bridge

Tem of Apo

Site of Hermit

Cascade

Top Wood

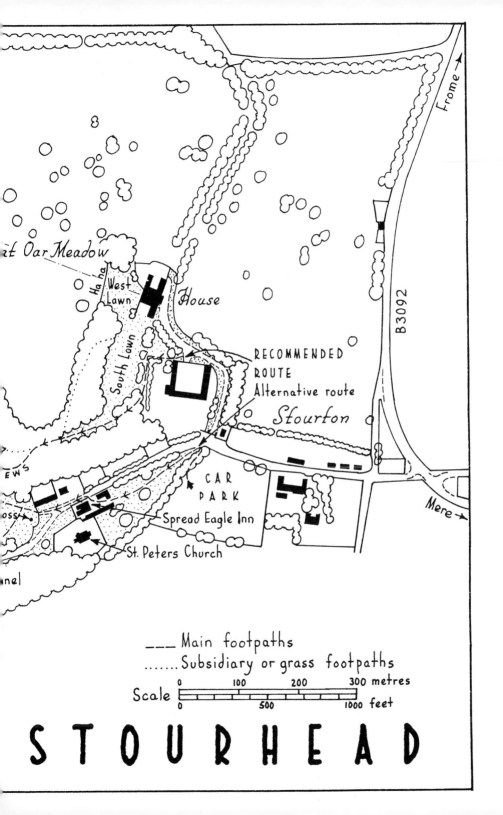

it Oar Meadow

Ha ha

West Lawn

House

South Lawn

RECOMMENDED
ROUTE
Alternative route

Stourton

Frome →

B3092

EWS

oss →

CAR
PARK

Spread Eagle Inn

St. Peters Church

Mere →

nel

___ Main footpaths
......Subsidiary or grass footpaths

Scale

| 0 | 100 | 200 | 300 metres |
| 0 | 500 | 1000 feet |

S T O U R H E A D

from the melancholy and the sublime to the arcadian and the beautiful. The planned route goes anti-clockwise to the Pantheon and back by way of the Temple of Apollo on its hill. In eighteenth-century fashion, the landscape and each of its features were to be revealed gradually, beginning with the imposing sight of Apollo's Temple apparently floating in greenery on the opposite hill. Undoubtedly the best way to see Stourhead is to approach from the house so that the first glimpses of the lake are from above. 'Tis better to look up to wood and down to water . . . ' a principle that has been lost in this century since the habit has grown of entering from the village. Henry Hoare created the main features in two stages. First he made the Temple of Flora on the east bank, the dam, the Grotto and the Pantheon, all between 1745 and 1755, thereby completing the outward journey. Although he may have conceived the whole scheme earlier, he did not actually embark on the second stage, comprising the Temple of Apollo, Stone Bridge and Bristol Cross, until he could stand before his Pantheon and place them with care to form the 'Charming Gaspar picture'. In common with others of his age the main source of his inspiration was the study of classical art and literature; he was creating a classical ideal.

His grandson, Richard Colt Hoare, who succeeded him, continued the work and made many changes, especially in the area near the house. He elaborated the planting with exotic trees, laurels and rhododendrons and made the gravel path to encompass the north arm of the lake. Thereafter each succeeding generation has made its own changes and none more so than the last. Sir Henry and Lady Hoare, who gave the property to the National Trust, lived at Stourhead for 53 years, longer than any of their predecessors. They planted the main collection of hybrid rhododendrons and many of the conifers. During their time the separation of the house from the lake was emphasized, perhaps because they lived in the village for a while. Stourhead is not, then, entirely the work of one man or of the eighteenth-century but the product of a dynasty spanning 200 years. Conserving such a garden involves aiming at a broad concept, that gives unity to the whole, while attempting to reconcile each generation's contribution according to its relative importance. Since 1947 this awe-inspiring responsibility has been in the hands of the National Trust which alone, perhaps, has the continuity to formulate long-term objectives and the independence to pursue them.

Deep, lime-free soil and abundant moisture make Stourhead an ideal place for growing trees. Henry Hoare planted the hanging woods mostly with beeches and oaks, interplanted with conifers. He aimed at a subtle blending of greens. Many of the original beeches, now with towering boles, remain in 'The Shades' between the house and the lake. While they move towards the end of their life-span, their replacements are threatened

Stourhead. The Pantheon, designed as a focal point by Henry Flitcroft for Henry Hoare II, who conceived the original layout of the garden in the eighteenth century. *Iris Hardwick*

by the modern menace of grey squirrels. Henry Hoare had no such imported problem but neither did he have the new tree species from America that Richard Colt Hoare planted with such enthusiasm between 1791 and 1838. The magnificent Tulip Trees, Variegated Sycamores, the picturesque Weeping Ash near the bridge, Scarlet and Lucombe Oaks, Swamp Cypresses, Pink Chestnuts, Indian Bean Trees and many other exotics were planted by Colt Hoare and he began the conversion of the landscape into an arboretum. Many of his trees are now remarkable specimens of their kind. He also planted a variety of shrubs, including a large number of *Rhododendron ponticum* and added many more of the Cherry Laurels planted by his grandfather. The panoramic drawing in the house by Francis Nicholson is an unusually precise record of the appearance of the lakeside in 1811. Although it was already thickly planted, Colt Hoare continued to plant evergreens for another 25 years.

The next major period of planting was in this century, after the sixth Baronet, Sir Henry Hugh Arthur Hoare, had succeeded in 1894 at the age of 29. With many buildings in need of repair, he saved Stourhead from dereliction. By then the landscape was overgrown with Pontic Rhododendron and Cherry Laurel which he removed in quantity to be replaced with the latest kinds of hybrid rhododendron. At first he planted azaleas and the old hardy hybrids of the Waterer class such as 'Gomer Waterer', of which there is a large group near the Stone Bridge, and later the stronger-coloured varieties produced after the First World War like 'Britannia', which fit less easily into the eighteenth-century scene. He dotted them apparently indiscriminately around the lake and they have become progressively more exposed to view as older trees have fallen. The National Trust has been gradually re-grouping the more vivid kinds behind the trees. The long-term aim is to maintain Sir Henry's collection but to rearrange it in a sequence so that most of the modern varieties will be grown near the house and village. By late May the display is spectacular and even as late as July there is still the white *R. auriculatum* and 'Polar Bear'.

Perhaps Sir Henry's most conspicuous tree plantings are the Copper Beeches, their strong purple dominating the summer scene, but with conifers his impact on the garden was also considerable. There are many notable specimens among them. The Japanese White Pine, *P. parviflora*, at 21.3m (70ft) is the tallest recorded in Britain and the Macedonian Pine, *P. peuce*, is another champion at 33.5m (110ft). Several Noble Firs, *Abies procera*, and a Sitka Spruce soar to great heights while the rare Californian Nutmeg, *Torreya californica*, at 14.3m (47ft) is enormous by the standards of this country. The conifers are particularly effective where grouped together in their sombre majesty around the north arm of the lake, where replacement plantings will be concentrated.

No living thing can remain static and for more than 200 years Stourhead has been developing and changing; partly because of the biological laws of growth and decay but also in response to the whims of successive owners. Such is the strength of the design, so firmly keyed to the site, that it is still Henry Hoare's Elysium. No matter what the season, or the weather, it retains that magical ability to uplift the spirit which is the true quality of a great work of art.

Wedhampton Manor
Mrs E.L. Harris

Open for NGS in spring and summer. 8km (5 miles) SE of Devizes. Moderate-sized garden of general interest, remarkable chiefly for its fine specimen of the Cut-leaved Lime, Tilia platyphyllos 'Laciniata'. Fine Queen Anne house (not open).

Wilton House
The Earl of Pembroke

At Wilton, 4km (2½ miles) W of Salisbury on the A30 (Exeter) road. For opening arrangements see HHCG ; usually every day except Mondays, Easter to mid-October. Garden of 14ha (35 acres) part open, around Tudor house rebuilt by Inigo Jones and John Webb and altered later by James Wyatt; fine trees, river and Palladian Bridge. Light alkaline soil with high water-table in shallow valley of the rivers Nadder and Wylye, at 61m (200ft). Rainfall 914mm (36in.). Four gardeners. Guidebook available but little information on the garden.

There is a great sense calm at Wilton and it derives from the combination of the mature trees, the smooth, uncluttered lawns and the broad, shallow-banked river. For more than three centuries the garden has assimilated changes and additions but the result is curiously coherent; here is a blend of the formal and the informal, nineteenth-century Italianate and Classical landscape. The garden contains magnificent cedars including some of the earliest introduced from Lebanon, starting from about 1650. Many royal visits and family occasions have been commemorated by planting the progeny of the original cedars.

An engraving shows the immense and extraordinarily complex formal garden laid out by Isaac de Caus in 1633 for the brothers William, Earl of Pembroke, and Philip, Earl of Montgomery. Measuring 305m (1,000ft) by 123m (400ft) it straddled the river and ignored its awkward informality.

This was perhaps the finest garden of Charles I's time who 'loved Wilton above all places'.

It was Henry, ninth Earl of Pembroke, friend of Lord Burlington and William Kent, who turned against the formal garden. He replaced it in the fashion of the time with a landscape of classical simplicity and in 1737, with the help of Roger Morris, he designed and built the famous and beautiful Palladian Bridge across a widened River Nadder south of the house. Later in that century Sir William Chambers was commissioned to build the classical stone pavilion which so effectively acts as an eye-catcher on the hill beyond the river.

The present formality mostly dates from the first half of the nineteenth-century when Catherine, Countess of Pembroke, second wife of the eleventh Earl, employed Sir Richard Westmacott to make the extensive Italian terrace garden (not open to visitors) west of the house with its triple-arched loggia. He also made the broad, formal, gravel walk which forms an axis from the superb east front, between magnificent cedars and limes and tranquil lawns to a raised stone seat set in a formal arrangement of yew hedges, now embellished with 'Iceberg' roses.

Beyond is an attractive informal flower garden with a variety of shrubs

and bulbs, and still further east a beautiful stone summerhouse, which appears in Richard Wilson's painting 'Wilton House' in the Upper Cloisters. This little building has been linked to a column surmounted by a fine Egyptian statue of Venus from the Arundel collection, and thence to the river by another formal arrangement, a short avenue of the 'Allumii' form of Lawson's Cypress.

The most recent addition to the garden has been the formal garden in the forecourt, designed by David Vicary in 1971. Here, set in pleached limes, are two linked squares. One contains a circular pool, a really generous gushing fountain, and corners jostling with shrubs; the other has a simple four-square pattern of paths and borders with statues in the corners.

Index